8TH EDITION
COLLEGE TYPEWRITING

D. D. LESSENBERRY *Professor of Education, Emeritus
University of Pittsburgh*

S. J. WANOUS *Professor of Education, School of
Education, UCLA (Los Angeles)*

C. H. DUNCAN *Head, Business Education Department
Eastern Michigan University*

T 77
BASIC
COURSE

SOUTH-WESTERN PUBLISHING CO.
Cincinnati   •   Chicago   •   Burlingame, Calif.
Dallas • New Rochelle, N. Y. • Brighton, England

CONTENTS ▶ BASIC TYPEWRITING FOR COMMUNICATION

▶ PREFACE

The typewriter is a tool of written personal and business communication. The purpose of learning to type is to speed up the communication process. And the function of both the instructor and the textbook is to facilitate this learning.

PURPOSE AND ORGANIZATION OF THE TEXTBOOK

COLLEGE TYPEWRITING, Basic Course, Eighth Edition, has a threefold purpose: First, to develop the techniques of typewriter operation upon which all applied skills depend; second, to present procedures of problem solving that are basic to all typewritten applications; and third, to provide practice on those forms of typewritten communication that are basic for both personal and business use. This threefold purpose is implemented by 75 carefully planned lessons, a special business typing project, and a convenient reference guide to frequently needed typewriting information.

The 75 lessons are organized into 12 sections. Each section emphasizes one of the important phases of learning to typewrite: learning the letter keys, learning the figures and frequently used symbols, basic skill development, centering, word division, personal correspondence, tabulation, outlines and reports, business letters, among others. The student thus has an opportunity to concentrate his attention and effort on one phase of learning at a time without the frequent interference of mixed or diffused goals.

The first 5 sections (30 lessons) concentrate on developing high skill in typing alphabetic copy and copy containing figures and frequently used symbols. Right techniques of typing are given initially greater importance than the attainment of a certain number of words a minute, but both speed and accuracy are given appropriate emphasis at appropriate times. Beginning with Lesson 16, the technique of tabulating is introduced through specially designed drills. In addition, the frequently applied skill of typing from longhand (script) is initiated. At the end of Lesson 20, common correction symbols are presented so that rough-draft copy can be encountered in the following lessons. Other related skills are woven into the lessons in a similar way when appropriate.

Section 6 develops the skills of horizontal and vertical centering, the basis for all problem layouts. In addition, the problems require the application of centering principles to the typing of memorandums, announcements, and postal cards.

Section 7 is devoted to personal communica-ns: personal notes and letters, memorandums, e addressing, and composing at the typewriter.

Section 8 develops the important skills of tabulation and word division. Tabulation is presented as an extension of centering, using the backspace-from-center method.

Section 9 is devoted to typing business letters in modified block style. Other elements of related emphasis include: large envelope addressing, carbon pack assembly and insertion, erasing, centering tables in letters, and typing letters from rough-draft copy.

Section 10 emphasizes the typing of outlines and report manuscripts (with footnotes). It also continues the emphasis on composing at the typewriter that was begun in Section 7.

Section 11 provides a two-lesson review of the preceding 71 lessons in preparation for the two-lesson measurement of basic and problem skills provided in Section 12.

SPECIAL FEATURES OF THE LESSONS

1. Early emphasis on the most frequently used letters, words, and two-letter stroking combinations to build stroking facility quickly.
2. Electric typewriter information and variations in practice material to accommodate electrics.
3. Meaningful labeling of drills to give purpose to practice and of problem models to give quick orientation to problem layout.
4. Frequent technique practice activities to assure continuous emphasis on *how* to type.
5. Periodic guided writing and skill-comparison activities to motivate the typist to work toward progressively higher goals and to practice on progressively more difficult copy.
6. Triple-controlled copy (graduated in difficulty) in order to force students to move gradually and with certainty toward the copy level they will be using in the office.

ACKNOWLEDGMENTS

We express our grateful thanks to the instructors, students, and business workers who have contributed so generously of their ideas for the content and organization of this book.

Special recognition is made of the contribution of Dr. Jerry W. Robinson whose research into stroking combination frequencies, effects of copy difficulty, and teacher practices and preferences has significantly influenced the preparation of this new Eighth Edition of COLLEGE TYPEWRITING, Basic Course.

All these have helped us to make this book an effective aid to those who wish to learn to type with maximum skill in minimum time and to those who teach typewriting at the college level.

Lessenberry • Wanous • Duncan

Problem 12: Résumé (Data Sheet)

Full sheet; 1" top and side margins; 1 cc

Words

INTRODUCING

Charles G. Ford

1200 Juniper Drive   Telephone Number:
Billings, Montana 59102   (406) 871-2240

Education

Almost five years of cooperative work-study, Cascade University,
Billings, Montana. Degree of Bachelor of Business Administration
to be awarded June 7, 19--. Grade-point average: 3.7 ("A"). Have
been on Dean's Honor List during all study sessions. Major: Business Management. Minor: Economics.

Representative Advanced Courses

Business Statistics--study of the application of statistical methods
                    to the solution of business problems
Econometrics--advanced study of the quantitative aspects of eco-
                    nomics applied to business operations
Computer Applications--study of the application of computer science
                    to business operations

Representative Basic Courses

Principles of Economics, Principles of Management, Accounting Systems and Data Processing, Mathematics of Finance, Current Social
Forces, Psychology of Group Interaction, Survey of Classical Lit-
erature, Marketing Management, and others

Work Experience

19--   : Co-op in Data Processing (3 years) for Montana Light
                and Power Company, Billings
Summer, 19--: Salesman for Utilities Insurance Company, Denver
19-- to 19--: Clerk-Typist during 2 summers for Utilities Insur-
                ance Company, Denver

Memberships

Alpha Kappa Psi, business society; United Appeal (voluntary fund-
raiser); University YMCA (president of Youth Club)

Personal Details   Hobbies

Birthplace: Denver, Colorado   Skiing, boating, fishing,
Birth Date: February 18, 19--   bridge, reading, debating
Height: 5' 10"
Weight: 170   References
Health: Excellent   (by request)

Words:
2
6
13
21
25
38
52
65
79
87
99
113
121
134
141
155
159
171
184
197
210
219
225
238
244
257
270
274
279
292
302
312
323
324
338
346
353

LESSON 1

1A Get Ready to Type

1. ARRANGE YOUR WORK AREA

a. Clear the work area of unneeded books and papers.

b. Place this textbook to the right of the typewriter on a bookholder, or put something under the top to raise it to better reading position.

c. Have the front of the frame of the typewriter even with the front edge of the desk or table.

2. INSERT THE PAPER

a. Adjust the **paper guide (8)** as directed on page iii.

b. Place a full-size sheet of paper on the desk to the left of the typewriter, turned so the long side of the paper is close to you.

c. Pull the **paper bail (11)** forward—toward you—with your right hand.

d. Grasp the paper with your left hand, the thumb under the sheet, as illustrated at the right.

e. Bring the paper to the **cylinder** or **platen (14)** and drop it between the cylinder and the **paper table (10)**, against the **paper guide (8)**; *at the same time*, bring the right hand to the **right cylinder knob (19)** and twirl the knob with a quick movement of the fingers and the thumb.

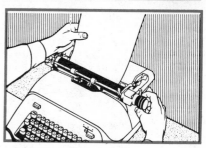

f. Snap the paper bail back with the thumb to hold the paper firmly against the cylinder. Place the **paper-bail rolls (13)** about 1½ inches from the side edges of the paper.

3. KNOW YOUR TYPEWRITER

• The numbers shown in boldface in the text above are those assigned to the machine parts illustrated below and on the diagrams presented on pp. i-ii.

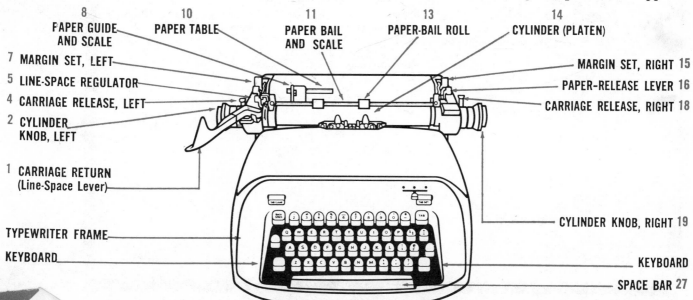

8 PAPER GUIDE AND SCALE
10 PAPER TABLE
11 PAPER BAIL AND SCALE
13 PAPER-BAIL ROLL
14 CYLINDER (PLATEN)

7 MARGIN SET, LEFT
5 LINE-SPACE REGULATOR
4 CARRIAGE RELEASE, LEFT
2 CYLINDER KNOB, LEFT
1 CARRIAGE RETURN (Line-Space Lever)

MARGIN SET, RIGHT 15
PAPER-RELEASE LEVER 16
CARRIAGE RELEASE, RIGHT 18

CYLINDER KNOB, RIGHT 19

TYPEWRITER FRAME
KEYBOARD

KEYBOARD
SPACE BAR 27

Problem 11: Application Letter

Plain sheet; line: 65; begin on Line 10; 1 cc

1200 Juniper Drive
Billings, Montana   59102
March 1, 19--

Mr. Elmer G. Kaising
Rocky Mountain Insurance Co.
1515 Cleveland Place
Denver, Colorado   80202

Dear Mr. Kaising

Mr. Neil J. Simms, Director of Cascade University Placement Center, has told me that you can use a young man who has a demonstrated skill in data processing and programming, a working knowledge of statistics, and a strong background in economics and business management. I have those qualifications, and I should like to apply for the position you have available.

An honor student in Cascade's College of Business Administration, I shall be graduated in June with a major in management. My program of studies has emphasized the quantitative aspects of business operations. Some of my areas of study are: principles of data processing, managerial accounting, computer theory and application, and statistical methods of business operation.

Recently I have gained valuable experience in data processing, systems analysis, and procedural administration as a co-op student with Montana Light and Power Company here in Billings. On the basis of an analysis I made of that firm's data processing system as a requirement for one of my college courses, the Company replaced its unit record system with a computer system.

Additional information summarized on the enclosed resume will give you the opportunity of comparing my qualifications with the requirements of the position you have to fill.

May I have an interview at your convenience? Since I shall be in Denver during the period April 2-10 to visit my family, perhaps an interview could be arranged then. You can reach me by mail at the address given above. I should like to prove personally that I am the man for the job.

Sincerely yours

Charles G. Ford

Charles G. Ford

Enclosure

Words:
4
9
12

16
22
26
31

34

48
61
74
86
99
108

121
134
147
160
173
184

197
210
223
235
249
260

274
288
296

309
322
334
347
353

357

360

362

4. ADJUST THE LINE-SPACE REGULATOR

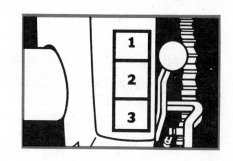

Set the **line-space regulator (5)** on "1" for single spacing the lines you are to type in this lesson.

(Set the regulator on "2" for double spacing and on "3" for triple spacing when such spacing is needed.)

The first two lines shown below are single-spaced (SS); the next line is a double space (DS) below the second line; and the last line is a triple space (TS) below that.

Line 1	This line and the next are single-spaced. SS
2	This line and the next are double-spaced.
3	(one blank line) DS
4	This line and the next are triple-spaced.
5	
6	(two blank lines) TS
7	Set the regulator for correct spacing.

5. SET THE MARGIN STOPS

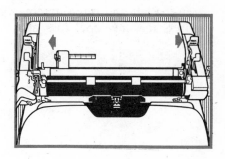

Move the **left margin stop (7)** to approximately 25 spaces to the left of the center of the paper. Move the **right margin stop (15)** to the end of the scale. You will type the copy line for line and do not need the right margin stop to indicate the line ending.

6. TAKE CORRECT TYPING POSITION (as illustrated)

EYES ON COPY

FINGERS CURVED;
WRISTS LOW

ELBOWS NEAR THE BODY;
FOREARMS PARALLEL TO
SLANT OF KEYBOARD

SIT BACK IN CHAIR;
BODY ERECT

TEXTBOOK AT RIGHT OF
MACHINE, ELEVATED FOR
EASY READING

TABLE FREE OF UNNEEDED
BOOKS

FEET ON FLOOR, ONE
JUST AHEAD OF THE
OTHER

Special Personal Communications

Problem 8: Letter on Half-Size Paper (5½″ x 8½″)

Half sheet; begin on Line 10; 3 blank line spaces after the date; ¾″ side margins; indented paragraphs; mixed punctuation; correct your errors; envelope

Type the letter from the illustration at the right. Set a tabulator stop for the paragraph indentions and a second tabulator stop at the center point of the sheet. Tabulate to this second stop to type the return address, date, and closing lines.

Indent the quoted paragraph 5 spaces from the left and right margins. After you address the envelope, fold and insert the letter.

	Words
¾-inch side margins	
6601 Hardy Drive	3
Austin, Texas 78757	8
August 27, 19--	11
Science Research Associates, Inc.	17
1256 Michigan Boulevard	22
Chicago, Illinois 60607	27
Gentlemen:	30
For my term paper, "Beginning Posi-	37
tions for Office Workers," I am quoting	45
Humphreys and Taxler as follows:	51
Because so much depends	56
on impressions made by the job	62
seeker in his interview, the	68
guidance worker may well arrange	75
for groups of students to learn	81
job-finding techniques.	86
If you have other books or pamphlets	94
on job-finding techniques for beginning	102
office workers, please send me a price	109
list.	110
¾-inch side margins	
Sincerely yours,	114
Mary Moore	
(Miss) Mary Moore	118/144

Letter Typed on a Half-Size Sheet

Problem 9: Lengthening a Letter

Use Problem 8 directions when typing the letter given below. After typing the complimentary close, look at the letter to see if its placement seems too high on the sheet; if so, leave 4 or 5 line spaces between the complimentary close and the writer's name to add the appearance of length to the completed letter.

	Words
(Return address and date of Problem 8) dr	11
frank e liguori, dean department of business	21
administration cuyahoga community college	29
cleveland, oh 44114 dear dr liguori. (¶1)	37
You are quoted as saying in your dissertation,	46
"Few high school graduates had adequate	54
understanding of the details of the job applica-	64
tion." (¶2) Will you please send me the exact	72
reference for the quotation or tell me where I	82
can get access to your research. I shall be	91
most grateful for this help. sincerely yours	100
(miss) loretta m king	104

Problem 10: Letter on Half-Size Paper (8½″ x 5½″)

Insert the paper with the short width at the left. Use 1″ side margins. Begin on Line 5. Type the letter of Problem 9.

1B Finger Position

Look at the keyboard shown below and locate **asdf** (*the home keys for the left hand*) and **jkl;** (*the home keys for the right hand*).

Look at your typewriter keyboard and locate the home keys. Place the fingers of your left hand on **asdf** and the fingers of your right hand on **jkl;** with your fingers curved and positioned upright (not slanting or leaning to the outside of the keyboard).

Remove your hands from the keyboard; then place your curved fingers in home position again, holding them *lightly* on the keys. *Repeat two or three times.*

1C Key Stroking and Spacing

For electric typewriters, turn ON-OFF switch to ON position.

Type **f** with the *left first finger*; then type **j** with the *right first finger*. Strike each key with a down motion and with the finger pulled slightly in to the palm of the hand, as illustrated below.

Type **fj** four times: **fjfjfjfj** Next, read how to space after typing a letter or group of letters.

To SPACE after typing a letter or between groups of letters, operate the **space bar (27)** with a quick down-and-in motion of the right thumb.

On the line on which you typed **fj** four times, type **f** (space) **j** (space) five times:

f j f j f j f j f j

Then on the same line, type:

asdf jkl; asdf jkl;

1D Carriage (or Element Carrier) Return

To space the paper forward and return to the beginning of the line, use the **lever (1)** on a non-electric (manual) typewriter or the **key (1)** on an electric one. Locate this part on your typewriter; then make the return as directed and illustrated below.

Nonelectric (Manual). Move the hand, fingers bracing one another, to the carriage return lever and move the lever inward to take up the slack; then return the carriage with a quick wrist and hand motion. Drop the hand to typing position without letting it follow the carriage across.

Electric and Selectric. Reach the little finger of the right hand to the return key, flick the key lightly, release it quickly, and return the finger to its typing position.

On the Selectric the return key returns the element carrier (*not the carriage*) to the left margin.

RETURN the carriage (or carrier). Then, operate the space bar several times and return again.

Telegrams

Services Available. Two basic types of telegraph services are used: (1) *domestic* (for messages communicated within the continental United States) and (2) *international* (for overseas messages).

Classes of Domestic Service. Only two classes of domestic telegraph service are now available: (1) the *telegram* (which is given priority of transmission) and (2) the *overnight telegram* (which is less expensive but subordinated in transmission time).

Telefax. Western Union provides businesses having a large volume of telegraph messages a special sending-receiving machine called Desk-Fax. The form used with Desk-Fax is called Telefax.

Each company that uses this service is assigned a series of call letters to identify the Desk-Fax station. These letters should be typed opposite the heading CALL LETTERS on all Telefax messages transmitted. The class of service should be indicated by typing FR (for telegram) or NL (for overnight telegram) in the appropriate space. The name of the subscriber to Desk-Fax service is typed in the CHARGE TO blank.

Point of Origin and Date. Type the sender's city and state and the date on the same line a DS below the last line of the printed heading.

Addressee's Name and Address. Double-space from the date to type the addressee's name and address in block and single-spaced form; include all information that will facilitate delivery of the telegram. The title *Mr.* before the addressee's name will not be transmitted, but *Miss* and *Mrs.* will be transmitted and should be used. Western Union does not charge for the necessary address and a 2-line signature or signature and address.

Body of the Message. Begin the message a double space below the address. Use single spacing. Line length is unimportant so long as the message is typed within the ruled area of the blank. Use punctuation marks as there is no charge for them.

Sender's Name; Address. Type the sender's name a double space below the message. The company name, if used, is typed below the sender's name. If the sender's address is to be transmitted, type it on the line directly below his name or the company name. If the company name or the sender's address is not to be transmitted, type it at the left margin a double space below the reference initials (if used).

Carbon Copies. Usually a minimum of three copies are prepared—the *original copy* (for transmittal), the *file copy*, and the *billing* or *accounting copy*. Sometimes a fourth copy, the *confirmation copy*, is prepared and mailed to the addressee with a covering letter to make certain that the message was transmitted correctly.

Problem 7: Telefax

1 Telefax; 1 cc on a half sheet; type from the model; correct your errors

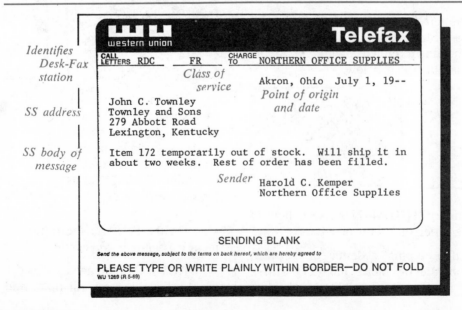

1E Home-Key Stroking Practice

DO: Type the typescript lines below. Single-space (SS) the two lines of copy; double-space (DS) between two-line groups, as shown.

Stroking Cue: Strike each key with a quick, snap stroke and release it immediately; then strike the next key without pausing.

1	f j d k	ff jj ff jj fj fj fj dd kk dd kk dk dk dk fj dk fj
2		ff jj ff jj fj fj fj dd kk dd kk dk dk dk fj dk fj

DS (operate the return twice)

3	s l a ;	ss ll ss ll sl sl sl aa ;; aa ;; a; a; a; sl a; sl
4		ss ll ss ll sl sl sl aa ;; aa ;; a; a; a; sl a; sl

DS (double-space)

5	Home keys	a; sl a;sl dk fj dkfj a;sl dkfj a;sldk a;sldkfj a;
6		a; sl a;sl dk fj dkfj a;sl dkfj a;sldk a;sldkfj a;

DS

7		a as ask ad lad ask lad all fall add lass all fall
8		a as ask ad lad ask lad all fall add lass all fall

DS

9	Space once	a lad; ask dad; a lad asks dad; ask all; all fall;
10	after ;	a lad; ask dad; a lad asks dad; ask all; all fall;

TS (triple-space)

Return without looking up

Space with a down-and-in motion

1F Stroking Technique for H and E

1. Locate the new key on the keyboard chart.
2. Locate the new key on the typewriter keyboard.

3. Study the reach illustration for the new key.
4. Type the tryout drill for that key.

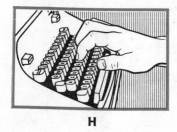

H

E

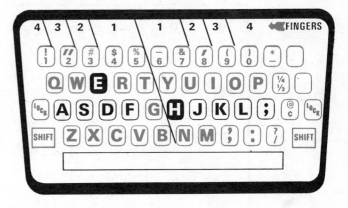

Reach the *right first finger* to the left to type **h** without moving the other fingers from their home keys.

Reach the *left second finger* up to **e**, lifting the first finger slightly to free the controlling finger.

Tryout Drills *type the lines as shown*

1	h	hj has hash lash dash hj half all hall shall shall
2		hj has hash lash dash hj half all hall shall shall

DS

3	e	ed led fled sale lake fled ee feel seek keel sleek
4		ed led fled sale lake fled ee feel seek keel sleek

DS

5	h e	he led a lad; he has a sled; he seeks a safe deal;
6		he led a lad; he has a sled; he seeks a safe deal;

TS (triple-space)

Keep thumb close to the space bar

Problem 5: Voucher Check

ADAMS AND DAWSON, INC.
3602 Wilshire Blvd.
Los Angeles, CA 90005

16–310
1219

April 1, 19 -- No. 198

Words

2

PAY to the order of California Suppliers, Inc. $ 125.00   9

One hundred twenty-five and no/100----------------------------------- Dollars   23

WEST COAST NATIONAL BANK
LOS ANGELES, CALIFORNIA 90006

⑆1219⑈0320⑆ 143 0602 46⑈

Treasurer, ADAMS AND DAWSON, INC.

Detach This Stub Before
Cashing This Check

TO   California Suppliers, Inc.
     1682 Vine Street
     Los Angeles, CA 90028

IN PAYMENT OF THE FOLLOWING INVOICES:

28
32
36

Date	Invoice	Amount
3/17/--	1269	125.00

40

ADAMS AND DAWSON, INC.
3602 Wilshire Blvd.
Los Angeles, CA 90005

Problem 6: Ruled Card Fill-in

TO CHANGE YOUR ADDRESS . . . REQUEST SUBSCRIPTION

☐ Please change my address.
My present label is attached.
My new address is below.

ATTACH NAME LABEL FROM THIS ISSUE
FOR COMPUTER CHANGE OF ADDRESS

Words

0

☒ If you do not get your own copy of MOP, do you
want to receive MOP free?   YES ☒   NO ☐

Signature_____
You must sign here to receive MOP.

0

Date February 14, 19--   4

Name Mr. David Vowells   Title Asst. Office Manager   12

Company Lone Star Development Company   18

Street 4200 Broadway Avenue   22

City Fort Worth   State Texas   ZIP 76117   27

BOTH NEW AND OLD SUBSCRIBERS MUST GIVE INFORMATION REQUESTED BELOW.

MAJOR JOB FUNCTION
(Check one)

☐ Corporate Executive
☐ Technical Office

☐ Financial
☐ Purchasing

☐ Administrative Office
Other_____

MAJOR BUSINESS
AT ABOVE
ADDRESS:

☐ Agriculture
☐ Mining
☒ Construction
☐ Manufacturing

☐ Transportation
☐ Communications
☐ Utilities
☐ Wholesale Trade
☐ Retail Trade

☐ Finance
☐ Insurance
☐ Real Estate
☐ Services/Education
☐ Government

27

Other_____

Primary Product Business buildings   31

EMPLOYEES AT
THIS ADDRESS: ☐ 1-10   ☐ 11-19   ☐ 20-49   ☐ 50-99   ☐ 100-249   ☐ 250-499   ☐ 500-999   ☐ over 1000

1G Stroking Technique Practice *type the lines as shown*

SPACING CUE: Space once after ; when it is used as a mark of punctuation.

Stroking Cue: Snap the finger quickly toward the palm of the hand as you release the key.

1	Home keys	ask a lad; a lad asks dad; a fall fad; ask a lass;
2		ask a lad; a lad asks dad; a fall fad; ask a lass;

Return without spacing at end of line

DS

3	h e	she has jade; he has a safe lead; he seeks a deed;
4		she has jade; he has a safe lead; he seeks a deed;

DS

5	All keys	lease a hall; sell all desks; a shelf held a safe;
6		lease a hall; sell all desks; a shelf held a safe;

DS

7		he held a lead; she sells jade; he has had a sale;
8		he held a lead; she sells jade; he has had a sale;

1H Remove the Paper and Center the Carriage

──────── **TO REMOVE THE PAPER** ────────

1. Raise or pull forward the **paper bail (11)**.
2. Operate the **paper-release lever (16)** with your right hand.
3. Remove the paper with your left hand. Return the lever to its position (or leave it in forward position if so directed).

TO CENTER THE CARRIAGE

Depress **right carriage release (18)** and hold it down. *At the same time,* grasp the **right cylinder knob (19)** firmly and move carriage to center.

LESSON 2

2A Get Ready to Type *for each lesson in this section*

1. Move the typewriter so the front of the frame is even with the edge of the desk.
2. Adjust **paper guide (8)** and **paper bail (11)**.
3. Have **paper release (16)** engaged.
4. Set **line-space regulator (5)** on "1" for single spacing (SS).
5. Set the **left margin stop (7)** about 25 spaces to left of center of paper; move the **right margin stop (15)** to end of scale. *Note the numbers on the margin scale or* **paper-bail scale (11)** *for stop settings and use these stop settings for this lesson and remaining lessons of this section.*

2B Preparatory Practice *type the lines as shown*

Correct Typing Position: Sit erect; feet on the floor; wrists low and relaxed; fingers curved. (See illustration on page 2.)

Stroking Cue: Begin to type at a slow, even pace. Strike the keys sharply; release them quickly. Hold your eyes on the copy as you type.

1	Home keys	fj dk sl a; fd jk fds jkl fdsa jkl; asdf ;lkj a;sl
2		fj dk sl a; fd jk fds jkl fdsa jkl; asdf ;lkj a;sl

Eyes on copy as you return

DS

3	h e	hj ed he she shed hj ed held hall shall sell shell
4		hj ed he she shed hj ed held hall shall sell shell

DS

5	All keys taught	he fled; she leads; he has a desk; she sells jade;
6		he fled; she leads; he has a desk; she sells jade;

TS

Problem 3: Invoice with Ruled Columns

TENNESSEE SUPPLIERS, INC.

INVOICE

111 Aberdeen Road • Nashville, Tennessee 37205 • Telephone 615-321-9987

				Words
Sold to	Henderson and Sons 3001 Broad Street, South Chattanooga, TN 37401	Date March 17, 19--		7 12 18
		Our Order No. B-37126		
		Cust. Order No. CN-2097		20
Terms	2/10,n/30	Shipped Via Tennessee Transport		26

Quantity	Description	Unit Price	Total	Words
1	Steel card file	3.40	3.40	31
1	Tenfile check case	1.95	1.95	37
4	Foam rubber stamp pads	.80	3.20	44
1	Moderne ash stand	14.95	14.95	51
2	Trendline staplers	6.25	12.50	58 59
			36.00	60

Problem 4: Statement of Account

Statement of Account

Date June 1, 19--

To   Lawrence Appliance Co.
271 Commonwealth Avenue
Boston, MA 02115

Kramer-Cummins Corporation
597 Cumberland Avenue
Portland, Maine 04101
Telephone 891-6467

Words
3

7
12
16

Date	Items	Debits	Credits	Balance Due	Words
May 1	Balance			365.00	
4	Credit Memorandum #3324		125.50	239.50	20
9	Payment on account		239.50	00	28
23	Invoice #3379	721.00		721.00	35
25	Invoice #3401	255.05		976.05	42 48

2C Shifting for Capitals: Left Shift Key

LEARN: To type a capital letter controlled by a finger of the right hand, as **H**, depress the **left shift key (28)** with the *left fourth (little) finger* without moving the other fingers from typing position. Hold the shift key down until the key for the capital has been *struck and released*; then release the shift key and return the finger to typing position quickly.

Tryout Drill. Study the illustration; then watch your left hand to see that it does not move out of position as you type **Hal** three times: Hal Hal Hal then type the following lines:

```
Ha Ja Ka La Ha Hal Ja Jake Ka Kahl La Ladd Ha Hall
                                                  DS
La Lake Ka Kale Ja Jade Ha Hale Jeff Leff Les Hess
                                                  TS
```

2D Continuity Practice

DO: Type each line twice, single-spaced (SS); then double-space (DS) before typing the next line. To double-space when the line-space regulator is set for single spacing, operate the return *twice*.

SPACING RULE: Space once after ; when it is used as a mark of punctuation except that you will make the return without spacing if ; is the last stroke in the line.

1 *All letters taught are used*   Ha Hale Hall Ja Jake Jeff La Ladd Ka Kale Les Jess   *Return without looking up*

2   Hal leads; Jeff led all fall; Hal has a safe lead;

3   Lee led; Les fled; Jeff had a sale; he sells jade;

4 *Type on—one key at a time; do*   Jake feels he has a safe lease; Jeff seeks a deed;

5 *not pause or stop*   Hal Hall heads all sales; Jake Hess asks less fee;

6   Les Kade has had a fall sale; he has a sales lead;

7   Lee held a jade sale; Hal Leeds seeks a safe deal;

2E Know Your Typewriter

LEARN: The first line illustrated below and at the right is in *elite* type; the second, in *pica* type. Look at *your* typed lines. Does your typewriter have *pica* type? or *elite* type?

```
12 elite spaces to a horizontal inch

10 pica spaces to a horizontal inch
```

LEARN: *Center Point*, 50 for elite; 42 for pica.

Tryout Drill. Remove the paper from the machine. Place the left and right edges together. Make a slight crease at the exact center at the top.

```
12 elite spaces to a horizontal inch
```

1		2		3	
1		2		3	

```
10 pica spaces to a horizontal inch
```

Reinsert the paper with the center at 50 for elite type or at 42 for pica type (unless your instructor directs you to use another center point).

Move the paper guide against the left edge of the paper. Check to see that it is in this position at the beginning of each practice period.

Tabulated Business Forms

Use printed forms if they are available, or half sheets of paper with the typewritten material arranged as it would be on printed forms. *Do not type the headings that would ordinarily be printed on the forms.*

Number of Copies. At least two copies (an original and a carbon) are made of invoices, credit memorandums, and similar forms. As a rule, single copies are made of statements of account.

Tabulator Mechanism. Make full use of the tabulator mechanism to insure proper alignment of figures in the columns and to speed up your work. For a column of numbers, set a tabulator stop at the point that requires the least forward and backward spacing. Space forward for short amounts; backspace for long amounts.

Abbreviations. Periods may be omitted after abbreviations, and they may be omitted in columnar tabulations of figures where the ruling separates the dollars from the cents. It is customary to use abbreviations such as *gal., ft., ea., %* for *percent,* @ for *at,* C for *hundreds,* M for *thousands,* # for *No.,* and other similar special abbreviations. Names of months may be abbreviated when limited space on the form makes this desirable.

Spacing. Single-space invoices, statements, and similar forms (such as credit memorandums, purchase requisitions, purchase orders, etc.) unless you have three or fewer lines, in which case use double spacing. Many companies require business forms to be typed with double spacing.

For business forms having items that require more than one line for the description, type the description on successive lines (single-space and indent the second line 3 spaces).

Items in Columns. There is no hard-and-fast rule on spacing data in columns. Generally, the longest line in each column, except the one in which the items are listed or described, is centered by eye measurement under the column heading. Centering by exact methods is not required or recommended. Begin the description items about 2 spaces to the right of the ruled line.

Problem 2: Purchase Order with Ruled Columns

LESSON 3

3A Get Ready to Type ⑤*

Review Get Ready to Type, page 5:

1. Align machine with edge of desk.
2. Adjust paper guide.
3. Insert paper; adjust paper bail.
4. Set machine for SS (on "1").

5. Set margin stops at the numbers noted on the scale when you set machine for 2B, page 5 (25 spaces to left of center and at the end of the scale).

*A time schedule for the parts of this lesson and following ones is given as a guide for your minimum practice. If time permits, retype selected lines from various drills.

3B Preparatory Practice ⑦ *each line twice*

DO: Type the first line twice SS (single-spaced); DS (double-space), then type the next line twice; DS and type the final line twice.

Stroking Cue: Type with a light, quick motion and with the finger pulled slightly toward the palm of the hand as the key is released.

```
a; sl a;sl fj dk fjdk ed hj edhj Ha Ja Ka La Ha He     Return quickly

he she held all hall jell sell dell heed feel seek
```
Space once
after ;
```
Hal fell; Lee led all; Jeff Hall held a fall sale;
```

3C Stroking Technique for I and T ⑩ *each line twice SS; DS after second typing of line*

I

T

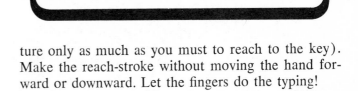

Reach the *right second finger* up to **i**; lift the first finger slightly for improved stroking control.

Straighten the *left first finger* slightly and reach up to **t** without arching the wrist or moving the hand forward.

Curved Fingers. Keep the fingers curved and in home-key position except when a reach-stroke is to be made; then extend the controlling finger (relaxing the curva-

ture only as much as you must to reach to the key). Make the reach-stroke without moving the hand forward or downward. Let the fingers do the typing!

Tryout Drills

i
```
k i ik if is his did side like life fill said file
```

t
```
f t tf at let set the tell take tale last that ate
```

i t
```
i t it fit its this list still; if it is; if I did
```
All reach-strokes
taught are used
```
I had a list; Keith has left his list at the lake;
```

SUPPLEMENTARY PROJECT ▶ SPECIAL COMMUNICATION FORMS

(Prepare an original copy of each form.)

Interoffice Correspondence

An interoffice letterhead form is used for correspondence between offices or departments of a company. Printed headings on the form enable the typist to set up information quickly. *If an interoffice form is not available, type the direction headings* (TO:, FROM:, etc.) *in positions similar to those illustrated in Problem 1 below.*

Omissions in Interoffice Correspondence. Personal titles (*Mr., Mrs., Dr., Miss,* etc.), salutation, complimentary close, and signature are usually omitted.

Margins; Spacing. One-inch side margins are used. Short messages may be double-spaced; longer ones are single-spaced with a double space between paragraphs. Triple-space between last line of heading and first line of message body.

Reference Initials; Notations. Type reference initials a double space below the last line of the message at the left margin. All other notations (enclosure, carbon copy, etc.) are typed in the same position they occupy in regular correspondence.

Envelopes for Interoffice Correspondence. Envelopes of a special color may be used for interoffice correspondence. When such envelopes are not used, type the words COMPANY MAIL in the space normally used for the postage stamp.

Use a personal title with the name when addressing the envelope. Type the address on two lines, unless the envelope is to go to a company office in some other city, in which case the complete address must be typed. Note the way to type an envelope used for interoffice correspondence. ▶

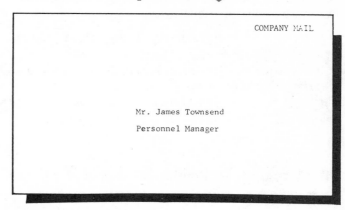

Problem 1: Interoffice Memorandum on Chain Feeding Envelopes

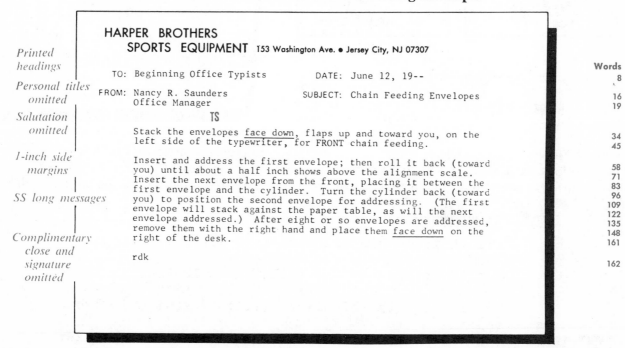

3D Stroking Technique for C and . (Period)

(10) *each line twice SS;*
DS after second typing of line

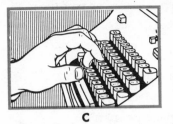

C

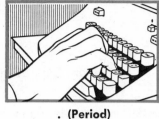

. (Period)

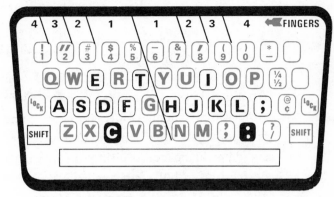

Reach down to **c** with the *left second finger* without twisting the elbow in or out or moving the hand down.

Extend the *right third finger* down to type **.** (period) without moving the hand downward or the elbow outward.

SPACING RULE: Space once after **.** (period) used at the end of an abbreviation; twice after **.** at the end of a sentence, except when it is the last stroke in the line; then return without spacing.

Tryout Drills

c	d c dcd cd cash call case lack deck each face sick
.	l . l.l .l adj. del. La. Ill. Lt. Jeff set a date.
c .	Jack called. He is sick. Lt. Heck has his check.
Review	Keith has cashed the checks. Jack is at his desk.

3E Continuity Practice (18) *each line twice SS; DS after second typing of line*

Home-Row Stroking: Strike each key firmly, release it quickly, and pull the finger toward the palm of the hand.

Third-Row Stroking: Reach to the third row (just above home row) with the finger without arching the wrist or moving the hand forward.

First-Row Stroking: Make the reach to the first (bottom) row without swinging the elbow out or changing the hand alignment.

All keyboard characters taught are used.

1	h and e	he she shed shelf heads shall fee feed feeds feels	Return without pausing
2	i and t	it is; he hit it; he is still ill; take this list;	
3	c and .	all call cash check chief cite each adj. etc. Ill.	
4	All letters taught are in Lines 4-8	I shall take the deed. I see Jack lists the cash.	
5		I see Keith is at his desk. Kit has a shelf safe.	
6		Let Jack take the file. He has set the lease fee.	
7		Kit Hale has a late date. Jeff has the last list.	
8		Lt. Keith said he cashed the checks that Kit left.	

TS

Problem 6: Report Manuscript

Side margins: 1½" left, 1" right;
top margin: 1½" pica, 2" elite

Type the following copy as a two-page leftbound manuscript.

Prepare a carbon copy. Erase and correct errors as you type.

Words

THE RETURN OF MAN | 4

At 10:42 a.m. (EST) Saturday, December 21, 1968, from Cape Kennedy, Florida, | 19
Apollo 8 burst the bonds of earth, riding a mighty Saturn 5 rocket and carrying | 35
American astronauts Borman, Lovell, and Anders into interplanetary space on man's | 51
first voyage around the moon.[1] At 10:51 a.m. (EST) the following Friday, after | 67
six days in space (orbiting the moon ten times), the Apollo 8 astronauts blazed | 83
perfectly to a bull's-eye predawn splashdown about a thousand miles from Honolulu | 100
and only 2½-3 miles from the aircraft carrier U.S.S. Yorktown, the pickup vessel. | 116
The astronauts were safe, sound, and happy at the end of the half-million-mile | 132
Christmas journey, an odyssey unprecedented in the annals of man.[2] Man had indeed | 149
gone to the "forbidding, desolate moon" and returned safely to the "good earth." | 165

In their six-day voyage, the Apollo 8 crew established a flock of new space- | 180
travel records, including: | 186

1. First men to travel so far from earth (233,000 miles) SS | 197
2. First men to enter moon's gravitational pull SS | 207
3. First men to orbit moon and see its back side SS | 217
4. A new speed record for man (nearly 25,000 mph)[3] | 227

Not since the voyage of Columbus (epitomizing the Renaissance) has any single | 243
exploration done so much to enlarge the horizons of man. But aside from the fact | 259
that this epic achievement will be celebrated for as long as men honor the bravery | 276
and skill of other men, we earthlings can only guess at the long-range significance | 293
of the flight. | 296

The central lesson of Apollo 8 seems clear and unmistakable, however: If man | 311
can elevate his moral and ethical concepts to reach his scientific achievements, | 327
then no problems of famine, disease, or war are insoluble. The central difficulty | 344
in solving these human problems is that a relatively limited number of thinkers and | 361
technicians working with sophisticated electronic computers and mechanical devices | 378
are not sufficient to create an equally needed public conscience. Only education | 394
can do that––from kindergarten through college. Such education must be provided | 410
by an army of teachers who are capable of harmonizing an idealistic philosophy with | 427
a realistic understanding of and point of view toward the problems in relation to | 443
our economic, political, and technical ability to solve them. | 456

| 459

---

[1] The Cincinnati Post and Times–Star (December 21, 1968), p. 1. | 479

[2] Ibid. (December 27, 1968), p. 1. | 487

[3] Fred M. Harmon, "The Great Triumph in Space," U.S. News & World Report, | 506
Vol. 66, No. 1 (January 6, 1969), p. 9. | 514

● Self-Improvement Practice

DO: Type the first line twice SS; then DS and type the next lines in the same way.

Return Cue: Return without spacing after the last stroke in the line; begin next line immediately.

```
1        he she the aid did is his it hit let jet tile till

2        as has led lead head each teach at ate hate checks

3        face late last desk sees fate heed seed this scale

4        last all fall ice side less fit add like fell tell

5        case call fill life list still skid had field felt

6        fill the case; he let it fall; each has had a desk
```

LESSON 4

4A Get Ready to Type ⑤

Follow steps in Get Ready to Type, page 5. Center the paper; set the left margin stop 25 spaces to the left of the center of the paper for the beginning of a 50-space line; move right stop to end of scale.

4B Preparatory Practice ⑦ *each line twice SS; DS after second typing of line*

All letters taught are used

```
a;sl edhj tfik cd.l it fits he she sick deck still

Jeff called; Lee is ill.  Jed cashed these checks.      Space quickly

I shall take the case.  I see Jeff heads the list.
```

4C Stroking Technique Practice ⑮ *each line twice SS; DS after second typing of line*

First-Row Stroking: When typing a key in the first (lowest) row, make a direct finger reach without swinging the elbow out or changing the hand alignment with the keyboard.

Third-Row Stroking: When typing a key in the third (third from bottom) row, reach with the finger without arching the wrist or moving the hand forward. Snap the finger toward the palm of the hand.

All letters taught are used.

1	Curve your fingers	`he flies a jet; he feels ill; she had aid; he held`	Eyes on copy as you return
2	Strike and release quickly	`cite the date; he leads the class; face this side;`	
3		`it sticks; if she dials it; the chief has the file`	
4		`Kit takes the checks; Jake seeks a safe cash deal.`	
5	Shift firmly	`Jeff called it a chief skill; Keith has the facts.`	
6		`Jack called.  I had his list.  Kit cashed a check.`	
7		`Lee said Lt. Hill left the chief file at his desk.`	

Problem 4: Business Letter

Modified block; blocked ¶s; mixed punctuation; line: 60; date on Line 16; 2 cc's; correct errors; envelope

Note. A color bar (|) has been given to aid you in arranging the opening and closing lines.

	Words
January 4, 19--	Mrs. Kathryn Townsend	John Marshall Junior High School		14
Noble and Marion Streets	Houston, TX 77009	Dear Mrs. Townsend:	27

After many years of extensive research and study by eminent scientists throughout	44
the world, we are pleased to announce the publication of our richly illustrated	60
series	61

THE MYSTERIES OF THE EARTH — 66

This series was designed especially for junior high school students. The text	82
has been written in easy, concise language so the ideas can be grasped quickly	98
by young students. Your students will find this series exciting and interesting.	115

We are sure you will want this series for your library. We are, therefore, send-	131
ing you, free of charge, a copy of the first volume. Examine it carefully; then	147
order the series quickly so you will have the books for the beginning of your	163
next school year.	166

Sincerely yours,	J. Mark Atkinson	Assistant Sales Manager	*your initials*		179
cc Dr. Elwood J. Foley, Principal	185

Problem 5: Table

Reading position on full sheet; 4 spaces between columns; SS each pair of lines; DS between pairs of lines

Center the columnar headings over the longest line in each column. Prepare a carbon copy; correct errors.

Words

DAY-BY-DAY LOG OF APOLLO 8 — 5

(December 21-27, 1968) — 10

Activity	EST	Date	Words
Blastoff from Cape Kennedy	7:51 a.m.	December 21	26
Left earth's gravity for moon	10:41 a.m.	December 21	37
Passed the midpoint of flight	3:08 a.m.	December 22	47
First live telecast from spacecraft	3:01 p.m.	December 22	58
Second telecast from spacecraft	2:58 p.m.	December 23	69
Entered moon's gravitational field	3:30 p.m.	December 23	80
Engine fired to drop craft into orbit	4:05 a.m.	December 24	92
Telecast on ninth orbit of moon	9:31 p.m.	December 24	102
Engine fired to boost craft out of orbit	1:10 a.m.	December 25	115
Fifth TV transmission from spacecraft	4:15 a.m.	December 25	126
Made midcourse correction	7:09 a.m.	December 26	136
Final live telecast from spacecraft	3:52 p.m.	December 26	147
Spacecraft reentered earth's atmosphere	10:41 a.m.	December 27	160
Splash down in Pacific off Honolulu	10:51 a.m.	December 27	171

4D Shifting for Capitals: Right Shift Key ⑧

LEARN: To type a capital letter controlled by a finger of the left hand, as **A**, depress the **right shift key (26)** with the *right fourth (little) finger*. Hold the shift key down until the key for the capital has been *struck and released*; then release the shift key and return the finger to typing position without pausing.

Tryout Drill. Study the illustration. Watch your right hand to see that it does not move out of position as you type **Alf** three times: Alf Alf Alf then type the following lines twice each:

```
Al Sl Al Diehl Di Fl Dick Flack El Taft Ceil Slade
                                                   DS
Alf has the list.  Seth is sick.  Cal called Dick.
```

4E Continuity Practice ⑮ *each line twice SS; DS after second typing of line*

Continuity Cue: Begin to type at a slow, even pace. Increase your stroking rate gradually. Move from one letter to the next without pausing.

Shift-Key Cue: Hold the shift key down firmly until the capital letter is typed; then release the shift key and return the finger to home position.

All reach-strokes taught are used.

1   he held the dial; file each lease; date this side;   Hold the wrists low

2   a fast field; he cites the fact; Dee fits it least

3   if I see; she had a safe lead; Ed heads his class;

4   The staff sheet is late; Dick still takes the cash

5 Shift firmly Jack steals the last act. I shall tell his staff.

6   Ceil has a check. Kit said it. Jeff flies a jet.

● Self-Improvement Practice *each line twice SS; DS after second typing of line*

Stroking Cue: Type with easy, rhythmic stroking. Move from letter to letter without pausing between strokes.

Space-Bar Cue: Operate the space bar with a short, quick, down-and-in thumb stroke in rhythm with the typing without pausing between words.

All letters taught are used.

1 Relax—but   Dick held a jade sale at Delf Lake late last fall.
   don't slouch

2   Cliff asked Seth if he had set the last test date.

3   This is the file case that Cal let Lee Leith take.

4   Fae Dahl said Jack has left the test at Lake Heid.

5   Jack has the file that Cal said he left last fall.

Problem 1: Memo Announcement

Use a half sheet; line: 60; top margin: 1½". Correct your errors as you type memo at the right.

Problem 2: Card Announcement

Type the message of Problem 1 as a postal card announcement. Type the talk title in cap and lower-case letters enclosed in quotation marks as part of the final sentence of ¶ 1. As a signature line use Ron Allen, PDK Secretary. Use your college residence address for the card address.

January 3, 19-- 3

A distinguished educator, Dr. Raymond S. McNeil of Educational Technology, Inc., will be the speaker at the next regular meeting of Phi Delta Kappa. His subject will be

11
20
30
37

INSTRUCTIONAL STRATEGIES 42

The meeting will be on Wednesday, February 15, at 4:30 p.m. in the Little Theater of the Cathedral of Learning. Be certain to hear this eminent scholar.

51
60
69
73

Problem 3: Personal Letter

Prepare a corrected copy of the following letter. Use modified block style; blocked ¶s; mixed punctuation; line: 60; *date* on Line 16. Prepare a carbon copy. Address a small envelope. Correct your errors as you type. **Note.** The use of parentheses with "Miss" or "Mrs." in a typewritten signature is optional.

Words

2920 Scioto Hall 3
Cincinnati, Ohio   45219 8
January 3, 19-- 11

College

L.
Mr. Paul Ritchie 15
~~School~~ of Education 20
University of Cincinnati 25
Cincinnati, Ohio 45219 29

Dear Mr. Ritchie: 33

My word record for the month of December is given below. It includes time spent typing course outlines and lecture notes as well as time devoted to reading final examinations.

45
58
69

December 10	2 hours	73
December 11	3 hours	77
December 14	8 hours	81
December 16	5 hours	85
December 17	6 hours	89

Since I shall be doing full-time student teaching next quarter and will not often be on campus, will you please have my check mail to me at the address shown above?

101
114
122

I appreciate the opportunity very much of working with you as a teaching and office assistant. That experience will be almost as valuable, I believe, as my student teaching activity.

135
147
160

Sincerely yours, 163

Miss Mary Riga 166

5A Get Ready to Type ③ *use standard procedure, page 5*

5B Know Your Typewriter ②

LEARN: The **ribbon-control lever (22)** can be set to type on the upper, middle, or lower part of the ribbon if there are four adjustments on the typewriter for this control. If there are just three adjustments, the typing will be on the upper or lower part of the ribbon. When the lever is set in stencil position, the ribbon is disengaged. This position is used to type stencils.

DO: Set the ribbon-control lever to type on the upper part of the ribbon.

5C Preparatory Practice ⑦ *each line twice SS; DS after second typing of line*

DO: As you type the line the first time, note the awkward or difficult letter combinations. In the next writing of the line, try to smooth out the typing pace so you can type with continuity. Type a letter; turn loose of it; and type the next letter. Get rid of typing jerks or pauses; just keep on typing.

All letters taught are used in each line.

if it is; she called; Cliff sells jade; I like it.   Eyes on copy

Cal let Lee take all the jade; he is at Fell Lake.

Dick said that Cliff let Jack Hill take the files.

5D Stroking Technique for O and R ⑩ *each line twice SS; DS after second typing of line*

O

R

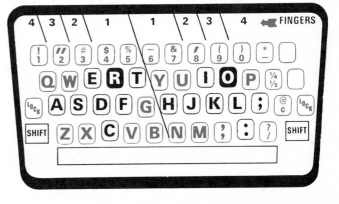

Reach the *right third finger* up to type **o** without moving the hand forward or the elbow outward.

Reach the *left first finger* to **r** without moving the other fingers from home-key positions.

Tryout Drills

o   l o lol so do to old sold fold told cold took look

r   f r frf air far sir are car cars heard clear chair

o   r   or for cord road rock role frock force chord floor

Review Carl Ford left the horse for Dr. Rod Cole to ride.

LESSON 75

75A   Preparatory Practice ⑤ *each line twice; then 1' writings on Line 4*

Alphabet   Jack Hibler may request the new ZIP Codes from Gwen Jevon next Monday.

Figures   Pay Invoice No. J2148375, but be sure to deduct Credit Memo No. C6490.

Figure-symbol   This 9- by 12-foot carpet is marked $587 but sells for $463 this week.

Fluency   He is aware of the unusual contract to be awarded the big trade union.

    | 1 | 2 | 3 | 4 | 5 | 6 | 7 | 8 | 9 | 10 | 11 | 12 | 13 | 14 |

75B   Skill-Comparison Typing ⑦ *each line for a 1' writing; compare gwam*

Balanced-hand   The six girls may go to the city to work with the auditor of the firm.

Double letters Ella was puzzled by the letter that followed the offer of a free book.

Adjacent keys   I saw Lew Polk strike out on a pop fly, but he still leads all others.

One-hand   Rated only average, my test car drew no awards in a few races at Lynn.

Row 1   Zeal or zest can bring much more success next time than luck ever can.

Consecutive   To excel my gym record, Cecil must surpass my skill in the broad jump.

    | 1 | 2 | 3 | 4 | 5 | 6 | 7 | 8 | 9 | 10 | 11 | 12 | 13 | 14 |

75C   Growth Index ⑧ *DS one 5' writing; determine gwam and errors*

All letters are used.

		1'	5'	
¶ 1 1.4 SI 5.4 AWL 85% HFW	Will you be a dropout, or will you hang tight and finish college?	13	3	45
	A high percentage of students who enter college do not stay to complete	28	6	48
	a degree. A majority of these leave college during the first year or	42	8	50
	two after entry. Most of those who make it through the first two years	56	11	53
	manage to stay with it until they have met all diploma requirements.	70	14	56
¶ 2 1.4 SI 5.4 AWL 85% HFW	Students give a wide variety of reasons for dropping out of school.	14	17	59
	Among them are marriage, lack of money, and desire for a well-paying	28	19	61
	job. Not so often given but just as real are: not seeing how the	41	22	64
	courses being offered prepare for life goals, not adjusting to a new	55	25	67
	kind of society, and not getting passing grades in all courses.	67	27	69
¶ 3 1.4 SI 5.4 AWL 85% HFW	Are you content with college now and pleased with all you have so	13	30	72
	far accomplished? If not, compare your personal goals with the aims	27	33	75
	of the program of courses you are now pursuing. If the two don't mesh,	41	36	78
	try some other program before you give up. The prize of success and	55	38	80
	satisfaction may be as near as the next section of the general catalog	69	41	83
	of your college.	73	42	84

1' GWAM | 1 | 2 | 3 | 4 | 5 | 6 | 7 | 8 | 9 | 10 | 11 | 12 | 13 | 14 |
5' GWAM | 1 | 2 | 3 |

75D   Problem Typing Measurement ㉚ *continue typing the problems on pages 131-133*

5E Stroking Technique for Z and N ⑩ *each line twice SS; DS after second typing of line*

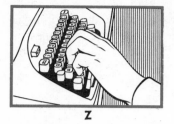

Z

N

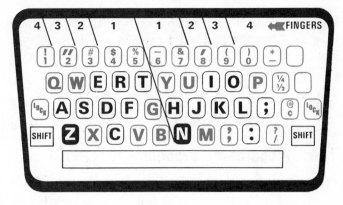

Reach the *left little finger* down to type **z** without moving the hand down or the elbow in or out.

Move the *right first finger* down to type **n** without moving the other fingers from their home keys.

SPACING SUMMARY: Space once after . (period) used at the end of an abbreviation; do not space after . within an abbreviation; space twice after . used to punctuate a sentence; and once after ; (semicolon) used as punctuation. At the end of the line, make the return without spacing after the final stroke whether this is a mark of punctuation or a letter.

Tryout Drills

z   a z aza za zeal haze size daze jazz raze doz. doze

n   j n jnj an can and hand not note once think chance

z n   Zoe has lots of zeal and zest; this drill is done.

Review   Dr. Nietz is in this first zone. The zoo is near.

5F Continuity Practice ⑱ *each line twice SS; DS after second typing of line*

Continuity Cue: Type at a steady pace without pausing between strokes, words, or lines.

Stroking Cue: Type with your fingers and with minimum hand or arm motion. Use snappy strokes.

All reach-strokes taught are used.

1   to do so; of the code; took a loss; food does cost

2   it is hers; take her car; it is fair; if there are

3   the food fair is here; their stock is off; too far

4   it is here to do; take her to the fair; do so here

5   an old hand; a size ten; in the end zone; seize it

6   The hard freeze forced the school to close at ten.

7   Roz and Liz think this last act has a fine chance.

8   Zahn had it sent there C.O.D. Jake left at three.

SECTION ▶12◀ MEASUREMENT: Basic and Problem Skills

LESSONS 74–75

Purpose. The purpose of this section of two lessons is to measure the basic and problem skills you have developed as well as your knowledge of problem layout and machine manipulations.

Machine Adjustments. Unless otherwise directed, use a 70-space line and SS. Be alert to required changes in line length and spacing in the measurement portions of the lessons.

LESSON 74

74A   Preparatory Practice ⑤ *each line twice; then 1′ writings on Line 4*

Alphabet	Helga Veek expects just as sizable a drop in my new quota as in Fay's.
Figures	Process the following orders immediately: M127485, M304621, and N219.
Figure-symbol	Invoices #B4178 and #L3956 (less 2%) require a net payment of $697.40.
Fluency	They may award the contract to a downtown auditor at the minimum rate.

| 1 | 2 | 3 | 4 | 5 | 6 | 7 | 8 | 9 | 10 | 11 | 12 | 13 | 14 |

74B   Growth Index ⑩ *DS one 5′ writing; then 1′ writings as time permits*

All letters are used.

	GWAM 1′	GWAM 5′

¶ 1
1.4 SI
5.4 AWL
85% HFW

You have learned a great deal about typing in only a few months. You may not be striking all keys as rapidly or as precisely yet as you want to, but you have begun a sturdy foundation upon which you can build even more skill. Like any other skill, typing demands continued effort to be maintained or improved; so set aside daily practice time.

13	3	44
27	5	47
41	8	49
55	11	52
69	14	55

¶ 2
1.4 SI
5.4 AWL
85% HFW

If you proceed with the typing sequence in college, your practice time will be scheduled for you. Even so, you will find that a bit of extra practice each day may be just enough to push your new skill into a prize grade category. Even if you do not continue with formal typing instruction, you can add greatly to your skill all by yourself.

13	16	58
27	19	61
41	22	63
56	25	66
68	27	69

¶ 3
1.4 SI
5.4 AWL
85% HFW

A timed effort is superior to an untimed one. Timing supplies a little desirable pressure; it also helps to inform you just how well you are doing. In school, your teacher times you. If you practice on your own, you ought to work under time pressure then, too. A timing record or tape is an effective device to use for this very fine purpose.

13	30	71
27	33	74
41	36	77
55	38	80
69	41	83

1′ GWAM | 1 | 2 | 3 | 4 | 5 | 6 | 7 | 8 | 9 | 10 | 11 | 12 | 13 | 14 |
5′ GWAM | 1 | 2 | 3 |

74C   Problem Typing Measurement ㉟

Get Ready to Type . . . . 4′
Timed Production . . . . 25′
Final Proofreading . . . . 6′

Supplies Needed: half sheet, 1; postal card, 1; letterhead, 1; full sheets, 4

Turn to page 131 and begin to type the problems given there. When time is called, complete the line you are typing, remove the paper from the machine, and retain all your work. In Lesson 75 you will continue with the problems at the point you stopped in Lesson 74. *Erase and correct all errors as you type.*

● **Self-Improvement Practice** *each line twice SS; DS after second typing of line*

TYPING DOUBLE LETTERS / Nonelectric: Use a short, quick stroke. Do not allow full return of the key between strokes. **Electric:** Allow time for the key to return to position before striking it again.

TYPING ONE-HAND WORDS: Type by stroke response (one letter at a time) but pass from one letter to the next quickly. Speed up the typing by eliminating the pauses between strokes.

All letters taught are used.

1	Double letters	soon took fool tool root cook door cool noon floor
2	One-hand, double-letter words	see seed ill hill feed kill tree hook freed street
3	One-hand words	in as no at on are oil far kin set nil car ink add
4	Drill on z	zest size zone haze zinc raze daze fizz jazz sized
5	Drill on o and n	to do on no nor not note ton tone in kind one torn

LESSON 6

6A Get Ready to Type ③ *use standard procedure, page 5*

6B Preparatory Practice ⑦ *each line twice SS; DS after second typing of line*

All reaches
taught are
used

Liz called; Ron heard her. Ed thinks Jan is fine.

in it; as on; to do so; can find; Roz can find it;

o r n

Fritz and Frank North do not like to ride at noon.

6C Stroking Technique Practice ⑮ *twice as shown*

Lines 1–2. Adjacent-key controls, such as **tr, oi, re**, and the like, need special attention. *Think* each letter vigorously.

Lines 3–4. Make a direct reach from **c** to **e**, **e** to **c**, and the like, without returning the controlling finger to home position.

Lines 5–6. Use a short, quick stroke. Center the stroking action in the fingers. Do not pause between strokes or between words.

All reach-strokes taught are used.

1	Adjacent	has said are her soil coil short trade heads sales
2	keys	Kier has a fine tire on sale; it has a safe tread.
		DS
3	Direct	once force checks led deal lot old sold kits likes
4	reaches	Zach liked all the desks. Ceil checked each once.
5	Double	off add look fall need less staff loss steel skill
6	letters	He took a loss on the steel desk and lost the fee.
7	Speed-up	if it is he to do so or for the tie did then field
8	words	Jan lent a hand to Ken. Rod did it for Sid Field.

LESSON 73

73A Preparatory Practice ⑤ *each line twice; then 1' writings on Line 4*

Alphabet Vaughn Dixon acquired the prize job with a large firm just like yours.

Figures Order 25 each of Cat. Nos. 273J, 596C, 3140V, and 836M from Eban, Inc.

Figure-symbol Send payment notices on these accounts: #4128, $57.90; #6329, $84.50.

Fluency Hand the proxy statement to the chairman so their title can be signed.
| 1 | 2 | 3 | 4 | 5 | 6 | 7 | 8 | 9 | 10 | 11 | 12 | 13 | 14 |

73B Basic Operations Checkup ⑬

1. **Centering Vertically and Horizontally.** Center the following announcement vertically and each line horizontally on a half sheet (8½" by 5½"). Use double spacing.

BUSINESS-ECONOMICS CLUB

Regular Monthly Meeting

January 23, 3 p.m.

Royce Hall, Room 132

Speaker: Dr. L. N. Reeves

Topic: "Business in Education"

2. **Centering on Special-Size Paper.** Insert a half sheet with the long side at the left. Center the announcement of Item 1 again both vertically and horizontally. Use *triple* spacing and place the copy in *reading* position.

3. **Centering on a Postal Card.** DS and center the Item 1 announcement vertically and horizontally on a postal card (or paper cut 5½" x 3¼").

4. **Centering Columnar Headings.** First, on a half sheet, type the 3 columnar entries shown below, leaving 8 spaces between them. Then center the following headings over Columns 1, 2, and 3, respectively:

Advertising Medium	1960	1970
Radio-Television Spots	$ 75,000	$100,000

5. **Listening for the Bell; Word Division.** Use a half sheet and double spacing. Set the margin stops for a 60-space line, adding 5 spaces to the right margin for the ringing of the bell. Be guided by the bell to return the carriage as you type the following paragraph. Use the margin release, and divide words as necessary to maintain a reasonably uniform right margin.

Listening for the typewriter bell as a guide for returning to start the new line requires that you know the fundamental guides for dividing words. Without this important knowledge, you are quite likely to have less-than-attractive right-hand margins.

73C Problem Layout Review ㉜

Supplies Needed: half sheets, 2; full sheets, 2; envelopes: large, 2; small, 1; letterheads, 2

Make a typewritten list of the problems listed at the right in order of textbook page number. Put the list in a convenient place for easy reference.

Type each problem as directed, except that you will prepare a carbon copy of each one and correct any errors you make as you type.

Problems To Be Typed

Page No.	Lesson Part No.	Problem No.
94–95	54C	2
101	57D	1
103	58D	2
104	59D	1
119	67D	—

6D Sentence Guided Writing ㉕

DO: Type each sentence three times without the guide. Increase the speed of stroking slightly when typing the sentence the second and third times.

DO: Type each sentence for a half minute. Pace your typing to complete the sentence in exactly a half minute (with the guide).

DO: Type each sentence as a 1' writing, trying to type the sentence twice. Your gross words a minute (*gwam*) are shown in Column 2 below.

Position Cue	Sit erect; feet on floor; fingers curved; wrists low.

Shift-Key Cue	Depress and hold shift key down firmly until capital letter has been typed.

All reach-strokes taught are used.

		Words in Line*	GWAM 30" Guide
1	Joe thinks I can do the drill.	6	12
2	Keith has laid all the tile he can.	7	14
3	Al can lend a hand to all those in need.	8	16
4	Zoe can teach Rod to dance; she said she can.	9	18
5	Ken has done one line of the drill for his friend.	10	20

| 1 | 2 | 3 | 4 | 5 | 6 | 7 | 8 | 9 | 10 |

---

*HOW TYPEWRITTEN WORDS ARE COUNTED

Five strokes are counted as one standard typewritten word. The figures in the first column at the right of the copy show the number of 5-stroke words in each of the lines. The scale beneath the copy shows the word-by-word count (5 strokes at a time) for each of the lines.

TO DETERMINE TOTAL WORDS TYPED

(1) List the figure at the end of each complete line typed during a writing. **(2)** Note in the scale the figure directly below the point at which you stopped typing. **(3)** Add these figures to determine the total gross words typed. (Gross words are the same as *gwam* for a 1-minute writing.)

● **Self-Improvement Practice**   *two or three times as shown*

All letters taught are used.

1 2	j and z	jet zinc jest zoo jazz join jade jot zeal oz. doz. Zeke joins their jet set for jazz at the lake zoo.
3 4	k and c	coke risk lack check stock clerk thanks think once Jack thinks a clerk needs to check the coke stock.
5 6	f and n	find facts off nine staff then front and of friend All the staff think Fran can find half of the ink.
7 8	Double letters	fell tell sell jell call tall hall soon tool class Nell can soon tell if the class did all the drill.

| 1 | 2 | 3 | 4 | 5 | 6 | 7 | 8 | 9 | 10 |

SECTION 11 ▶ REVIEW: Basic and Problem Skills

LESSONS 72–73

Purpose. The purpose of the two lessons of this section is to review the work of the preceding 71 lessons in preparation for the measurement activities of Section 12.

Machine Adjustments. Unless otherwise directed, use a 70-space line and SS. Be alert to required changes in line length and spacing in the checkup and review portions of the lessons.

LESSON 72

72A   Preparatory Practice ⑤ *each line twice; then 1' writings on Line 4*

Alphabet   Jud Vance says the quest for great power may take extra zeal by Irwin.
Figures   Our store has three locations: 38-40 Main; 2756 Oakland; 1396 Beamer.
Figure-symbol Jay insured his car, Engine #P41738295J, on Mutual Policy #A2134-J-67.
Fluency   She works with great vigor on the eight land forms for the city panel.
            | 1 | 2 | 3 | 4 | 5 | 6 | 7 | 8 | 9 | 10 | 11 | 12 | 13 | 14 |

72B   Basic Operations Checkup ⑬ *line: exactly 50; each item on a separate half sheet*

1. **Shift Keys and Shift Lock.** Begin on Line 10. DS the following paragraph:

    Dr. Gail Evans is the author of TEACHERS ALL. In addition, she has contributed numerous articles to the periodical <u>Modern Education</u>. Her latest is entitled "The Current Status of Auto-Instruction." She will lecture tonight at 8 p.m. in Hinkle Hall.

2. **Typing Outside the Margins.** Type on Line 17. Begin the sentence given below 7 spaces outside the left margin. When the bell rings, continue typing and complete the sentence on one line.

    Are you drinking at the fountain of knowledge or merely gargling?

3. **Typing Roman Numerals.** Begin on Line 8. DS the Roman numerals **I.** through **X.** in a column at the left margin.

4. **Margin Release and Backspacing.** Reset the left margin 4 spaces to the right. Begin on Line 12. SS the following numbered items; DS between them. Use the margin release and backspacer to position the numbers.

    1. Operate the margin release key, then backspace four times to type the number.
    2. Begin the second line of an enumerated item at the same point where the first line begins.

5. **Automatic Line Finder.** Reset the left margin for a 50-space line. Begin on Line 12. DS the following sentence, using the line finder (ratchet release) to type the superscripts and the subscripts.

    Decrease the temperature of the H_2SO_4 to 0° centigrade or 32° Fahrenheit.

6. **Aligning and Typing Over.** Reinsert the paragraph typed as Item 1; gauge the line and letter; type over the first and last lines.

72C   Problem Layout Review ㉜

Supplies Needed: half sheets, 2; postal cards, 2; full sheets, 1; small envelopes, 1

Make a typewritten list of the problems listed at the right in order of textbook page number. Put the list in a convenient place for easy reference.

Type each problem as directed, except that you will prepare a carbon copy of each one and correct any errors you make as you type.

Problems To Be Typed

Page No.	Lesson Part No.	Problem No.
59	34C	1
61–62	36C	2
70–71	41C	1, 3
87	51C	1

LESSON 7

7A Preparatory Practice ⑧ *each line twice SS; DS after second typing of line*

● Beginning with this lesson and for all following lessons, getting ready to type will be a part of typing the Preparatory Practice.

All letters taught   Jack took the disk; Fitz needs it to send to Carl.

Direct reaches   led sled ode code once check tried shirt free tree

Shifting   Jeff Stone and Jack Firth stood drill in the rain.
| 1 | 2 | 3 | 4 | 5 | 6 | 7 | 8 | 9 | 10 |

7B Sentence Guided Writing ⑤

DO: Type each of the following sentences as two 1' writings, or type each one three times if 1-minute timing is not used.

Reading Cue: Think and type the easy two-letter words, such as **to**, **do**, and **it**, as *words*. Think the word (not the letters) vigorously.

	Words in Line	GWAM 30" Guide
Jane is to aid Hale as soon as she can do so.	9	18
Tod can do the three lines of the drill for Keith.	10	20

| 1 | 2 | 3 | 4 | 5 | 6 | 7 | 8 | 9 | 10 |

7C Stroking Technique for U and W ⑩ *each line twice SS; DS after second typing of line*

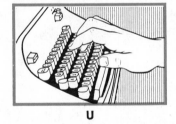

U

W

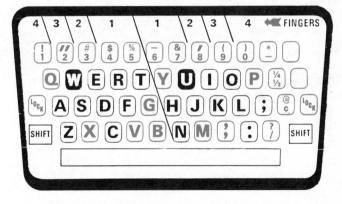

Reach the *right first finger* up to **u** without moving the other fingers from their home keys.

Reach the *left third finger* up to type **w** without moving the hand forward or arching the wrist.

Tryout Drills

u   j u juj us use due jut sue fun sun cut cue hue nut

w   s w sws wit with worn sworn how show sow sown when

u w   four sure just turn thus with work wish want would

Review   We know June wants to show the house to us at two.

	Words
duplicators, copiers, and calculators | 253
—the secretary uses regularly in her | 261
work. Others—punched-card equip- | 267
ment, tape-activated machines, and | 274
the electronic computer—may or | 281
may not be operated by the secre- | 287
tary, but they are important to her | 294
work.[4] | 296

Data processing is not a new process; it | 304
has been operating for centuries. Nor is the | 313
mechanical processing of data a new develop- | 322
ment. In fact, from the digital computer on | 331
his hands and feet, man has progressed | 339
through the abacus, the simple adding ma- | 347
chine, the electric calculator, and the elec- | 355
tronic calculator to the modern electronic | 364
computer. | 366

Increasing dependence upon data is a | 374
phenomenon of modern business. Information | 382
from all parts of an industrial complex are | 391
channeled into its central offices. Other data | 401
are researched and collected, statistics are | 410
organized into meaningful tables and graphs, | 419
and reports are prepared for others to study, | 428
evaluate, and act upon. Few areas offer the | 437
secretary greater opportunity to prove her | 446
value as an administrative assistant.[5] | 454

[1]E. Wainright Martin, Jr., Electronic Data Processing (Rev. ed.; Homewood, Illinois: Richard D. Irwin, Inc., 1965), p. 3. (*33 words*)

[2]Clarence B. Randall and Sally Weimer Burgley, Systems & Procedures for Business Data Processing (2d ed.; Cincinnati: South-Western Publishing Co., 1968), p. 79. (*42 words*)

[3]Data Processing Management Association, Automatic Data Processing (Englewood Cliffs, N.J.: Prentice-Hall, Inc., 1966), pp. 11-14. (*31 words*)

[4]J Marshall Hanna, Estelle L. Popham, and Esther K. Beamer, Secretarial Procedures and Administration (5th ed.; Cincinnati: South-Western Publishing Co., 1968), p. 428. (*44 words*)
[5]Ibid., p. 427. (*4 words*)

Problem 2: Outline

Half sheet, long side at left; line: 45; 1" top margin

	Words
PROCEDURES OF DATA HANDLING | 6
I. RECORDING DATA | 9
  A. Original Source Documents | 15
  B. Preparing Cards and Tapes | 21
II. CLASSIFYING DATA | 27
  A. Using Alphabetic Code | 32
  B. Using Numeric Code | 37
  C. Using Alphanumeric Code | 42
III. CREATING NEW DATA | 48
  A. Programming to Manipulate Data | 55
  B. Performing Arithmetic Operations | 63
    1. Addition | 66
    2. Subtraction | 70
    3. Multiplication | 75
    4. Division | 78
IV. SORTING DATA | 83
V. SUMMARIZING DATA | 88
  A. Consolidating Data | 92
  B. Providing for Information Retrieval | 100

Problem 3: Composing

Compose as you type in unbound manuscript form a two- or three-paragraph statement of your understanding of the effects of computers and automation on your chosen field of work. Proofread and correct your copy; then type a final copy using THE COMPUTER AND I as a heading.

● Self-Improvement Practice

If you complete the problem typing any day before the period ends, select from the following statements a topic for an interpretative composition.

For each topic selected, *compose as you type* one or two paragraphs giving your interpretation of the statement. If time permits, type a corrected copy.

1. The years teach much which the days never know. —Emerson

2. Thoughts are but dreams till their effects be tried. —Shakespeare

3. At any age, to be only a member of a group is to be less than a complete person. —Stoddard

4. Responsibility is the price every man must pay for freedom. —Hamilton

5. There are two kinds of fools. One says, "This is old, therefore it is good." The other says, "This is new, therefore it is better." —Inge

7D Stroking Technique for B and , (Comma) ⑩ *each line twice SS;*
DS after second typing of line

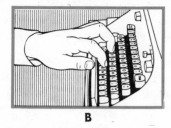

B　　　　**, (Comma)**

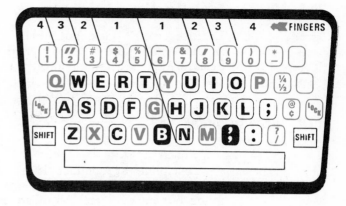

Reach the *left first finger* down to type **b** without moving the hand from its typing position.

Reach the *right second finger* down to type , (comma). *Space once after a comma in a sentence.*

Tryout Drills

b　　　f b fbf bid fib fob rob rib job fbf both born bond

,　　　k, k, Kit, Fitz, and Ken took the bus; I can, too.

b ,　　to be, we can be, on the job, be sure, it is best,

Review　Burt, not Bud, cashed the Club checks at the bank.

7E Continuity Practice ⑰

DO: Type the copy as shown except that you are to type the last line of each group twice, double spacing after the second typing of the line. If time permits, use Line 10 for as many 1' writings as possible. Type without hurry, but type!

Reach Cue: Keep the correct hand alignment with the keyboard. As you make the down reach to **,** or **b,** for example, let the finger make a short, low, direct movement to the key without twisting the hand or the elbow out of position.

All reach-strokes taught are used.

1		but we job cut our wish both work just debts would
2	w u b ,	if we knew, cut our dues, four jobs, back to work,
3		Buck wants a job with the new branch of this bank.
4		jot kind down or for zone size their line short in
5	o r n z	jot it down; he has ten stores; he is a trade czar
6		Liz went to France in June; Zoe can join her soon.
7		of just task off face joke silk act jest code free
8	j k c f	face the fact; just file it; of the code; act fast
9		Jack has to face the fact that the job takes work.
10	1' writings	Buzz does not need luck to win if he works to win.

| 1 | 2 | 3 | 4 | 5 | 6 | 7 | 8 | 9 | 10 |

LESSON 7　　　　　　**Section 1: Letter Keys**　　　　　　**16**

LESSON 71

71A Preparatory Practice ⑦ *each line three times; then 1' writings on Lines 3 and 4*

Alphabet   Laziness vexed Jack, but he built his physique by lifting more weight.
Figures   A survey on June 7, 1968, listed the population of the town at 23,540.
Figure-symbol   Serial #81547 was stamped on the engine; Model #2193 (R) was below it.
Fluency   Of the six major elements, I think the first is most important by far.

| 1 | 2 | 3 | 4 | 5 | 6 | 7 | 8 | 9 | 10 | 11 | 12 | 13 | 14 |

71B Growth Index ⑦ *a 5' writing; determine* gwam *and errors*

All letters are used.

		GWAM 1'	GWAM 5'

¶ 1
1.4 SI
5.4 AWL
85% HFW

Discipline of conduct is a condition of life that will be with us — 13 | 3 | 51
as long as we live. When we are children, our parents and our teachers — 28 | 6 | 54
guide our conduct and establish our discipline. A boy, for instance, who — 42 | 8 | 57
wishes to become an expert athlete must be made to discipline himself — 56 | 11 | 60
through daily practice and work to perfect his style. Also, a girl who — 71 | 14 | 63
has a desire to become a fine pianist must be urged to discipline her- — 85 | 17 | 65
self to follow set hours and methods of practice in order to do well. — 99 | 20 | 68

¶ 2
1.4 SI
5.4 AWL
85% HFW

As the years pass, however, each of us realizes more and more that — 13 | 22 | 71
the discipline must come from within. No longer can we depend upon our — 28 | 25 | 74
parents and teachers to goad us into appropriate action; we must employ — 42 | 28 | 77
our own self-discipline. To be successful in college, for example, we — 56 | 31 | 79
must develop good study habits and stay with them. To be a success in — 71 | 34 | 82
business, we must plan our own work and make that plan work. As we grow — 85 | 37 | 85
older, we must discipline ourselves to put work before personal enjoy- — 99 | 40 | 88
ment. There is a time for work and a time for play, and each requires — 113 | 42 | 91
its own discipline of conduct. Finally, the time comes when we must — 127 | 45 | 94
discipline ourselves to the freedoms as well as to the demands of our — 141 | 47 | 96
own old age. — 144 | 48 | 97

1' GWAM | 1 | 2 | 3 | 4 | 5 | 6 | 7 | 8 | 9 | 10 | 11 | 12 | 13 | 14 |
5' GWAM | 1   2   3 |

71C Problem Typing Measurement: Outline and Manuscript ㊱

Get Ready to Type	. . . .	2'
Timed Production	. . . .	30'
Final Proofreading	. . . .	4'

Problem 1: Two-Page Leftbound Manuscript

Full sheets; top margin: 1½"
pica; 2" elite; errors corrected

THE MACHINE AGE OFFICE   *Words* 5

Automation, which greatly increases 14
man's ability to use tools, and computers, 24
which multiply his ability to do mental work, 33
must rank with nuclear energy as the most 42
important developments of our age. Com- 50
puters were originally developed by scientists 59
and engineers to aid in the solution of prob- 68
lems involving large amounts of computation.[1] 77
Today, computers are being utilized in data 86
processing departments in business to the 94

                                Words

great benefit of everyone. This is true because 104
"the tremendous speed and accuracy of data 113
processing equipment make possible the pro- 121
duction of the myriad reports and documents 130
required in a modern business operation."[2] 139
Everyone in today's business world is af- 147
fected in some way by computers and elec- 155
tronic data processing. According to the Data 164
Processing Management Association, elec- 172
tronic data processing has become a necessary 181
and integral part of our existence.[3] Those who 191
work in business offices are affected by 199
mechanical and automated processes both 207
directly and indirectly. As an example, Hanna, 217
Popham, and Beamer point out: 223

      The modern office uses many 228
machines and facilities in processing 238
data. Some of them--typewriters, 246

● **Self-Improvement Practice** *each line three times SS; DS after third typing of line*

All reach-strokes taught are used.

Beth wrote a card to Nan and Sue, a note to Keith.

Dan said Ed is a whiz; and Jan, I know, thinks so.

A lad can be what he likes if he likes what he is.

It is their bid for the work. She held it for us.
| 1 | 2 | 3 | 4 | 5 | 6 | 7 | 8 | 9 | 10 |

LESSON 8

8A Preparatory Practice (8) *each line three times SS; DS after third typing of line*

All reach-strokes taught are used in the first line.

Bud, Tod, and Liz worked for an hour; so did Jack.

but who bad true blue when built black doubt board

We want to do all our work just as well as we can.
| 1 | 2 | 3 | 4 | 5 | 6 | 7 | 8 | 9 | 10 |

8B Tab Mechanism Control (12) *three times*

SETTING TABULATOR STOPS

1. Move the carriage as far to the left as possible.
2. Clear previous settings to eliminate false stops by depressing the **tab clear key (31)** as you pull the carriage all the way to the right. *To remove a single stop without canceling other stops, tabulate to the stop and* operate the tab clear key. *Smith-Corona and Olympia typewriters have a Total Tab Clear key that clears all stops at one time without moving the carriage.*
3. To set a tabulator stop, move the carriage to the desired position; then depress the **tab set key (23)**. Repeat this procedure for each stop needed.

TABULATING TECHNIQUE

Nonelectric (Manual) Machines: Depress and hold the tab bar (right first finger) or key (right fourth finger) down until the carriage has stopped.

Electric Machines: Flick the tab key lightly with the little finger; return the little finger to its home position at once.

SET TAB STOPS FOR THE DRILL:

1. Clear all tab stops. (See directions given above.)
2. For Column 2, set a tab stop 15 spaces from the left margin.
3. For Column 3, set a tab stop 15 spaces from first tab stop.
4. For Column 4, set a tab stop 16 spaces from second tab stop.

and	Tab	set	Tab	with	Tab	then
did		oil		work		wish
the		was		down		town
aid		ink		both		hand
wit		saw		lend		burn

Tab bar

Tab key

KEY | 3 | 12 | 3 | 12 | 4 | 12 | 4 |

LESSON 70

70A Preparatory Practice ⑦ *each line three times; then 1' writings on Lines 3 and 4*

Alphabet   Five quick zebras formed a phalanx, viewing a young jackal with alarm.

Figures   Invoice Nos. 4571 and 8692 were both paid last month by Check No. 301.

Figure-symbol   I am requesting 9 seats @ $2.60, 8 seats @ $3.20, and 7 seats @ $4.15.

Fluency   To look for the right job is far better than to look for just any job.

| 1 | 2 | 3 | 4 | 5 | 6 | 7 | 8 | 9 | 10 | 11 | 12 | 13 | 14 |

70B Technique Practice: Machine Manipulation ⑧ *each line at least three times*

Tabulator   automation ⟦5⟧ computers ⟦5⟧ probability ⟦5⟧ prediction ⟦5⟧ electronic

Shift lock   Order the magazine Saturday Review and two copies of the book ELECTRA.

Backspacer   Be careful of your use of Ibid., loc. cit., and op. cit. in footnotes.

Ratchet release   Raise the temperature of the H_2O to 212°; lower the H_2SO_4 to just 72°.

Margin release   It is not enough to think that you can; you must take the next step and prove it.

| 1 | 2 | 3 | 4 | 5 | 6 | 7 | 8 | 9 | 10 | 11 | 12 | 13 | 14 |

70C Skill-Transfer Typing ⑤ *each paragraph repeated for a 1' writing; compare gwam*

	1' GWAM

Straight copy
        Striking the keys when you type is not the same thing as striking   13
a golf ball, for in typing you do not follow through.   24

Rough draft
In typing, you must use a quick, sharp stroke and pull the finger   13
just slightly toward the palm of your hand.   22

Script
You should realize the power that is yours by typing with quiet hands and arms that are almost free of motion.   12 / 22

Statistical
        If you are typing 35-45 gwam, can you add 2 or 3 gwam to your   12
rate by the end of the term? Just 5 days remain!   22

70D Problem Typing Review ㉚

Get Ready to Type . . . . 2'
Timed Production . . . . .23'
Final Proofreading . . . . 5'

DO: Type each of the problems listed at the right. Type the problems as directed, except that you will prepare a carbon copy of each one and will correct errors as you type.

Problems To Be Typed

Page	Lesson Part No.	Problem No.
109	62D	—
111	63D	1
115	65C	2
117	66D	2
118	67C	—
120	68C	—

8C Stroking Technique Practice ⑮ *twice as shown*

STROKING CUE / Home Keys: After striking the key firmly, pull finger slightly toward palm of hand.

Third-Row Keys: Reach with the finger; do not move the hand forward.

First-Row Keys: Make a direct reach without moving the elbow out or changing hand alignment.

Space-Bar Stroke: Use a quick, down-and-in motion. Release the bar quickly.

All reach-strokes taught are used.

1	Home keys	all fall hall shall as ask had fad half dash flash
2		shall add; had half; has a hall; ask all; as a fad
3		J. K. Dahl asks half. D. J. Hall adds a fall fad.
4	Third-row keys	work tire wit out oil sure tried forth trust weeks
5		use that route; write it; there were; short street
6		We were told to take the truck route for the tour.
7	Bottom-row keys	nice back zinc bond corn zone branch czar none can
8		has been in town, count the bonds, check the blank
9		Roz sent cash to the bank; the bank wants a check.

Space with down-and-in thumb motion

| 1 | 2 | 3 | 4 | 5 | 6 | 7 | 8 | 9 | 10 |

8D Paragraph (Continuity) Typing ⑮ *type the ¶s as directed; determine gwam*

DO: Clear tab stops; then set a stop for a 5-space ¶ indention. Use DS.

DO: Depress tab bar or key to indent the first line of each ¶.

DO: Type the ¶s as shown; then type 1′ writings on each of the ¶s.

All letters taught are used.

		Total Words 1′ GWAM
¶1 *1.0 SI 4.2 AWL 97% HFW	Tab ⟶ All of us need to know how to talk and write	9
	well, as we now do a lot of both. We are sure to	19
	need these skills in the world of work, too.	28
¶2 1.0 SI 4.2 AWL 97% HFW	If we do not talk and write well now, we can	37
	learn to do both well. We will need these skills	47
	on the job if it is a job of the size to cause us	57
	to show our worth.	61

| 1 | 2 | 3 | 4 | 5 | 6 | 7 | 8 | 9 | 10 |

*COPY DIFFICULTY: The ease or difficulty of copy to be typed is influenced greatly by three factors: (1) Syllable intensity (SI) or average number of syllables per word; (2) Stroke intensity or average word length (AWL); (3) Incidence of high-frequency words (HFW) or the percent of words used from among the 1,254 most-used words. In this section of lessons, the paragraphs are "very easy."

TO DETERMINE GWAM: The ¶s are marked with the 4-word count shown in figures and with an in-between count of 2 words shown by a dot (.) to aid you in determining your 1-minute *gwam*. If ¶ 1 is typed and a part or all of ¶ 2 in the 1-minute writing, use the cumulative total word count given in the column at the right plus the count for the incomplete line shown beneath the second paragraph.

69D Problem Typing: Poem, Outline, and Unbound Manuscript ㉕

Problem 1: Poem

Half sheet, long side at left;
line: 35; begin on Line 13

	Words
A SERMON IN RHYME	4

	Words
If you have a friend worth loving,	11
Love him. Yes, and let him know	17
That you love him, ere life's evening	25
Tinge his brow with sunset glow.	32
Why should good words ne'er be said	39
Of a friend till he is dead?	45
If you hear a song that thrills you,	52
Sung by any child of song,	58
Praise it. Do not let the singer	65
Wait deserved praises long.	71
Why should one who thrills your heart	78
Lack the joy you may impart?	84

        --Daniel Webster Hoyt   88

Problem 2: Outline

Half sheet, long side at left; begin on
Line 10; line: 40; spread the heading

	Words
SEEDING A LAWN	6

	Words
I. PREPARING THE SOIL	10
A. Breaking Up and Pulverizing Soil	18
1. Spade	20
2. Power tiller	23
B. Soaking Area To Be Planted	29
C. Adding Nutrients	34
II. SMOOTHING OUT THE SEEDBED	41
A. Leveling the Soil	45
B. Cutting Off High Spots	50
1. "Homemade" drag	55
2. Roller	57
3. Rake	59
III. SEEDING AND PROTECTING THE LAWN AREA	68
A. Using Mechanical Seeder	74
B. Adding Protective Cover	79
1. Straw	82
2. Cloth	84
C. Sprinkling To Set Seed	89

Problem 3: Unbound Manuscript

Full sheet; DS; 5-space ¶ in-
dention; 1½" or 2" top margin

● Underline italicized items.

	Words
TYPING SPECIAL SYMBOLS AND SIGNS	7

(¶ 1) Type the hyphen with a space before 14
and after it for a minus sign (6 – 2). The 23
small x with a space before and after it can be 32
used for the multiplication sign (2 x 6). Use 42
the quotation mark (") for inches, seconds, 51
and ditto; and the apostrophe (') for feet or 60
minutes. Type the symbol for "Care of" with 69
the small c, diagonal, and small o (c/o). Type 79
the dash with two hyphens without spacing 87
before or after them (May 6--Wednesday). 96
(¶ 2) Many symbols or signs not on the stan- 103
dard typewriter keyboard can be made by 111
combining characters. To type the exclama- 119
tion point, type the period; backspace; and 128
type the apostrophe (!). For a plus sign, type 138
the diagonal; backspace; and type the hyphen 146
(+). For a division sign, type a hyphen; 154
backspace; and type a colon (÷). (¶ 3) Sym- 162
bols are raised (superscripts) or lowered (sub- 171
scripts) from the writing line by using the 180
ratchet release and the cylinder. To type the 190
degree symbol, for example: Operate the 198
ratchet release; turn the cylinder *toward* you 208
slightly; then type a small o (68°). (¶ 4) 216
When typing chemistry symbols, the sub- 224
scripts must be lowered from the line of writ- 233
ing. Type the symbol in all capitals, *leaving* 243
space for the subscripts; then backspace to the 258
space for the first subscript; operate the 266
ratchet release; and turn the cylinder a half 276
space *away* from you; type the first subscript 286
--then space to the second blank space and 294
type the second subscript; and so on. Type 303
the following chemistry symbols: $MgSO_4$ and 312
Na_2CO_3. 313

Note. One-page manuscripts are not numbered.

LESSON 9

9A Preparatory Practice ⑧ *each line three times SS; DS after third typing of line*

All reach-strokes taught Bud, John, and Cliff work with zest; so does Bill.

Double letters Nell and Bill Hess will soon see Lee and Rob Reed.

Easy It is just luck that Dick Burns can be with Keith.
| 1 | 2 | 3 | 4 | 5 | 6 | 7 | 8 | 9 | 10 |

9B Sentence Guided Writing ⑦

DO: Type each sentence as a 1' writing or type each three times if the 1' timing cannot be used. Study the Stroking Cue at the right before beginning to type the sentences.

Stroking Cue: Think the easy two- and three-letter words, such as **is, to, the,** and **and,** as words. Slow down slightly for such words as **was, were, looks, scared,** and so forth.

		Words in Line	GWAM 30" Guide
Easy	The work is to be done in an hour or so.	8	16
Difficult	We were sad when we saw that Fred was scared.	9	18
Easy	The suit is a fine fit, and it looks well on Jane.	10	20

| 1 | 2 | 3 | 4 | 5 | 6 | 7 | 8 | 9 | 10 |

9C Stroking Technique for Y and X ⑩ *each line three times SS; DS after third typing of line*

Y

X

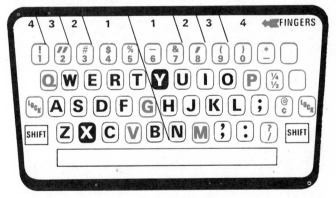

Reach the *right first finger* up to type **y**. Do not arch the wrist or move other fingers from their home keys.

Reach the *left third finger* down to type **x** without moving the hand downward. Reach with the finger!

Tryout Drills

y jyj yj yet say jay hay jay lay jy fly way hay day

x sxs xs xs ax six fix fox box nix next sixth fixed

y x yes dry cry boy hay bay they next jinx lynx sixth

Review Jayne Clay can fix the next tax list for Rex Knox.

LESSON 69

69A   Preparatory Practice ⑦ *each line three times; then 1' writings on Lines 3 and 4*

Alphabet   John had a puzzled look when Bix requested a very special song for me.

Figures   Precincts 29, 30, and 31 report 1,928, 754, and 637 votes cast so far.

Figure-symbol   Cindy asked Dick, "Doesn't the sum of 8 3/4 and 9 4/5 equal 18 11/20?"

Fluency   Television woos many a person away from the things he should be doing.
                | 1 | 2 | 3 | 4 | 5 | 6 | 7 | 8 | 9 | 10 | 11 | 12 | 13 | 14 |

69B   Skill-Transfer Typing ⑧

1. Type a 2' writing on each ¶ below. Determine *gwam*. Compare rates. Identify slower ¶.

2. Type two 1' writings on the ¶ on which you had fewer *gwam*. Try to equal the better 2' rate.

| | | GWAM | |
| | | 1' | 2' |

¶ 1
1.4 SI
5.4 AWL
85% HFW

It is true that there is just as much competition in business 12 | 6 | 52
today as fifty years ago? A lot of great many folks do not think there is. 25 | 13 | 58
They say competition is much less (nl) in evidence now than before. 38 | 19 | 65
They allude to what they consider to be a great growth in companies that 53 | 26 | 72
once were small, and to the increasing merging of firms one with another. They point, 70 | 35 | 80
also, too, to the boom rise in government control and in taxes, two factor that limits com- 86 | 43 | 88
petition to some extent. 91 | 45 | 91

¶ 2
1.4 SI
5.4 AWL
85% HFW

Yet, one point of view stands out. Competition in the last few decades 14 | 7 | 53
seems to have become more intense: in terms of prices, in terms of services, 30 | 15 | 61
and in terms of products. Is it because of huge firms or in spite of them? That 46 | 23 | 69
is a moot question. However, a demand for better products and a need to refine 62 | 31 | 77
the methods of production have made more acute the need for firms to combine 78 | 39 | 85
all resources in a unique way to produce products at competitive prices. 92 | 46 | 92

69C   Composing and Typing from Rough Draft ⑩

DO: Type the portion of the manuscript as given; then describe what happens to you when you type a timed writing. Make corrections; then retype the manuscript from your corrected copy.

MIND AND BODY

(¶ 1) If proof is needed that the mind has a far-reaching influence upon the body, just watch me type. The psychiatrists must have had my typing in mind when they wrote:

(¶ 2) The relationship between body and mind is continuous and intimate. . . . Mind and body are so closely connected . . . not even a single thought or mood can come into existence without being reflected in the physical organism.[1]

(¶ 3) I type quite well, as a rule; but when I hear, "Get ready for a 5-minute writing, please," my emotions take over my typing motions and *(Describe how you feel and how you type when taking a timed writing.)*

---

[1]Edward A. Strecker and Kenneth E. Appel, <u>Discovering Ourselves</u> (New York: The Macmillan Company, 1962), pp. 12-13.

9D Stroking Technique for V and P ⑩ *each line three times SS; DS after third typing of line*

V

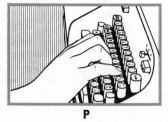

P

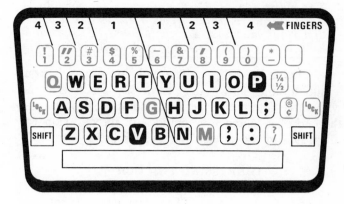

Reach the *left first finger* down to type **v.** Hold the elbow in position and the hand in alignment.

Straighten the *right fourth finger* slightly and move up to type letter **p.** Avoid twisting the elbow out.

Tryout Drills

v   fvf vf vie view vow vows five live rove love have

p   ;p; p; up cup pay pen spend spent help paid prize

v p   van zip vote solve prove peace pound strive poise

Review   Steve and Paul say they leave for Spain next week.

9E Continuity Practice ⑮

DO: Type the six lines of drill twice as shown. (DS between two-line groups.) Use the ¶ for two or more 1' writings or type the ¶ twice if the 1' timing is not used.

Stroking Cue: Type with finger action. Hold the hands and arms quiet, almost motionless. Reach—don't hop—to the keys. Keep typing at a smooth and steady pace.

All reach-strokes taught are used.

1   by say yet year your why try six box tax next jinx
2 y and x   Dwayne will help Rex file his sales tax next year.

3   put part paid shop type keep five live have twelve
4 p and v   Van pays in cash and saves; it proves a fine plan.

5   you vex plans serve wax prove yes dye please price
6 y x p v   You and Paul have typed just five of the six jobs.

		1' GWAM
1.0 SI	Tab · 4 · 8	
4.5 AWL	----→ As you work to learn, you will learn to work	9
95% HFW	· 12 · 16	
	in such a way that skill will be yours. Work for	19
	20 · 24 · 28	
	speed with zest now and then, but know that speed	29
	32 · 36 · 39	
	is just a part of the plans you want to have next.	39

| 1 | 2 | 3 | 4 | 5 | 6 | 7 | 8 | 9 | 10 |

Problem 1: Two-Page Leftbound Manuscript

Top margin: pica, 1½"; elite, 2"; indent quotations and enumerated items 5 spaces from left and right margins; SS quotations; SS lines of each enumerated item, but DS between items.

Typing the Ellipsis: The omission of words from a quotation is shown by an *ellipsis*, which is typed with three alternating periods and spaces, or four if the end of a sentence is included in the omission (as illustrated in the quoted paragraphs below).

	Words
ADDRESSING FOR OCR	4

The ZIP Code system of mail sorting was started by the Post Office Department on July 1, 1963. After only a few years, ZIP Codes are now being used in envelope addresses by a vast majority of mailers, both business and personal. The widespread use of ZIP Codes has helped to hold down mailing charges. As President Johnson has said:
(12, 20, 29, 36, 45, 54, 63, 71)

> The ZIP Code system is effective, efficient, and essential to a modern postal system . . . . By holding down the cost of handling each individual piece of mail, ZIP Code benefits not only mail users, but also the taxpayers . . . .[1]
(78, 85, 93, 100, 108, 114, 118)

ZIP has now been combined with the Optical Character Reader (OCR) to provide electronic mail sorting for a sizable portion of business mail in several major cities.[2]
(125, 134, 143, 151)

According to the Post Office Department, OCR's are now in use in eight major cities: Boston, Chicago, Detroit, Houston, Los Angeles, New York, Philadelphia, and San Francisco.[3] Some of these cities have more than one OCR.
(159, 168, 176, 184, 193, 196)

The POD suggests the following general guides for addressing envelopes to be compatible to OCR's reading habits:[4]
(204, 212, 219)

1. The address must be prepared in a type style the OCR can read accurately. Both pica and elite typewriter type are ideal; script-like type is not.
(226, 233, 239, 247, 249)
2. All lines of the address should be blocked at the left.
(257, 263)
3. All addresses are preferably single-spaced (including two- and three-line ones for uniformity).
(272, 279, 284)
4. The bottom line of the address must contain the city and state names and the ZIP Code. The state name may be spelled in full or abbreviated according to the standard abbrevia-
(292, 300, 306, 314, 320)

	Words

tions or the special two-letter abbreviations.
(326, 330)

5. The next-to-last line of the address should be reserved for the street address or the Post Office box number, if either is known.
(338, 345, 352, 357)
6. The address should be surrounded by white space, as follows: 1/2 inch above, 5/8 inch to the left, and the entire space below and to the right. In other words, the OCR read zone must be clear of all but the address.
(364, 372, 379, 387, 393, 401)

Some purists have lamented such "tampering" with long-observed rules of envelope addressing, suggesting that the POD recommendations represent too great a departure from "convention." In overall effect, however, the changes are not really drastic; at the same time, they result in quite readable addresses. Furthermore, as Robinson has pointed out:
(408, 417, 426, 434, 444, 453, 463, 472)

> If the foregoing guides result in address placement that is less artistically balanced than functional, remember that speed and accuracy in mail handling are more important than beauty of envelopes . . . .[5]
(478, 486, 493, 500, 506, 513)

[1]*National ZIP Code Directory*, POD Publication 65 (Washington, D.C.: Post Office Department, 1968), p. iii. (*31 words*)

[2]Jerry W. Robinson, "The Marriage of ZIP and OCR," *Typewriting News* (Spring, 1969), p. 3. (*21 words*)

[3]*Addressing for the Optical Character Reader*, POD Publication 114 (Washington, D.C.: Post Office Department, 1968), p. i. (*33 words*)

[4]Ibid., pp. 3-6. (*4 words*)

[5]Robinson, op. cit., p. 4. (*10 words*)

Problem 2: Manuscript with Table

Retype page 2 of Problem 1, adding the following copy to make a three-page manuscript:

	Words

The following table may be used as a guide for addressing envelopes and postal cards. Its use will result in acceptable address placement for OCR sorting. Column 1 gives the kind of mailing piece (small envelope, large envelope, or postal card); Column 2, the distance between the top of the envelope or card and the first line of the address; and Column 3, the distance from the left edge of the envelope or card to the horizontal beginning of the address.[6]
(302, 310, 320, 329, 337, 347, 355, 365, 374, 383, 387)

			Words
Small Envelope	2"	2½"	391
Large Envelope	2½"	4"	395
Postal Card	2"	2"	399

[6]Robinson, loc. cit. (*20 words*)

● **Self-Improvement Practice** *each line three times SS; DS after third typing of line*

v Dave Volp will have a leave of four or five weeks.

x Rex fixed the box for Liz; next, he did your desk.

y Kaye said you should stay with Faye for five days.

p Pete has the pep, push, and poise for the top job.

Double letters Lee will call Bill Cook to see if he has the book.

LESSON 10

10A Preparatory Practice ⑧ *each line three times SS; DS after third typing of line*

All letters taught are used.

Clay Kane proved this size sox will just suit Dan.

in at on was you far kin eve hop red lab just zinc

Their work is done; they can leave when they wish.

| 1 | 2 | 3 | 4 | 5 | 6 | 7 | 8 | 9 | 10 |

10B Tab Mechanism and Return Controls ⑫ *type twice*

1. Clear all tab stops.
2. For Column 2, set tab stop 15 spaces from left margin.
3. For Column 3, set a tab stop 15 spaces from first tab stop.
4. For Column 4, set a tab stop 16 spaces from second tab stop.

TABULATING CUE

Nonelectric (Manual): Depress and hold tab bar or key down until the carriage has completed its movement.

Electric: Flick the tab key lightly with the little finger; return the finger to home position quickly.

RETURN CUE

Nonelectric: Move lever inward to take up the slack; return with a quick wrist and hand motion. Do not follow carriage across.

Electric: Reach the little finger to the return key, flick the key lightly, and release it quickly.

for	Tab	act	Tab	hand	Tab	live
lay		lop		corn		your
but		wet		lend		have
cot		oil		lays		year
six		car		torn		vote
fox		pin		turn		size
win		sea		they		hunt
box		lop		wish		zone
fit		ate		laid		next

KEY | 3 | 12 | 3 | 12 | 4 | 12 | 4 |

Tab bar

Tab key

LESSON 10 **Section 1: Letter Keys** **21**

LESSON 68

68A Preparatory Practice ⑦ *each line three times; then 1' writings on Lines 3 and 4*

Alphabet   As the bus sped away, Dave Jantz made a quick lunge for the exit door.

Figures   They asked each of us to type these formulas: H_2O, H_2SO_4, and Na_2CO_3.

Figure-symbol   She told everyone to type math formulas like this: $X^2 = 3Y - (Z + 5)$.

Fluency   Every chairman can save a lot of effort if he will just plan his work.

| 1 | 2 | 3 | 4 | 5 | 6 | 7 | 8 | 9 | 10 | 11 | 12 | 13 | 14 |

68B Skill-Transfer Typing ⑧

1. Type a 2' writing on each ¶ below. Determine *gwam*. Compare rates. Identify slower ¶.

2. Type two 1' writings on the ¶ on which you had fewer *gwam*. Try to equal the better 2' rate.

		GWAM 1'	2'
¶1 1.4 SI 5.4 AWL 85% HFW	One of the dreams of our present system of education is to bring	13	7
	the school to the student. A number of plans are being used to make	27	13
	this dream come true. First, the state university in each of many	40	20
	states has set up one or more local centers. Second, some states have	54	27
	added two or three new colleges to their state college systems. Third,	69	34
	a great number of junior colleges and technical schools have been	82	41
	started in both urban and suburban areas. Thus, more and more students	97	48
	can commute and do not have to live on the campus. The cost of going	111	55
	to school can thereby be reduced.	117	59
¶2 1.4 SI 5.4 AWL 85% HFW	In 1960 there were about 1,300 colleges in the U.S. in which one	13	7
	could earn a degree: universities, senior colleges, and special schools.	28	14
	In all, well over 3,500,000 full-time and part-time students were taking	43	21
	courses of one kind or another in such colleges. At the same time there	58	29
	were more than 500 two-year junior or community colleges in which more	72	36
	than 400,000 were enrolled for study. By the end of the decade the four-	87	43
	year colleges had grown so that just over 4,000,000 full-time and more	101	50
	than 1,000,000 part-time students were enrolled as the two-year colleges	115	57
	shot up to more than 1,500,000 full-time and part-time students.	128	64

1' GWAM | 1 | 2 | 3 | 4 | 5 | 6 | 7 | 8 | 9 | 10 | 11 | 12 | 13 | 14 |
2' GWAM | 1 | 2 | 3 | 4 | 5 | 6 | 7 |

68C Special Footnotes ⑤

When two footnotes contain references to the same work and one follows the other without intervening footnotes, use *Ibid.*, the abbreviation for *ibidem* (meaning in the same place), and the exact page number for the second footnote *if it differs from the first one.*

When a footnote refers to a different page in a work already cited and one or more footnotes separate it from the first one, use the author's name and the notation *op. cit.*, the abbreviation for *opere citato* (meaning in the work cited), with the appropriate page number. If the reference is to precisely the same page covered by a reference not immediately preceding, use the author's name and *loc. cit.*, the abbreviation for *loco citato* (meaning in the same place), without the page number.

DO: Use your page-end indicator behind a full sheet of paper. On Line 18 at the bottom of the page, type the underline and the following footnotes.

------

[3]Richard A. Lester, Manpower Planning in a Free Society (Princeton: Princeton University Press, 1966), p. 205.

    [4]Ibid.

    [5]Ibid., p. 210.

    [6]Haggblade, loc. cit.

    [7]Rohrer, op. cit., p. 56.

10C Stroking Technique Practice (15) *three times as shown*

Lines 1 and 2: When the same finger controls two keys in succession, as the first finger controls **fr** in **front** and **br** in **branch**, move the controlling finger directly to the second key. Type without pausing between strokes.

Lines 3 and 4: To type adjacent keys, such as **re** in **here**, **poi** in **point**, and the like, think each letter vigorously and make each motion precisely. Train your eyes to see quickly the correct sequence of letters to be typed.

All reach-strokes taught are used.

1	Direct	why led side front once branch lots like kind just
2	reaches	Zahn holds the checks; Herb left the wharf; I like
3	Adjacent-key	has poor suit buy oil cards talk klatch point Yule
4	reaches	start here; few buy silk; we hope you trade; as we
5	All letters	Vance hopes to work with Jane for a day next week.
6	taught	Cal had a job for Roz to do, but she did not stay.
7		The skills you build you can prize as well as use.

| 1 | 2 | 3 | 4 | 5 | 6 | 7 | 8 | 9 | 10 |

10D Continuity Practice (15)

DO: Type the six sentences three times each or use each sentence for two 1' writings with the 30" call of the line-ending guide. Use the ¶ for three or more 1' writings, or type it twice if 1' timing is not used.

Technique Summary: Sit erect, feet on floor. Curve the fingers. Hold eyes on the copy as you type. Type at a steady pace, with hands and arms quiet and stroking action centered in the fingers. Space quickly with a down-and-in motion of the right thumb.

All letters taught are used.

		Words in Line	GWAM 30" Guide
1	Vern fixed the barn for Clay Zilch.	7	14
2	Ruth wrote that you are to pay your way.	8	16
3	Jake said a lad fell when he rushed to class.	9	18
4	Do not put off for an hour what you should do now.	10	20
5	Keith paid for the work with his half of the cash.	10	20
6	Fred and Dave Hays have to pay a tax on the prize.	10	20

		1' GWAM
1.0 SI 4.4 AWL 93% HFW	Tab ----→If you work well, you can soon type what you	9
	have had to write with a pen up to now. Try hard	19
	to build a skill you can prize for years. On the	29
	next try just do your best to top your last speed.	39

| 1 | 2 | 3 | 4 | 5 | 6 | 7 | 8 | 9 | 10 |

67D Problem Typing: Two-Page Leftbound Manuscript with Footnotes

Side margins: 1½″ left, 1″ right; top margin on page 1: 1½″ pica, 2″ elite; top margin on page 2: 1″ for both pica and elite type

Type the following copy as a two-page manuscript to be bound at the left. Center the title over the *line of writing*.

Use your page-end indicator sheet to guide you in placing the heading on the first page, the page number on the second page, and the footnotes.

	Words
PROBABILITY IN BUSINESS	5

Probability is the likelihood of the occurrence of any particular form of an event. For example, if a fair coin is tossed into the air, one of two events will occur––the coin will turn up either heads or tails. Most persons would assume that these two events are equally likely to occur.

There are many instances in which it is impossible to determine the probabilities so readily in advance. If a number of trials are made, however, the analysis of the experimental data will give a relative frequency that can be used as an estimate of the probability.

The concept of probability is particularly useful in business when there is a situation for which the outcome is uncertain: the likelihood that a new product will be successful or that rain will prevent the scheduled completion of a new building. Each of these situations involves uncertainty, and each of them is essentially a prediction of an outcome.

"The study of probability began around three hundred years ago."[1] According to Encyclopaedia Britannica, Jakob Bernoulli–– a Swiss mathematician––"can be regarded as the father of probability theory as a branch of mathematics."[2]

In an article entitled "It's More Probable Than You Think," Martin Gardner illustrated some remarkable examples of probability. One of them is what mathematicians call the birthday paradox. The birthday paradox pre-

(word counts: 15, 25, 34, 43, 52, 62, 65, 73, 82, 92, 100, 110, 119, 128, 137, 146, 155, 163, 173, 182, 190, 198, 206, 220, 228, 238, 241, 250, 259, 267, 276, 284)

	Words

dicts that out of a group of 23 people, the chances are more than even that of their 23 birthdays, two will fall on the same date.[3]

In another illustration of probability, the Life Science Library on Mathematics cites coincidental deaths of three presidents of the United States. John Adams, James Monroe, and Thomas Jefferson, for example, all died on the Fourth of July––Adams and Jefferson in 1826, Monroe in 1831.[4] Furthermore, two of our presidents share the same birth dates: James K. Polk and Warren G. Harding–– November 2.

Among the first applications of probability were those involving games of chance, and we still study "gaming theory." One of the first business applications of probability was made by insurance companies whose risks were determined by mortality tables.

Modern business management depends heavily upon the predictions of probability studies for such decisions as:

1. Determining desirable inventory levels.
2. Planning new products.
3. Estimating rate of growth.
4. Determining market potential.

(word counts: 293, 302, 311, 320, 336, 346, 353, 362, 371, 380, 389, 396, 399, 406, 415, 424, 433, 442, 450, 457, 465, 472, 479, 481, 486, 493, 500)

---

[1]George W. Snedecor and William G. Cochran, Statistical Methods (6th ed.; Ames, Iowa: The Iowa State University Press, 1967), p. 199. *(34 words)*

[2]"Probability," Encyclopaedia Britannica (1968), XVIII, 570. *(17 words)*

[3]Martin Gardner, "It's More Probable Than You Think," Reader's Digest (November, 1967), p. 108. *(26 words)*

[4]David Gergamini, Life Science Library on Mathematics (New York: Time, Inc., 1963), p. 143. *(25 words)*

LESSON 11

11A Preparatory Practice ⑧ *each line three times SS; DS after third typing of line*

All reach-strokes taught are used.

The boy played jazz for Vic for six weeks in June.

to be; for us; can do; we like; pay the; they can;

He can do the drill in an hour or so, I feel sure.
| 1 | 2 | 3 | 4 | 5 | 6 | 7 | 8 | 9 | 10 |

11B Stroking Technique Review ⑩ *each line three times SS; DS after third typing of line*

All letters taught are used.

1   boy axe owns says drop hue seeks laws top two yard

2   puff bulb lieu bulk fraud writes yield width snail

3   Jay can pay the two debts or seek a new bank loan.

4   Len felt that the size of the vote would help Ned.

5   Its style and tone have kept this harp at the top.
| 1 | 2 | 3 | 4 | 5 | 6 | 7 | 8 | 9 | 10 |

11C Stroking Technique for Q and M ⑩ *each line three times SS; DS after third typing of line*

Q

M

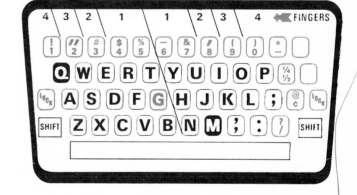

Reach the *left fourth finger* up to type **q** without swinging the elbow out or arching the wrist.

Reach the *right first finger* down to type **m**. Do not move the hand down or swing the elbow out.

Tryout Drills

q   qa quit qa quit quiz quack quick quell quote quite

m   mj am jam ham sum rum mix firm form harm come much

q m   quiz quack quest qualm much must myth mixed mosque

Review   Max made out a quiz for me to mail to Mr. Squires.

67A Preparatory Practice ⑦ *each line three times; then 1' writings on Lines 2 and 4*

Alphabet — Just how much should Greg Zahn expect to pay for five weeks in Quebec?

Figures — The ZIP Codes are: Alan, 53190; Dwayne, 74104; Ed, 27403; Sam, 60178.

Figure-symbol — Interest accumulated in 1968 to $432.57 when the rate increased by $\frac{1}{2}\%$.

Fluency — As you get to know a man, you get to know his good points most of all.
| 1 | 2 | 3 | 4 | 5 | 6 | 7 | 8 | 9 | 10 | 11 | 12 | 13 | 14 |

67B Typing from Rough Draft ⑧ *type twice with 1" top and side margins*

Words

The following guides ~~that follow~~ will be useful in ~~the~~ preparing — 10

of manuscripts of two pages *or more*: — 17

1. Never end a page with a hyphened word *or have* ~~Avoid having~~
   more than two consecutive lines end with a hyphen*ed word*. — 27 / 39

2. *Never have* ~~Avoid having~~ only one line of a paragraph at the bottom or at the top of a page. — 50 / 56

3. Type each footnote on the *same as* page ~~with~~ it*'s* reference
   figure. (Another acceptable practice is to place *all*
   footnotes at the end of the manuscript.) — 67 / 78 / 87

4. Type the page number on the s*e*cond *page* ~~sheet~~ and subsequent ones at the right margin a half inch from the
   top, unless the report is to be topbound, in which case
   center the number a half inch from the bottom edge
   of the sheet. — 98 / 108 / 120 / 130 / 133

67C Centering Over the Line of Writing ⑩

TO CENTER OVER LINE OF WRITING

To center over the line of writing (as a title in a leftbound manu-script), follow these steps:

1. Determine the center of the line:
   a. Note on the platen or paper-bail scale the numbers where the left and right margins are set.
   b. Add these two figures.
   c. Divide the sum by 2.

2. From the center of the line, backspace *once* for each *two* typewriter characters and spaces

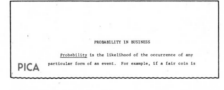

in the heading to be centered; begin to type where backspac-ing ends.

DO:

1. Set margin stops for typing a leftbound manuscript.

2. Beginning on Line 13, type two lines from the copy given below.

3. Using Steps 1 and 2 at the left, center the heading PROBABILITY IN BUSINESS over the line of writing.

4. Compare your copy with the appropriate model at the left.

5. Repeat Steps 1-4, above. See if you can complete the drill more quickly this time.

Probability is the likelihood of the occurrence of any particular form of an event. For example, if a fair coin is tossed into the air,

11D   Stroking Technique for G and ? (Question) ⑩

each line three times SS;
DS after third typing of line

G

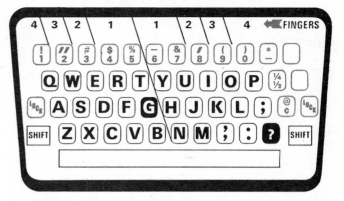

? (Question)

Reach the *left first finger* to the right to type **g** without moving the other fingers from their home keys.

Type **?** with the *right fourth finger*. Remember to shift to type **?** *Space twice after* **?** *at the end of a sentence.*

Tryout Drills

g   fgf gf go got fog fig rug dug big flag right fight

?   ;?; ?; ?; Is he? Is he next? Did Sam go to town?

g ?   Is Mat right? May Tom and I go? Am I to see Max?

Review Has Zeke packed my box with just five grown quail?

Do not space after ? at end of line

11E   Continuity Practice ⑫

DO: Type the first four lines three times each; DS after the third typing of the line. Use the ¶ for three or more 1' writings, or type it twice if 1' timing is not used.

Technique Summary: Sit erect. Curve the fingers. Space quickly. Strike each key with a quick, sharp stroke; release it quickly. Snap the finger slightly toward the palm of the hand as you release the key.

All letters are used.

    my gym fog rug put eggs must mark hymn guess eight

    large small quote square quick growth valves sighs

    terms dodge bring length slight lymph signs flings

q m g ?   May Gregg make a quick trip to the square for Meg?

1.0 SI
4.2 AWL
93% HFW

                                                              1' GWAM
Tab
----→The man who wants to get to the top must pay   9

a high price. It may take work to learn to type;   19

but if you just keep on and do not quit, the next   29

try may add a word. Have you the zeal to make it?   39

| 1 | 2 | 3 | 4 | 5 | 6 | 7 | 8 | 9 | 10 |

66D Problem Typing: Letter with Table; Portions of Second Page of Manuscript

Problem 1: Letter with Table

Modified block, blocked ¶s; mixed punctuation;
line: 65; date on Line 16; center listed items
with 6 spaces between columns; address envelope

Words

(*Current date*) Mr. Philip G. Morris | Quality   9
Foods, Inc. | 67 Canterbury Street | Worches-   17
ter, MA 01610 | Dear Mr. Morris: | (¶ 1)   24
Several weeks ago you asked me to let you   32
know when we increased the number of food   41
lines we are able to offer our customers. Just   50
this month we secured the franchise to sell   59
many of the products of Top Foods, Ltd.   67

Words

(¶ 2) Early next week I shall stop to see you   75
to explain the delivery schedule for these new   85
products. In the meantime, the two items   93
listed below will illustrate that the products   102
are priced right.   106

24-can case of yellow cling peaches $6.50   115
48-can case of creamed white corn   7.50   123

(¶ 3) If you need additional information be-   130
fore I arrive, please write me or call me collect   140
at (617) 821-3940. | Sincerely yours, | Richard   149
B. Higgenbotham | Assistant Sales Manager | 157
xx   158

Problem 2: Drill on Typing Portion of Second Page of Manuscript with Footnote

PICA

    In an article entitled "It's More Probable Than You
Think," Martin Gardner illustrated some remarkable examples
of probability. One of them is what mathematicians call the
birthday paradox. The birthday paradox predicts that out of
a group of 23 people, the chances are more than even that of
their 23 birthdays, two will fall on the same date.[3]

    Modern business management depends heavily upon the pre-
dictions of probability studies for such decisions as:

    1. Determining desirable inventory levels.
    2. Planning new products.
    3. Estimating rate of growth.
    4. Determining market potential.

    [3]Martin Gardner, "It's More Probable Than You Think,"
Reader's Digest (November, 1967), p. 108.

ELITE

    In an article entitled "It's More Probable Than You Think," Martin
Gardner illustrated some remarkable examples of probability. One of them
is what mathematicians call the birthday paradox. The birthday paradox
predicts that out of a group of 23 people, the chances are more than even
that of their 23 birthdays, two will fall on the same date.[3]

    Modern business management depends heavily upon the predictions of
probability studies for such decisions as:

    1. Determining desirable inventory levels.
    2. Planning new products.
    3. Estimating rate of growth.
    4. Determining market potential.

    [3]Martin Gardner, "It's More Probable Than You Think," Reader's
Digest (November, 1967), p. 108.

Type the following copy as page 2 of a leftbound manuscript (1″ top margin with the page number on Line 4). Use your page-end indicator sheet.

Since this second page is not full, space down appropriately to type the footnote in order to maintain a 1″ bottom margin.

Words

    In an article entitled "It's More Probable Than You Think," Martin Gardner   15
illustrated some remarkable examples of probability. One of them is what mathe-   31
maticians call the birthday paradox. The birthday paradox predicts that out of   47
a group of 23 people, the chances are more than even that of their 23 birthdays,   63
two will fall on the same date.[3]   70

Space down to Line 20 of your indicator sheet.

    Modern business management depends heavily upon the predictions of proba-   84
bility studies for such decisions as: 92

    1. Determining desirable inventory levels.   101
    2. Planning new products.   107
    3. Estimating rate of growth.   113
    4. Determining market potential.   120
   124

    [3]Martin Gardner, "It's More Probable Than You Think," Reader's Digest   141
(November, 1967), p. 108.   146

Line 1: Clear all tab stops. Set tab stops to have 5 blank spaces between words.

Tabulator   make   held   hand   work   them   eight

Space bar   he we am up as it or an by to of my on and few man

Shift keys   Don Ames and Zoe Foss played May Janz and Tod Hay.

Alphabet   May Vern Fox help Jack Wolds on the next big quiz?

LESSON 12

12A Preparatory Practice ⑧ *each line three times SS; DS after third typing of line*

Alphabet   Joe gave my boy five quick trips with Max and Liz.

q m g   Gus quit my team. Doug may go to Rome quite soon.

Easy   George said Tom Squires is the man to do the work.
| 1 | 2 | 3 | 4 | 5 | 6 | 7 | 8 | 9 | 10 |

12B Know Your Typewriter: Backspacing ⑤

Backspacing: To fill in an omitted letter or to position the carriage, depress the **backspace key (30)**. Locate the key on the keyboard.

Electric: Reach with the little finger; make a light, quick stroke. Release the key quickly to avoid a double backspace. Hold the key down for repeat backspacing.

Nonelectric (Manual): Straighten the finger and reach it to the backspace key with minimum hand motion. Depress the key firmly; release it quickly.

1. TYPE the first word; backspace and type over the final letter. Type the other words in the same way.
2. Type the first word again; backspace and type over the first letter. Type the other words in the same way.

it go by up as on we my am of cue fix pay men quit

12C Stroking Technique Review ⑫ *each line three times SS; DS after third typing of line*

1   z j q x   fix jobs quit size next quite jazz quote jinx quiz

2   k v b g   bank like have big kind gave talk serve black save

3   w p m f   firm hope know flip owns put from zip few my views

4   y u c d   cut why did buy act day used your type court place

5   Alphabet   Del Fox just quit my show and gave back his prize.
| 1 | 2 | 3 | 4 | 5 | 6 | 7 | 8 | 9 | 10 |

LESSON 66

66A Preparatory Practice (7) *each line three times; then 1' writings on Lines 3 and 4*

Alphabet
Sidney will keep the olive jaguar if he acquires extra cash from Buzz.

Figures
The new numbers are: Janet, 841-2937; Fred, 261-5200; Eric, 831-4129.

Figure-symbol
The 6½% interest of $81.08 on my $1,247.35 note (dated May 29) is due.

Fluency
Most of us, whether young or old, have potential that is never tapped.
| 1 | 2 | 3 | 4 | 5 | 6 | 7 | 8 | 9 | 10 | 11 | 12 | 13 | 14 |

66B Control Building: Long Words (5) *each line three times at your control rate*

Ken has described several business applications of probability theory.
Probability studies are particularly helpful in effective forecasting.
Analysis of the experimental data provides an estimate of probability.
| 1 | 2 | 3 | 4 | 5 | 6 | 7 | 8 | 9 | 10 | 11 | 12 | 13 | 14 |

66C Growth Index (8) *one 5' writing; determine* gwam *and errors*

All letters are used.

	GWAM	
	1'	5'

¶ 1
1.4 SI
5.4 AWL
85% HFW

A good business letter is a work of art, and the knack of writ-   13 | 3 | 54
ing such a letter is usually learned best through actual experience.   27 | 5 | 57
But experience does not always teach with zeal, and quite often this   41 | 8 | 60
is a very slow way to learn. In order to add to this vital skill more   55 | 11 | 63
quickly, therefore, the wise student will study what those who are   68 | 14 | 65
judges in the field have found to be the basic rules for effective   82 | 16 | 68
letter writing.   85 | 17 | 69

¶ 2
1.4 SI
5.4 AWL
85% HFW

The first such rule tells you to present in each statement just   13 | 20 | 71
one principal or main thought. This is the way to assure unity in your   27 | 22 | 74
letters. The next rule suggests that you connect all parts of your   41 | 25 | 77
message clearly and logically by the expert use of words; that is, make   55 | 28 | 80
the entire message stick together. The final rule urges you to direct   69 | 31 | 82
the attention of the reader to the key points of the letter; that is,   83 | 34 | 85
to give your message power.   89 | 35 | 86

¶ 3
1.4 SI
5.4 AWL
85% HFW

To apply the basic rules with success, it is imperative that you   13 | 37 | 89
plan your letter by developing a topic outline of what you wish to   26 | 40 | 92
say. At the beginning of the outline include a strong, hard-hitting   40 | 43 | 94
sentence that will quickly grasp the attention of the reader. At the   54 | 46 | 97
end of the outline add a sentence that will end the letter on a warm,   68 | 48 | 100
friendly note. Throughout the plan, try to see the situation as the   82 | 51 | 102
reader does.   84 | 52 | 103

1' GWAM | 1 | 2 | 3 | 4 | 5 | 6 | 7 | 8 | 9 | 10 | 11 | 12 | 13 | 14 |
5' GWAM | 1 | 2 | 3 |

12D Paragraph (Continuity) Typing ⑮

Each ¶ is marked with the 4-word count shown in figures and with an in-between count of two words shown by a dot (.) to aid in determining your 1′ *gwam*. (Use figure or dot nearest last word typed.)

¶ **1:** TYPE two 1′ writings. The figure or dot (.) above the last word typed (ignoring errors temporarily) will be your 1′ *gwam*.

¶ **2:** TYPE as directed for ¶ 1.

¶**s 1 and 2:** TYPE a 2′ writing, beginning with ¶ 1 and typing as much of ¶ 2 as you can. Divide 1′ *gwam* (figures at right plus incomplete sentence, if any) by 2 for your 2′ *gwam*.

All letters are used.

		1′ GWAM
¶ 1 1.0 SI 4.6 AWL 95% HFW	Make up your mind to put first things first;	9
	and if you try to mix work and fun, be quite sure	19
	you do the work first; then do what you wish, for	29
	you did first that which was first.	36
¶ 2 1.0 SI 4.6 AWL 95% HFW	When you work, work as hard as you can; when	45
	you play, you can do just what you wish. Do both	55
	with zest to be at your best. Right now let your	65
	work come first, and you will learn to type well.	75

| 1 | 2 | 3 | 4 | 5 | 6 | 7 | 8 | 9 | 10 |

12E Stroking Skill Checkup ⑩

DO: Type each sentence as a 1′ writing, typing it as many times as you can until time is called.

DO: Type Sentences 1, 3, and 5 for 1′ each; compare the *gwam** for the writings.

Stroking Cue: Make low, quick reach-strokes. Keep the hands and arms quiet—almost motionless.

All letters are used.

		Words in Line
1	Is there work for each of us to do?	7
2	Do you think you can learn to type well?	8
3	Wish for what you want, but work for it, too.	9
4	The six girls do not have quite the zeal you have.	10
5	All of them know they must put first things first.	10
6	He needs to know just the way to write your check.	10

| 1 | 2 | 3 | 4 | 5 | 6 | 7 | 8 | 9 | 10 |

*TO DETERMINE GWAM:

1. List the figure at the end of each complete line typed during the timed writing.

2. Note in the scale the figure directly below the point at which you stopped typing.

3. Add these figures to determine the total gross words typed, known as *gwam*.

Problem 2: Portion of a Manuscript Page with Footnotes

TYPING SUPERIOR FIGURES FOR FOOTNOTE REFERENCES

DO: Type the first line opposite Line 25 of the bottom half of the indicator sheet to maintain a 1″ bottom margin. Follow the steps given at the right in typing reference figures for footnotes.

1. Move the ratchet release (automatic line finder) forward.
2. Move the cylinder back (toward you) a half space.
3. Type the superior figure.
4. Return the ratchet release and cylinder to their regular positions.
5. Continue typing.

• *Do not type copy line for line; listen for bell to return at line endings.*

PICA

```
     new building.  Each of these situations involves uncertainty,    25
                                                                       24
     and each of them is essentially a prediction of an outcome.      23
                                                                       22
          "The study of probability began around three hundred        21
                                                                       20
     years ago."¹  According to Encyclopaedia Britannica, Jakob       19
                                                                       18
     Bernoulli--a Swiss mathematician--"can be regarded as the        17
                                                                       16
     father of probability theory as a branch of mathematics."²       15
                                                                       14
                                                                       13
          ¹George W. Snedecor and William G. Cochran, Statistical     12
     Methods (6th ed.; Ames, Iowa:  The Iowa State University         11
     Press, 1967), p. 199.                                            10
                                                                        9
          ²"Probability," Encyclopaedia Britannica (1968), XVIII,       8
     570.                                                               7
                                                                        6
                                                                        5
                                   1                                    4
                                                                        3
                                                                        2
                                                                        1
```

ELITE

```
     scheduled completion of a new building.  Each of these situations in-   25
                                                                             24
     volves uncertainty, and each of them is essentially a prediction of an  23
                                                                             22
     outcome.                                                                21
                                                                             20
          "The study of probability began around three hundred years ago."¹ 19
                                                                             18
     According to Encyclopaedia Britannica, Jakob Bernoulli--a Swiss mathe-  17
                                                                             16
     matician--"can be regarded as the father of probability theory as a     15
                                                                             14
     branch of mathematics."²                                               13
                                                                             12
          ¹George W. Snedecor and William G. Cochran, Statistical Methods    11
     (6th ed.; Ames, Iowa:  The Iowa State University Press, 1967), p. 199.  10
                                                                              9
          ²"Probability," Encyclopaedia Britannica (1968), XVIII, 570.        8
                                                                              7
                                                                              6
                                                                              5
                                   1                                          4
                                                                              3
                                                                              2
                                                                              1
```

Begin Elite Line with ↓   Begin Pica Line with ↓

	Words
scheduled completion of a new building. Each of these situations involves	13
uncertainty, and each of them is essentially a prediction of an outcome.	30
"The study of probability began around three hundred years ago."[1] According	44
cording to Encyclopaedia Britannica, Jakob Bernoulli—a Swiss mathematician—	64
"can be regarded as the father of probability theory as a branch of mathe-	79
matics."[2] SS	81
_____	85
DS	
[1]George W. Snedecor and William G. Cochran, Statistical Methods (6th	101
ed.; Ames, Iowa: The Iowa State University Press, 1967), p. 199.	114
DS	
[2]"Probability," Encyclopaedia Britannica (1968), XVIII, 570.	131

Problem 3: Portion of a Manuscript Page with Footnotes

Retype the copy of Problem 2 as an unbound manuscript with footnotes. If the last page of a manuscript is less than a page, place footnotes at bottom of page.

SECTION 2 ▶ IMPROVING BASIC SKILLS
LESSONS 13–15

Purpose. The purpose of this section is to improve your typing techniques and stroking skill. You will also learn to type longer words. *All letters are used in every drill of this section.*

Machine Adjustments. Line: 60—left margin stop 30 spaces to left of center, right stop at end of scale. Single-space (SS) word and sentence drills; double-space (DS) and indent paragraphs 5 spaces.

LESSON 13

13A   Preparatory Practice ⑧ *each line three times SS; DS between groups*

Alphabet	My friend Jack would just love to pass up his next big quiz.
2-syllable words	Begin typing at a very easy pace. Speed up as you go along.
Fluency	Do the work you like to do and like the work you have to do.

| 1 | 2 | 3 | 4 | 5 | 6 | 7 | 8 | 9 | 10 | 11 | 12 |

13B   Manipulative Parts Drill: Shift Keys ⑩ *each line at least twice SS; DS between groups*

1	Left shift	Kathy and Nat Kelso left for Nepal; the Harts went to Japan.
2	Right shift	C. Q. Roberts may open an office above A. X. Sill Supply Co.
3	Both shifts	Ask Jan Ellis, Don Maze, and Glenn Markel to help Mrs. Bell.
4	Both shifts	Will Clyde Coe or Rick Dye enter the race at Le Mans in May?
5	Both shifts	Use AL for Ala., WI for Wis., MA for Mass., and CO for Colo.

| 1 | 2 | 3 | 4 | 5 | 6 | 7 | 8 | 9 | 10 | 11 | 12 |

13C   Technique Practice: Response Patterns ⑮ *each line at least twice SS; DS between groups*

Word-Level Response. Some short, frequently used words (like **to**, **and**, **the**, and **work**) are so easy to type they can be typed as words instead of letter by letter. *Think and type the word.*

Letter-Level Response. Many words (like **only**, **state**, **exceed**, and **extra**) are not so easy to type even though they are often used. Such words are typed letter by letter. *Think the letter; type it.*

Combination Response. Most normal copy is composed of both word- and letter-level sequences that require variable speed: high speed for easy words, low speed for hard ones. *Learn to recognize the difference.*

1	Word-level response	is to for do an may work so it but an with and them she with
2		if he is to go; she did the work; he may work with the panel
3		He may go with us and make them do the work by the big dock.
4	Letter-level response	only state jolly zest date plump verve extra join rate taxes
5		you saw a great race; my only free dates are; get a tax case
6		You exceeded the stated rate; only the street guard saw you.
7	Combination response	it up so at for you may was but him work were they best into
8		the case is, the great city, date the card, quit my best job
9		If it is up to you to get the best rate, look into it today.

| 1 | 2 | 3 | 4 | 5 | 6 | 7 | 8 | 9 | 10 | 11 | 12 |

65A   Preparatory Practice ⑦ *each line three times; then 1' writings on Lines 2 and 4*

Alphabet   Kip Judge has a very large screen he will bring for my quiz next week.

Figures   In 1959, 302 clerks were working here; in 1964, 734; and in 1969, 928.

Figure-symbol   Zeno's sold 2,479 meals @ $1.75 per plate and 860 pieces of pie @ 35¢.

Fluency   The very time to try again and to do our best is when we want to stop.

| 1 | 2 | 3 | 4 | 5 | 6 | 7 | 8 | 9 | 10 | 11 | 12 | 13 | 14 |

65B   Preparing a Page-End Indicator ⑩

A page-end indicator is a standard 8½″ x 11″ sheet on which the numbers 1 to 33 have been typed vertically line by line from the top edge along the right side of the upper half while the numbers 33 to 1 are similarly typed on the lower half. Such an indicator is a useful device for typing manuscripts. It is particularly helpful in estimating the space needed for footnotes at the bottom of a page.

PROCEDURE

Insert a full sheet of paper. At the right edge of the sheet type the figure 1 in the first line space from the top edge, the figure 2 in the next space, and so on until you type the figure 33. In the next line space, repeat the figure 33; in the next space type 32, and so on down to figure 1 in the last line space on the page.

• *Keep your page-end indicator sheet for later use.*

DRILL

Place the page-end indicator sheet back of and extending slightly to the right of a full sheet. Insert these sheets into the typewriter and on the bottom half type the following words centered on Lines 24, 18, and 12, respectively:

> horizontal
> vertical
> center

65C   Problem Typing: Outline and Footnotes ㉝

Problem 1: Outline

Line: 70; SS; start on Line 20, using page-end indicator

	Words
LEFTBOUND MANUSCRIPTS WITH FOOTNOTES ᴛs	7
I. MARGINS FOR MANUSCRIPTS BOUND AT LEFT ᴅs	16
A. Top Margin	19
1. First page, 1½ or 2 inches	25
2. Other pages, 1 inch	30
B. Side and Bottom Margins (All Pages)	38
1. Left side, 1½ inches	43
2. Right side, 1 inch	48
3. Bottom, 1 inch	52
II. FOOTNOTES FOR ALL MANUSCRIPTS	60
A. Numbering	63
1. Reference figure at end of citation or quotation	74
2. Footnote (same reference figure) on page with quotation	86
B. Spacing	89
1. Separated from text or body by 1½-inch underline, preceded by a single space and followed by a double space	100 / 112
2. Single-spaced, separated by double spacing	122

13D Continuity Practice: Guided Writing ⑰ *½', 1', and 2' writings as directed*

Paragraph 1. Type two ½-minute writings. Determine *gwam* for the better writing (1' *gwam* times 2). Use this as your ½-minute base rate when setting a new goal. Ignore errors temporarily.

New Goal: Add 2 *gwam* to your ½-minute base rate; then type two ½-minute and two 1-minute writings at the new goal rate.
Paragraph 2. TYPE ¶ 2 as directed for ¶ 1.

Paragraphs 1 and 2. Type a 2-minute writing without the guides. Begin with ¶ 1 and type as much of ¶ 2 as you can. Determine *gwam*. Ignore errors. If time permits, type a second 2-minute writing.

All letters are used.

		GWAM *1'
¶1 1.2 SI 4.8 AWL 94% HFW	The person who cannot do at least one thing quite well	11
	finds it hard to move ahead in any job. So work on; do not	23
	give up. Value your new skill. Try daily to improve it.	34
¶2 1.2 SI 4.8 AWL 94% HFW	Size up the kind of job you want, and build the skills	45
	it requires. If typing is one of them, try to develop high	57
	speed next. Direct your effort to a new goal day by day.	69

1' GWAM | 1 | 2 | 3 | 4 | 5 | 6 | 7 | 8 | 9 | 10 | 11 | 12 |

*The figures in the GWAM Column at the right of the ¶s show the total words as well as the 1' *gwam*. The scale beneath the final ¶ indicates the 1' *gwam* for the incomplete line.

To Determine the 2' GWAM: Determine the 1' *gwam*, using the figures at the right of the ¶s and the scale beneath the final ¶; then divide the 1' *gwam* by 2.

LESSON 14

14A Preparatory Practice ⑧ *each line three times SS; DS between groups*

Alphabet — Karl and Jack served with Gus Fox in La Paz but quit in May.

2-syllable words — Cyrus will go into the city for the copy only if he is able.

Fluency — If we have the get up and go, can we go where we want to go?

| 1 | 2 | 3 | 4 | 5 | 6 | 7 | 8 | 9 | 10 | 11 | 12 |

14B Manipulative Parts Drill: Space Bar ⑩ *each line at least twice SS; DS between groups*

he was by the pier; call for my yacht; then get a quick deed

try to do your best now; send us an order; fold the end next

Just keep on, word by word. That is the way to build skill.

See if you can take the prize, for you must have skill then.

| 1 | 2 | 3 | 4 | 5 | 6 | 7 | 8 | 9 | 10 | 11 | 12 |

64E Problem Typing: Manuscripts ⑯

Problem 1: Unbound Manuscript

*Top margin: pica, 1½"; elite, 2";
side margins: 1" (10 pica spaces;
12 elite spaces); spacing: double;
SS and indent listed items 5
spaces from both margins*

Miniature models of both the pica
and the elite solutions are given at
the right. *Do not type from the models;*
work from the copy given at the bottom of the page.

Problem 2: Topbound Manuscript

If time permits, retype Problem 1 as
a topbound manuscript. Omit the last
sentence of ¶ 2, including the quotation.

PICA

ELITE

THE SPEAKER'S DILEMMA

	Words
	4

The inexperienced public speaker is faced with a real problem in deciding upon | 20

the method of delivery to use. The beginner usually feels more secure if he type- | 37

writes the speech in advance and actually reads the copy word for word. The big | 53

weakness in this, of course, is that audience contact is difficult to maintain. | 69

Most experienced speakers deliver their speeches extemporaneously from a pre- | 84

pared outline. The novice without a script, however, fears that he will "fall on | 101

his face." He is conscious of the point which was made so well by the orator | 117

Demosthenes of ancient Greece: "A vessel is known by the sound, whether it be | 132

cracked or not; so men are proved by their speech, whether they be wise or foolish." | 150

As a compromise, the beginner should probably use a typewritten script; but | 165

he should attempt to extemporize, and he should use the script only when he feels | 181

the need to do so. With experience, he will depend upon a script less and less. | 198

Aside from the decision regarding the form and the extent of notes to use, | 213

the speaker's dilemma includes other elements: | 222

    1. To gesture or not to gesture. | 227
    2. To inject humor or "play it straight." | 236
    3. To illustrate with examples or merely describe. | 246
    4. To visualize or merely vocalize. | 253

In general, visual aids and illustrative examples not only make a talk more | 269

interesting, but also encourage the speaker into natural animation and the use of | 285

spontaneous gestures. | 289

14C   Technique Practice: Stroking ⑭ *each line at least twice SS; DS between groups*

1	Home row	Alf Lakas had Sal add half a glass. I shall stash all cash.
2	Third row	Your typewriter is a useful tool; it helps you perform well.
3	Bottom row	Mac gave all six men a chance to act as foremen in my plant.
4	Adjacent keys	Mr. Leeds had his store open, but Sal quit buying art there.
5	Direct reaches	A host of friends is just a myth; true friends are numbered.
6	Double letters	Will Buzz and Lee carry the express carton to my booth soon?
7	One-hand words	After my new rate was set, a decrease in taxes was detected.
8	Balanced-hand words	It is right for them to sign the forms; Ken may do so, also.

| 1 | 2 | 3 | 4 | 5 | 6 | 7 | 8 | 9 | 10 | 11 | 12 |

14D   Continuity Practice: Guided Writing ⑱

DO: Type ½- and 1-minute writings on each ¶ as directed in 13D, page 28.

Then, type a 2-* and a 3-minute writing, beginning with ¶ 1 and typing as much of ¶ 2 as you can.

All letters are used.

		GWAM 1′	3′
¶1 1.2 SI 4.8 AWL 94% HFW	The major aim of this book is to help you learn how to	11	4 | 35
	type. Its second aim is to help you improve how you write,	23	8 | 39
	for you will not always be able merely to copy all the work	35	12 | 43
	you need to prepare. You will have to compose, also.	46	15 | 46
¶2 1.2 SI 4.8 AWL 94% HFW	As you practice to learn how to type, try to develop a	57	19 | 50
	writing skill, too. The next time you are asked to compose	69	23 | 54
	a paper for class, size up the job and set about writing it	81	27 | 58
	on the machine. It may be quite slow at first, but keep on.	93	31 | 62

1′ GWAM | 1 | 2 | 3 | 4 | 5 | 6 | 7 | 8 | 9 | 10 | 11 | 12 |
3′ GWAM | 1 | 2 | 3 | 4 |

*To determine the 2′ rate, divide the 1′ rate by 2.

LESSON 15

15A   Preparatory Practice ⑧ *each line three times SS; DS between groups*

Alphabet	Was Dale quick to give him a box just the size for my plant?
2-syllable words	Many of the women are away today to study a new money offer.
Fluency	A man can grow out of a small job and come to fit a big one.

| 1 | 2 | 3 | 4 | 5 | 6 | 7 | 8 | 9 | 10 | 11 | 12 |

64A Preparatory Practice ⑦ *each line three times; then 1' writings on Lines 3 and 4*

Alphabet   The qualities of the mined zinc keep varying with the job excavations.

Figures   Here is Rothman's order for 50M of Form CZ1234 and 20M of Form WX6789.

Figure-symbol   Perform the calculation of (134 x 569) – (127 x 45) on the calculator.

Fluency   It is easy to give advice to others but not always so easy to take it.

| 1 | 2 | 3 | 4 | 5 | 6 | 7 | 8 | 9 | 10 | 11 | 12 | 13 | 14 |

64B Technique Practice: Machine Manipulations ⑦ *each line at least twice*

Center
↓

Tabulator and return   Try not to pause at the end of the line before you return.

Tabulator   three ☐4☐ 3 ☐4☐ five ☐4☐ 5 ☐4☐ seven ☐4☐ 7 ☐4☐ eleven ☐4☐ 11 ☐4☐ fifteen ☐4☐ 15

Shift keys   Send Fields & Marshall ten copies of the new book by Niels and Atwood.

Space bar   If it is convenient, may I see you at the next meeting of the members?

Shift lock   Underline or ALL CAP addressee notations: Hold for Arrival, PERSONAL.

| 1 | 2 | 3 | 4 | 5 | 6 | 7 | 8 | 9 | 10 | 11 | 12 | 13 | 14 |

64C Composing at the Typewriter ⑩

1. Study the poem given as Problem 1, page 111, and decide what it means to you. Make notes.

2. Compose and type a paragraph, giving your interpretation of the poem. Proofread; correct; retype.

64D Typing Superscripts and Subscripts ⑩

A *superscript* is a figure or symbol typed above the line of writing; a *subscript*, a figure or symbol typed below. Use the ratchet release (automatic line finder) to position the carriage to the desired position.

To Type a Footnote Reference Figure (Superscript): (1) Operate the ratchet release; (2) turn the cylinder *backward* (toward you); (3) type the figure, then return the lever to normal position.

To Type a Chemistry Symbol (Subscript): (1) Operate the ratchet release; (2) turn the cylinder *forward* (away from you); (3) type the figure and return the lever to its position.

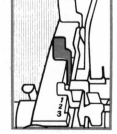

DRILL PROCEDURE

1. Type a 1" line, using the underline key.

2. Operate the ratchet release and move the cylinder *forward* (away from you) about 1".

3. Type another 1" line.

4. Return the lever to normal position; move the cylinder back to the first line; gauge the line and type over it.

5. Type the sentences given below, typing the superscript and the subscripts as directed at the left.

According to a Typewriting News article, "The ZIP Code should appear on the line with the names of the city and state."[1]

The symbol for sodium carbonate is Na_2CO_3.

15B Manipulative Parts Drill: Tabulator and Return ⑩ *twice as shown*

Machine Adjustments. Line: 60. Clear all tabulator stops, set a tab stop 5 spaces to the right of the left margin; then, set three additional tab stops 5 spaces apart.

Procedure. Begin the first line of the drill at the left margin. Tabulate once (5 spaces) to type Line 2; 10 spaces to type Line 3, and so forth. Learn to tab, release, and type quickly.

1	Margin→	Set a new goal for each drill and push yourself to reach it.
2	Indent 5 ----→	A new goal and renewed zeal may be all you need to win.
3	Indent 10 --------→	If more speed is your goal, keep your hands quiet.
4	Indent 15 ------------→	Do not quit; just keep on; give it your best.
5	Indent 20 ----------------→	Ask much of yourself; next, work for it.

15C Technique Practice: Stroking ⑮ *each line three times SS; DS between groups*

1	Long words	deftly together clarity express ideas puzzling message today
2	Weak fingers	exact size; top tax plan; quick stop; pop quiz; I was amazed
3	Awkward reaches	extra plaque; only jazz; excess nylon; was razed; exact copy
4	One-hand	Are you on my tax case? My tax rates are, in fact, average.
5	Balanced-hand	It is the duty of the six girls to work with the audit firm.
6	Combination	He based the case upon the data shown on the express ticket.

| 1 | 2 | 3 | 4 | 5 | 6 | 7 | 8 | 9 | 10 | 11 | 12 |

15D Growth Index ⑰ *three 3' writings; determine average gwam*

All letters are used.

		GWAM		
		1'	3'	

¶1
1.2 SI
4.8 AWL
94% HFW

How well you write means just how deftly you put words | 11 | 4 | 36

together to say what you want to say. It does not mean how | 23 | 8 | 40

well you can use a pen. If you learn to type well, you can | 35 | 12 | 44

improve the clarity as well as the manner of your writing. | 47 | 16 | 48

¶2
1.2 SI
4.8 AWL
94% HFW

When you next try to express an idea, reduce the haze; | 58 | 19 | 52

say what you want to say in such a way that the reader will | 70 | 23 | 56

know your meaning quickly. Do not leave him to puzzle over | 82 | 27 | 60

your message. A top typing job will help him on his way to | 94 | 31 | 64

what you mean, too. | 97 | 32 | 65

1' GWAM | 1 | 2 | 3 | 4 | 5 | 6 | 7 | 8 | 9 | 10 | 11 | 12 |
3' GWAM | 1 | 2 | 3 | 4 |

63D Problem Typing: Poem, "Spread" Titles, and Outline ㉕

Problem 1: Poem

Half sheet, long side at left; line: 45; SS; 2" top margin; center title in ALL CAPS

	Words
I Asked and Received TS	4
I asked for bread,	8
He gave me a field to plow --	14
A field to seed and tend and spray,	21
To care for day by day --	26
And I have bread now. DS	31
I asked for money,	34
He gave me work to do --	39
Work most exacting, demanding,	45
With horizons ever expanding --	52
Now I have money, too. DS	56
I asked for honors,	60
He gave me a choice to make --	67
The easy wrong or the hard right,	73
Honor or honors for which to fight --	81
He leadeth me: Honors without honor I forsake.	90

Problem 2: Centering "Spread" Titles

HOW TO CENTER A "S P R E A D" TITLE

1. From the center of the paper, backspace once for each letter except the last one in the heading and once for each space between words.
2. Type the title, spacing once between the letters and three times between the words.

Half sheet, short side at left; 2" top margin; DS; center each "spread" title shown below. The first one is given in correct form.

	Words
C E N T E R I N G H E A D I N G S	7
TYPING TITLES AND HEADINGS	13
TYPING REPORT OUTLINES	17
TYPING REPORT MANUSCRIPTS	22
CENTERING OVER WRITING LINE	28
CENTERING ON SPECIAL-SIZE PAPER	34

Problem 3: Outline of Manuscript Form

Full sheet; line: 70; SS; 2½" top margin

	Words
U N B O U N D A N D T O P B O U N D M A N U S C R I P T S TS	13
I. EASE OF READING AIDED BY MARGINS AND SPACING DS	23
A. Margins	25
1. Bottom and side: 1"	30
2. Top, first page: unbound, 1½ or 2"; topbound, 2 or 2½"	42
3. Top, other pages: unbound, 1"; topbound, 1½"	53
B. Spacing	55
1. Body of manuscript double-spaced	63
2. Paragraphs indented 5, 7, or 10 spaces uniformly	73
3. Quoted material of 4 or more lines single-spaced	84
a. Indented 5 spaces from both margins	93
b. Quotation marks permissible but not required	104
C. Page Numbers	107
1. First page: centered ½" from bottom edge of paper	119
2. Other pages, unbound: even with right margin ½" from top	131
3. Other pages, topbound: same as for the first page DS	142
II. CLARITY AIDED BY HEADINGS AND SUBHEADINGS DS	153
A. Main Headings	156
1. Centered in all capital letters	164
2. Followed by triple space	170
B. First-Order Subheadings	175
1. Typed on separate line even with left margin, underlined	188
2. Preceded by triple space and followed by double space	200
C. Second-Order Subheadings	205
1. Indented as first line of paragraph, underlined	216
2. Preceded by double space	222

Purpose. The basic purpose of this section is to develop your figure-typing skill. You will also build your basic skills to higher levels.

Machine Adjustments. Line: 60; SS all drills, unless otherwise directed; DS and indent ¶s 5 spaces.

Self-Improvement Practice. Select from page 39 material correlating with the appropriate lesson.

Copy Difficulty. Up to now you have typed very easy copy. You will now type longer, less frequent words that contain more syllables.

Some of the drills may be more difficult, but the straight-copy ¶s you will type are rated *Easy*.

You will also type some copy that contains figures and still other material in handwritten or script form.

LESSON 16

16A Preparatory Practice ⑧ *each line twice SS; DS between two-line groups*

Alphabet	Four jets zoomed up quickly, leaving six white trails below.
x and p	Rex put six stamps on a tiny box for the next postal pickup.
y and q	Ilya Myers quietly began her quest for quaint styles Monday.
Fluency	They kept the rug on the theory that they had a right to it.

| 1 | 2 | 3 | 4 | 5 | 6 | 7 | 8 | 9 | 10 | 11 | 12 |

16B Stroking Technique Practice for 5, 8, and 1 ⑮

5—Left first finger

8—Right second finger

1—Left fourth finger
(Special Figure 1)

1—Right third finger
(Letter *l* for 1)

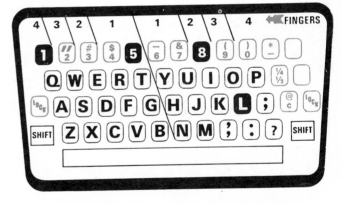

1. Locate the new key on the keyboard chart.
2. Find the key on your typewriter keyboard.
3. Study the appropriate reach illustration, at left.
4. Watch your finger make the reach a few times.
5. Type the tryout drill, below, for that key.

Tryout Drills *each line at least twice*

1	5	f f5f 5f 5f 551 555	All 55 students took 5 tests in 5 days.
2	8	k k8k 8k 8k 881 888	Kate may play the 88 from 8 until late.
3	Figure 1	a ala la la 111 111	My 11 men worked from May 1 to June 11.
4	Letter l as 1	1 11 .1 1. .11 1.1.	My 11 men worked from May 1 to June 11.
5		Is it Channel 5, 8, or 11? Was the score 5 to 8, or 8 to 5?	
6	Consolidation	Three of the 158 men are absent; the other 155 arrived at 8.	

| 1 | 2 | 3 | 4 | 5 | 6 | 7 | 8 | 9 | 10 | 11 | 12 |

63A Preparatory Practice ⑦ *each line three times; then 1' writings on Lines 2 and 4*

Alphabet   She will give any quaint excuse for making bold jaunts to polar zones.

Figures   I timed my 5 winners at 146, 137, 128, 116, and 109 wpm, respectively.

Symbols   Do not divide "don't" or "wasn't" (contractions) at the end of a line.

Fluency   You will find that you can do a lot of work if you will plan the work.
            | 1 | 2 | 3 | 4 | 5 | 6 | 7 | 8 | 9 | 10 | 11 | 12 | 13 | 14 |

63B Technique Practice: Response Patterns ⑩ *each line at least three times*

Balanced-hand   Six or eight of their men lent a hand with the work of the city audit.

Combination   Their union steward may draft a formal statement to the next chairman.

Double letters Lynn will see that Britt sends the letter to your office by next week.

One-hand   Did you arrive after I set the minimum rate based on average earnings?

One-hand   I was not at union headquarters when a new wage contract was defeated.
                | 1 | 2 | 3 | 4 | 5 | 6 | 7 | 8 | 9 | 10 | 11 | 12 | 13 | 14 |

63C Typing from Script ⑧ *line: 65; DS*

1. Type each of the following ¶s as a 1' writing. Determine *gwam* and errors.

2. Type a 3' writing on both ¶s combined. Repeat the first ¶ if necessary. Determine *gwam* and errors.

All letters are used.

	GWAM	
	1'	3'

To simplify your first typing of manuscripts, up to now all your reports were typed with a uniform 65-space line, regardless of whether your machine had pica- or elite-size type. Next, you will learn to arrange reports according to standard conventions of manuscript layout, based on number of inches in the margins instead of number of spaces in the writing line.

	1'	3'
	12	4	54
	25	8	58
	38	13	63
	51	17	67
	65	22	72
	73	24	74

When standard conventions are followed, pica and elite solutions will differ somewhat. If 1-inch side margins are used, for example, an elite line will contain 78 spaces while a pica line will contain only 65 spaces. As a result, considerably more copy can be placed on a page of elite type. Be quick to learn the placement points for reports just as you have for other problems.

	1'	3'
	12	28	78
	25	33	83
	38	37	87
	51	41	91
	64	46	95
	77	50	100

1' GWAM | 1 | 2 | 3 | 4 | 5 | 6 | 7 | 8 | 9 | 10 | 11 | 12 | 13 |
3' GWAM | 1 | 2 | 3 | 4 | 5 |

16C Tab Mechanism and Figure Practice ⑫ *type the drill three times as shown*

PROCEDURE FOR SETTING TAB STOPS

1. Clear all tab stops. (See page 17, if necessary.)
2. For Column 2, set a tab stop 8 spaces from the left margin.
3. For Column 3, set a tab stop 8 spaces from the first tab stop.
4. Set stops for remaining columns in similar manner.

TECHNIQUE EMPHASIS

Nonelectric: Depress and hold the tab bar or key down until the carriage stops. Move quickly back to home position and type the next item.

Electric: Flick the tab key or bar lightly; return the controlling finger to its home position at once.

Reach with the fingers	it	to	if	do	go	so	the	and	Eyes on copy during return
	85	15	88	55	51	18	581	858	
	we	in	as	no	be	on	was	pin	DS
	58	88	51	85	55	15	518	115	
	by	of	an	is	me	am	oz.	lb.	
	81	55	18	88	85	58	181	151	

KEY | 2 | 6 | 2 | 6 | 2 | 6 | 2 | 6 | 2 | 6 | 2 | 6 | 3 | 6 | 3 |

16D Skill-Transfer Typing ⑮

Skill-transfer typing is a procedure used to determine how well you are able to transfer your straight-copy skill to other types of copy: script (handwritten copy) and statistical copy, for example. **Goal:** To equal your straight-copy rate.

1. Type each ¶ as a 1' writing. Compare *gwam*. If your script rate does not equal your straight-copy rate, type two additional 1' writings on ¶ 2.
2. Type each ¶ again as a 1' writing. Compare *gwam*.
3. Type a 3' writing on ¶s 1 and 2 combined.

All letters are used.

		GWAM 1'	GWAM 3'	
¶1 1.3 SI 5.2 AWL 91% HFW	This is the age of numbers. Almost every adult has at	11	4	34
	least fifty numbers that are his and his alone. These range	23	8	38
	from the number of his birth record to the numbers of his	35	12	42
	credit cards, his car license, his accounts, and so on.	46	15	46
¶2 1.3 SI 5.2 AWL 91% HFW	It is important, next, that you master the top row on	11	19	49
	your machine. Whether you go to work in an office or just	23	23	53
	type your own letters, in years to come you will prize quite	35	27	57
	highly your number typing skill. Build it high today.	46	30	61

1' GWAM | 1 | 2 | 3 | 4 | 5 | 6 | 7 | 8 | 9 | 10 | 11 | 12 |
3' GWAM | 1 | 2 | 3 | 4 |

62D Problem Typing: Manuscript on Outlining ㉓

ALIGNING ARABIC AND ROMAN NUMERALS

Align columns of Arabic and Roman numerals at the right. To provide the proper spacing between the columns of Arabic and Roman numerals, set each tabulator stop for the number of spaces needed between columns *plus* the number of spaces required to type the longest line in the column.

SPACING BETWEEN RELATED AND UNRELATED COLUMNS

Spacing may vary between columns depending on their relationship. In the following manuscript, for example, related columns (1-2, 3-4, 5-6) are typed closer together for quick identification of the relationship between the columns; but unrelated columns (2-3, 4-5) are more widely separated.

Full sheet; 1½″ top margin; 65-space line; 5-space ¶ indention; DS the ¶s; SS the table and outline; spaces between columns as indicated

ARABIC AND ROMAN NUMERALS IN OUTLINES
TS

Use Roman numerals to identify major divisions of outlines; capital letters to identify subheadings; and Arabic numerals to identify items under subheadings. Study the Arabic and Roman numerals listed below:
DS

SPACING KEY									
	1	I		6	VI		15	XV	
	2	II		7	VII		40	XL	
9	3	4 III	10	8	4 VIII	10	50	4 L	9
	4	IV		9	IX		60	LX	
	5	V		10	X		100	C	

Type topic outlines without punctuation at the ends of lines (except for abbreviations), but type sentence outlines with appropriate punctuation at line endings.

There are several acceptable styles for capitalizing headings and subheadings. The style illustrated below (showing headings in descending order of importance) is one of the most widely used.
TS

TOPIC OUTLINE
TS

I. CAPITALIZING HEADINGS IN OUTLINES
DS
    Reset margin→A. Major Headings in All Caps
    B. Important Words of First-Order Subheadings Capitalized
    C. Only First Word of Second-Order Subheadings Capitalized
DS
II. SPACING OUTLINES
DS
    A. Horizontal Spacing
    Set tab→1. Title typed solid or as a spread heading
        2. Other headings typed solid
        3. Identifying numerals and letters followed by 2 spaces
    B. Vertical Spacing
        1. Title followed by a triple space
        2. Main headings (except the first) preceded by a double space, followed by a double space
        3. All subheading items single-spaced

Words
8
20
32
45
50
53
56
61
64
68
80
94
101
113
127
139
142
150
156
168
180
185
189
199
205
217
221
228
240
248
256

LESSON 17

17A Preparatory Practice ⑧ *each line twice SS; DS between two-line groups*

Alphabet   Having just made six quick points, we simply froze the ball.

z and o   Zed overshot their end zone, leaving the score zero to zero.

Figure   Her flight, No. 158, lands at 8 p.m. on Thursday, August 15.

Fluency   Did the firm pay the fares for the men, women, and children?

    | 1 | 2 | 3 | 4 | 5 | 6 | 7 | 8 | 9 | 10 | 11 | 12 |

17B Stroking Technique Practice for 2, 0 (Zero), and : (Colon) ⑮

2—Left third finger

0—Right fourth finger

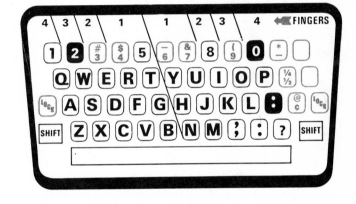

Typing : (Colon). Type : (the shift of ;) with the *right fourth finger*. Do not space after : used to separate hours and minutes in stating time. Space twice after : in other uses.

Tryout Drills *each line at least twice*

1   2   s s2s 2s 2s 22 222 Andrew is 21; Keith, 22; and Walter, 25.

2   0   ; ;0; 0; 0 00 000 Use 0, 00, or 000 steel wool for the job.

3   :   ; ;:; :; 1:15 8:01 5:10 Call me at 5:15 and arrive at 8:20.

4   Get there by 8:00 or 8:05; the opera begins at 8:15 or 8:20.

    Consolidation

5   Whether you are 20 or 50, each workday begins at 8:15 there.

17C Tab Mechanism and Figure Practice ⑮ *twice with SS; DS between typings*

Set left margin stop; set tab stops to leave 7 spaces between columns.

the	150	work	5810	eight	11,200
for	201	then	1580	handy	58,201
did	885	with	2285	right	21,822
and	551	town	2058	their	20,581
man	820	much	1150	girls	55,220
due	112	firm	8201	chair	18,250
aid	582	land	2805	field	52,815

KEY | 3 | 7 | 3 | 7 | 4 | 7 | 4 | 7 | 5 | 7 | 6 |

Purpose. The purpose of the 10 lessons of this section is to increase your communication skills through the medium of personal and business reports and to provide additional composing opportunities.

Machine Adjustments. Line: 70, unless otherwise directed; SS drills; DS timed writing ¶s and indent first line of each ¶ 5 spaces; DS manuscripts or reports.

Self-Improvement Practice. Type the script and rough draft items on pages 110, 111, 118, 122, or the Self-Improvement Practice items on page 126.

LESSON 62

62A Preparatory Practice (7) *each line three times; then 1' writings on Lines 2 and 4*

Alphabet — Professor Henry King announced a major quiz will be given next Monday.
Figures — These 80 scouts, 12 men, and 67 donkeys were loaded with 3,945 pounds.
Figure-symbol — Miller & Southby (local grocers) were selling bananas for 12¢ a pound.
Fluency — He will do well to try one or more of the very fine pens for the work.

| 1 | 2 | 3 | 4 | 5 | 6 | 7 | 8 | 9 | 10 | 11 | 12 | 13 | 14 |

62B Technique Practice: Stroking (10) *each line three or more times*

Balanced-hand — Did the chairman say the visit of the men will aid the endowment fund?
Adjacent — As Sadie has said, few can excel the many points Myrna Powell has won.
One-hand — In my opinion, it was foolish to race up that hill as fast as you did.
Hyphen — Here is an up-to-date reference for those out-of-this-world questions.
Roman numerals — Type Roman numerals in capital letters: I (1), IV, (4), V (5), X (10).

| 1 | 2 | 3 | 4 | 5 | 6 | 7 | 8 | 9 | 10 | 11 | 12 | 13 | 14 |

62C Speed and Control Building (10)

1. Type a 1' writing on the following ¶. Determine *gwam*. Then add 4 *gwam* to this rate for a new goal.
2. Type two 1' guided *speed* writings, trying to reach the new goal. If you attain it on the first or second attempt, add 4 more *gwam* for the next writing. Use a 15" guide call.

3. Reduce your last goal rate by 2 *gwam* for the next guided writing.
4. Type two 1' guided *control* writings on the ¶, trying to reduce your errors. If you make more than 2 errors on the first writing, reduce your speed by 2 more *gwam* for the next writing.
5. Type a 2' writing. Determine *gwam* and errors.

All letters are used.

1.4 SI
5.4 AWL
85% HFW

	2' GWAM	
Some workers can't do anything unless they are told just what to	7	53
do and how to do it. They may be good at routine jobs, but they are	13	60
limited by their lack of imagination, creativity, and the urge to ex-	20	67
plore new methods of doing things. Even great skill isn't adequate,	27	74
because quick hands must be guided by a reflective head––a fact many	34	80
workers often fail to recognize. Learn now to match your skills with	41	87
a desire to "find a better way" of doing your work.	46	93

2' GWAM | 1 | 2 | 3 | 4 | 5 | 6 | 7 |

17D Skill-Transfer Typing ⑮

DO: Type a 1′ writing on each ¶. Compare *gwam*. Then type another 1′ writing on each of the two slower ¶s.

DO: Finally, type a 3′ writing on ¶s 1, 2, and 3 combined. Determine *gwam*. Compare your 3′ *gwam* with your best 1′ *gwam* on each of the three ¶s.

All letters are used.

	GWAM 1′	3′	

¶1
1.3 SI
5.2 AWL
91% HFW

Will you enjoy working, or will you merely consider it — 11 | 4 | 42

something you must do? Your attitude may give the answer. — 23 | 8 | 46

Did you enter school to learn in order that you might go — 34 | 11 | 50

forth to serve? If so, you may well enjoy your work. — 45 | 15 | 54

¶2
1.3 SI
5.2 AWL
91% HFW

At what age will you begin work? If you attend college, — 11 | 19 | 58

you will probably be over twenty. Your next major effort may — 24 | 23 | 62

bring a sizable job. Will you quit, or will you keep on? — 35 | 27 | 66

¶3
1.3 SI
5.2 AWL
91% HFW

Even though the working life of most men is less than 50 — 11 | 31 | 69

years, more than a few plug along until they exceed 51 or 52. — 24 | 35 | 74

In about 18 years, our retirement age may drop by 10 percent. — 36 | 39 | 78

1′ GWAM | 1 | 2 | 3 | 4 | 5 | 6 | 7 | 8 | 9 | 10 | 11 | 12 |
3′ GWAM | 1 | 2 | 3 | 4 |

LESSON 18

18A Preparatory Practice ⑧ *each line twice SS; DS between two-line groups*

Alphabet — One judge was baffled as five boys quickly mixed the prizes.

c and y — Can you come by my office at once to approve your contracts?

Figures — Read: Unit 5, 8 pages; Unit 8, 20 pages; Unit 10, 12 pages.

Fluency — Did the auditor see the bids for this work on the city dock?

| 1 | 2 | 3 | 4 | 5 | 6 | 7 | 8 | 9 | 10 | 11 | 12 |

18B Tab Mechanism and Figure Practice ⑦ *twice as shown; DS between typings*

121	111	1582	12.50	8:15	11,500
212	222	2158	15.20	5:00	25,000
515	555	2085	28.00	2:50	85,205
818	888	8200	22.55	8:20	18,200

KEY | 3 | 7 | 3 | 7 | 4 | 7 | 5 | 7 | 4 | 7 | 6 |

18C Skill-Transfer Typing ⑫ *repeat 17D, above, as directed*

Problem 2

	Words
October 24, 19--	Miss Sally Hickenlooper	31 Pine Ridge Drive	Indianapolis,	15
IN 46260	Dear Sally:	20

Mrs. Lee has asked me to send you the following payroll record forms to be com- — 35
pleted before you report for work November 15: — 45

1. Employee's Withholding Exemption Certificate — 55
2. Health-Hospitalization Insurance Application — 64
3. Personal Data Card — 69

We certainly are pleased that you have decided to become an Office Aide when — 84
you move to Cincinnati next month. You will like Cincinnati, I know; and we — 100
shall do whatever we can to make your adjustment to new surroundings smooth — 115
and pleasant. — 118

As soon as your Cincinnati telephone is installed, please call and give me the — 134
number so that we can plan an unofficial welcome for you to the Queen City. — 149

Cordially yours, | (Miss) Shirley Biggs | Secretary to Mrs. Lee | xx | Enclo- — 163
sures | cc Mrs. Rhoda L. Lee — 168/181

Problem 3

Retype the letter of Problem 2, but address it to:

Miss Darlene Higgins
3800 Brentwood Court
Columbus, OH 43213

Supply an appropriate salutation and change the date in ¶ 1 to November 22. Prepare a carbon copy for Mrs. Rhoda L. Lee and type the carbon copy notation on the letter.

● Self-Improvement Practice *Line: 60; date on Line 16*

	Words
October 28, 19 -- (to 5)	3
Mr. Jay Bainbridge, *Manager*	9
54 Cleveland Avenue *Electrical Supply Company*	14
Milford, ~~Ohio~~ (OH) 45150	18
	22
Dear Mr. Bainbridge:	26

Here are the *hourly* pay rates for the ~~3 categories~~ *three classifications* of temporary employees we — 44
discussed on the telephone today: — 49

Senior Stenographer $3.00 — 54
Keypunch Operator 2.70 — 59
Clerk-Typist 2.60 — 63

As you indicated on the telephone, our rates are *somewhat* higher than those of some of the — 81
other agencies in this area. Apparently they *know* what their services are worth, and — 98
so do we. We have yet to have an employer tell us that an Office Aide did not — 114
give a day's work for a day's pay. ¶ May we have the opportunity of placing one or — 131
more of our highly trained workers in your company (soon) — 142

Sincerely yours, — 145

John D. Morganroth (Assistant Sales Manager) — 154/172

xx

18D Stroking Technique Practice for 3, 6, and / (Diagonal) ⑬

3—Left second finger

6—Right first finger

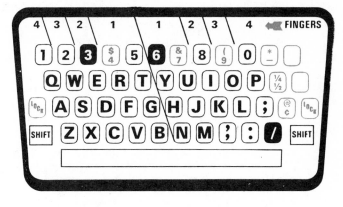

Typing the Diagonal (/). Move the *right fourth finger* down to **?** and *without shifting* type /. Use / to type fractions for which there are no keyboard symbols, as 2/3 and 3/4.

Tryout Drills *each line at least twice*

1   3   d d3d 3d 3d 3d 33 333 Type 31, 38, 53, 30, 23, 58, and 201.

2   6   j j6j 6j 6j 6j 66 666 Reach for 61, 56, 16, 26, 68, and 66.

3   /   ; ;/; /; / 1/8 or 1/5 Type these fractions: 1/8, 5/8, 2/5.

4   What is the sum of 136 and 63? of 20 and 58? of 3/5 and 2/3?

5   Consolidation   In 1868, we had just 215 workers; today, we have over 1,300.

18E Stroking Review and Skill Building ⑩

DO: Type each of the four drill lines twice: once for speed; once for control.

DO: Type two 2' writings on the ¶. Determine *gwam* on the better writing.

All figures taught   You must pay Edit, Inc., Invoices 163, 186, and 203 at once.

All figures taught   Order these items: 2 doz. 513A; 3 lbs. 268X; 10 gal. 360DC.

Alphabet   Dolly Webb seeks her next prize for quince jam at Big River.

Alphabet   Milford J. Zorn will give a trophy to the six quickest boys.

| 1 | 2 | 3 | 4 | 5 | 6 | 7 | 8 | 9 | 10 | 11 | 12 |

All letters are used.

	2' GWAM
1.3 SI	
5.2 AWL	
90% HFW	

The advice to write as you talk has a lot going for it,   6   48

provided you have an effective manner of speech. Some persons   12   54

who can talk in a clear, friendly way, however, will often   18   60

freeze up when they have to dictate a letter or report or   24   66

write one on the typewriter. The way to write as you talk is   30   72

really quite simple: Just forget about trying to impress or   36   78

express and simply try to inform with a free and easy manner.   42   84

2' GWAM | 1 | 2 | 3 | 4 | 5 | 6 |

61B Growth Index (13) *two 5' writings; determine gwam and errors for better writing*

All letters are used.

¶ 1
1.4 SI
5.4 AWL
85% HFW

What we say and how we say it influence the people to whom we talk
and write. Their reactions to us and our ideas are greatly influenced by
our language. Therefore, how we think and express our ideas will
vitally affect the success of our daily lives.

	1'	5'
	13	3	34
	28	6	37
	41	8	39
	51	10	41

¶ 2
1.4 SI
5.4 AWL
85% HFW

All major positions in the modern business world require an ability
to write well. The bigger the job, the more vital the writing skill.
Sooner than you expect, you may have an opportunity for such a job. Are
you ready to do the writing a top job demands?

14	13	44
28	16	47
42	19	49
52	20	51

¶ 3
1.4 SI
5.4 AWL
85% HFW

The flair some people seem to show in writing usually results from
years of careful effort. As you try to analyze the letters of others and
to write some yourself, you can develop your own flair. In fact, flair
may be little more than word skill well applied.

13	23	54
28	26	57
43	29	60
52	31	62

1' GWAM | 1 | 2 | 3 | 4 | 5 | 6 | 7 | 8 | 9 | 10 | 11 | 12 | 13 | 14 |
5' GWAM | 1 | 2 | 3 |

61C Problem Typing Measurement (30) *Line: 60; date, Line 16; 2 cc's; envelope; errors corrected*

Get Ready to Type . . . . . 4'
Timed Production . . . . 20'
Proofread . . . . 6'

1. Assemble needed supplies: 3 letterheads, 2 carbon sheets, 6 copy sheets, 3 envelopes.

2. Get ready to type; when told to begin, type as many problems as you can in 20 minutes.

Problem 1

	Words
October 24, 19--	Mr. J. Evan Richards	Apollo Tool & Die Works	1818 Sherman	15
Avenue	Norwood, OH 45212	Dear Mr. Richards:		24

Thank you for telephoning this morning to discuss with us the possibility of our providing some temporary secretarial help during the months of December and January. We shall be glad to work with you in any way that will be beneficial. — 40 / 56 / 72

The enclosed brochure describes our objectives and functions and outlines briefly our methods of operation. The table of pay rates for various classifications of employees will give you a good idea of the cost of the work you want to have done. — 88 / 104 / 121

Mr. Ronald J. Seybold, one of our work relations coordinators, will call you early next week to arrange an appointment to consider your job requirements in detail. You'll find him quite capable in matching the worker to the job. — 137 / 152 / 167

Sincerely yours, | John D. Morganroth | Assistant Sales Manager | xx | Enclosure | — 182
cc Mr. Ronald J. Seybold — 187/204

LESSON 19

19A Preparatory Practice ⑧ *each line twice SS; DS between two-line groups*

Alphabet   Pride in his work quickly gave Jim Fitz his next big chance.

Fractions   Type these fractions: 1/3, 5/6, 2/5, 3/8, 1/6, 8/15, 10/13.

Figures   Type these figures: 58, 20, 15, 11, 55, 38, 22, 10, 33, 85.

Fluency   She paid the firm the usual price for the six formal chairs.
            | 1 | 2 | 3 | 4 | 5 | 6 | 7 | 8 | 9 | 10 | 11 | 12 |

19B Stroking Technique Practice for 4, 9, and Shift Lock ⑬

4—Left first finger

9—Right third finger

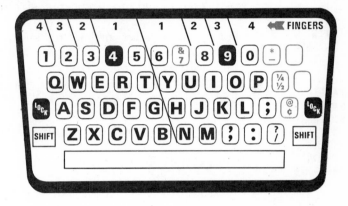

Using the Shift Lock (29). To type in ALL CAPS or to underline several words, use the shift lock. Depress the shift lock and leave it down until the typing is done. Operate the shift key to release it.

Tryout Drills *each line at least twice*

1   4   f f4f 4f 4f 14 44 444 Study Unit 14, pages 144 through 164.

2   9   l 191 91 91 91 99 999 All pools opened at 9:15 during 1969.

3   Shift lock   Vol. XXXVIII Check Vol. XXIX, No. 10, of the YMCA magazine.

4   Her ZIP Code is 49128. Did Jan and Ed say theirs was 63015?

    Consolidation
5   The clerk checked Items 24, 36, and 58 on pages 190 and 201.

19C Tab Mechanism and Figure Practice ⑫ *twice SS; DS between typings*

was	491	were	3649	after	13,462
yes	144	have	2992	yours	95,846
yet	191	best	3829	month	20,400
way	290	able	4059	today	16,396
let	490	next	1289	daily	52,609
off	958	plan	5395	story	41,200

KEY | 3 | 7 | 3 | 7 | 4 | 7 | 4 | 7 | 5 | 7 | 6 |

LESSON 60

60A   Preparatory Practice ⑦ *each line three times; then 1' writings on Line 4*

Alphabet   Max landed a few quick jabs, but they weren't enough to stop Vic Zola!

Figures   Check my record: May 7, 25 letters; May 8, 24; May 9, 28; May 10, 36.

Figure-symbol   Use 1/2 and 1/4--not ½ and ¼--with such fractions as 5/6, 3/8, or 7/9.

Fluency   To turn a fast buck is the only goal of a number of our newer members.
                 | 1 | 2 | 3 | 4 | 5 | 6 | 7 | 8 | 9 | 10 | 11 | 12 | 13 | 14 |

60B   Building Speed and Control ⑬ *two 1' writings on each ¶; then two 3' writings on both ¶s*

All letters are used.

		GWAM	
		1'	3'

¶ 1
1.4 SI
5.4 AWL
85% HFW

You would not expect a sizable response to a mailing late in the   13 | 4 | 40

spring of a letter promoting snow tires; nor should you expect a let-   27 | 9 | 44

ter written in less than standard language to be effective if it has   41 | 14 | 49

been mailed to a group of college professors.   50 | 17 | 52

¶ 2
1.4 SI
5.4 AWL
85% HFW

A good knowledge of words is vital, of course; but so is a clear   13 | 21 | 56

knowledge of the reader. It is quite important that you style your   27 | 25 | 61

message to your reader's taste and direct it to his vocabulary level.   41 | 30 | 65

The writer is just half of the communication process; the reader is   54 | 35 | 70

the other.   56 | 36 | 71

1' GWAM | 1 | 2 | 3 | 4 | 5 | 6 | 7 | 8 | 9 | 10 | 11 | 12 | 13 | 14 |
3' GWAM | 1 | 2 | 3 | 4 | 5 |

60C   Problem Typing Review ㉚

1. Make pencil notations of the problems and page numbers given at the right.
2. Type each problem once, correcting any errors you make, unless you are directed by your instructor not to do so.
3. Address an envelope for each letter typed. Fold and insert the letters.

Pages 98–99, 56C, Style Letter 2
Page 101, 57D, Problem 2
Page 103, 58D, Problem 2
Page 104, 59D, Problem 3

LESSON 61

61A   Preparatory Practice ⑦ *each line three times; then 1' writings on Line 4*

Alphabet   Jack Craven planned six spots for Roz, but she quit my show in August.

Figures   Industrial stocks moved up 5.89; rails, down 2.47; utilities, up 1.63.

Figure-symbol   Did Ned pay $4.81 to $4.95 (less 6% discount) for 37 ft. of #260 wire?

Fluency   If a job squeeze is on, get the most from the edge you have right now.
                 | 1 | 2 | 3 | 4 | 5 | 6 | 7 | 8 | 9 | 10 | 11 | 12 | 13 | 14 |

19D Skill-Transfer Typing ⑰

DO: Type a 1′ writing on each ¶. Compare *gwam*. Then type two 1′ writings on each of the two slower ¶s.

DO: Finally, type two 3′ writings on ¶s 1, 2, and 3 combined. Determine average *gwam*. Compare average *gwam* with your best 1′ *gwam* on each ¶.

All letters are used.

		GWAM 1′	3′
¶1 1.3 SI 5.2 AWL 91% HFW	How many GWAM can you type today: 16, 18, 19, 20, or 22?	12	4 | 49
	With thoughtful attention to your typing habits, you can soon	24	8 | 53
	type 25 to 30 GWAM. Try to improve your speed by at least 20	37	12 | 58
	to 24 GWAM before the end of this quarter.	45	15 | 60
¶2 1.3 SI 5.2 AWL 91% HFW	*A big secret to speed is to type without pausing, word by*	12	19 | 64
	word. As you complete a word, do not freeze to it. Instead,	24	23 | 68
	turn loose of it immediately, space quickly, and begin the next	37	27 | 73
	word at once. Force yourself to keep on.	45	30 | 75
¶3 1.3 SI 5.2 AWL 91% HFW	Have a special goal for each writing. If the immediate	13	34 | 79
	goal is to improve speed, move quickly from word to word. If	24	38 | 83
	the new aim is control, drop back in rate to type with greater	36	42 | 87
	ease. Adjust the rate to the purpose of practice.	46	45 | 91

1′ GWAM | 1 | 2 | 3 | 4 | 5 | 6 | 7 | 8 | 9 | 10 | 11 | 12 |
3′ GWAM | 1   2   3   4 |

LESSON 20

20A Preparatory Practice ⑧ *each line twice SS; DS between two-line groups*

Alphabet   Quig Flynn will have the boxes packed with my prize jellies.

Shift lock   Have you read THE PERSISTENT TRUTH and THE PRICE OF FREEDOM?

Figures   My test covers 156 pages in 4 chapters: 28, 29, 30, and 31.

Fluency   Major cities are rich with problems but poor with solutions.

   | 1 | 2 | 3 | 4 | 5 | 6 | 7 | 8 | 9 | 10 | 11 | 12 |

20B Skill-Transfer Typing ⑳

DO: Repeat 19D, above. Type the 1′ writings in reverse order: ¶ 3 first, then ¶ 2, and finally ¶ 1. Begin the 3′ writing with ¶ 1; *circle errors.*

GOALS: To improve skill in handling script and statistical copy; to increase percentage of transfer from straight copy to other kinds of copy.

59B   Skill-Transfer Typing ⑦   *Line: 60; each line for a 1' writing; compare* gwam

Words

Straight copy   Can their van move the six heavy zinc boxes for the foreman?   12

Statistical copy   My Order #736 totals $528.90 and must be shipped by June 14.   12

Rough draft   The artist worked (steadily on) in#spite of the stifling ~~intense~~ heat.   12

Script   *Ed expected the quiz to be very difficult for the nine boys.*   12

| 1 | 2 | 3 | 4 | 5 | 6 | 7 | 8 | 9 | 10 | 11 | 12 |

59C   Drill on Tabulating ⑥

USE: Half sheet; 60-space line; SS; 1½" top margin.
DO: Center horizontally the table of Problem 1, 59D, below, leaving 6 spaces between columns. As a cen-tered main heading, use MAILING CHARGES. Repeat, if time permits. **Goal:** To improve use of the tabulator and skill in aligning figures.

59D   Problem Typing: Business Letters and Postal Card ㉚

FOR LETTERS: Line 60; date on Line 14; 1 cc; envelope of appropriate size; errors corrected; sub-stitute your initials for xx in the reference line.

Problem 1

Words

October 23, 19-- | Dr. Michael R. Mc-   7
Donough | 6832 Dixie Highway | Hamilton,   14
OH 45014 | Dear Dr. McDonough: | 20

The letters introducing your new physical fit-   29
ness program to a selected sample of athletic   39
coaches were typed, folded, and mailed last   47
week. The various charges are listed below: 56

Typing Letters	$56.70	61
Addressing Envelopes	2.70	66
Folding, Stuffing, and Stamping	1.75	76
Postage	9.00	79
	$70.15	79

We are pleased to have had the opportunity   88
to assist you. The changes we worked out   96
together should result in a greater number of   105
responses. Please let us know how many re-   114
turns come in.   117

By the time you are ready to prepare a com-   125
plete promotion, we shall have a battery of   134
four Auto-Typists installed. The cost per letter   144
should therefore be less. In addition, the Auto-   154
Typists eliminate the need for error correction   163
on the final copies.   168

Sincerely yours, | John D. Morganroth | 175
Assistant Sales Manager | xx   180/193

Problem 2

Words

October 23, 19-- | Miss Jean G. Hanna, Dean | 8
Tri-State College of Business | 15 N.W. River-   17
side Drive | Evansville, IN 47708 | Dear   25
Miss Hanna: 27

We are pleased to send you today a compli-   35
mentary copy of our communications layout   44
guide   45

STYLED TO THE READER'S TASTE   51

This little booklet has become a popular item   60
on the shelves of many college bookstores.   69

After you have used the guide as a reference   78
for a few days, you will probably want each of   87
your secretarial students to have one. It is   96
obtainable at $1.50 a copy from Business   105
Books, Inc., 5101 Madison Road, Cincinnati,   113
Ohio 45227.   116

Thank you for your interest in our communi-   124
cations practices. We shall be pleased to re-   133
ceive any comments and suggestions you may   142
have for the improvement of our layout guide.   151

Sincerely yours, | Randall B. Parkhurst | Com-   160
munications Director | xx   164/184

Problem 3

Type and address a postal card to *Mr. R. B. Dunn, Manager | Central College Store | Louisville, KY 40212.* Use the date and ¶s 1 and 2 of Problem 2 for the message. Supply an appropriate salutation; omit the complimentary close and type OFFICE AIDES, INC. in all caps a triple space below the message.

20C Stroking Technique Practice for 7, – (Hyphen), and –– (Dash)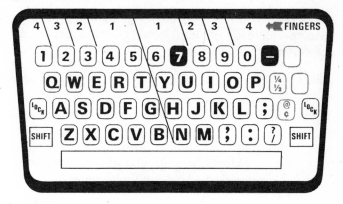

7—Right first finger

––—Right fourth finger

Typing the Dash (––). Type the dash with two hyphens without spacing either before or after; as in:

a 6-room house--2 bedrooms--at 12 Elm Ave.

Tryout Drills *each line at least twice*

1   7   j j7j 7j 7j 17 77 777 On May 27, 1970, 77 tags were issued.

2   –   ; ;-; -; co-op This up-to-date edition is first-class work.

3   ––   ; -- ; -- Use a 6-inch line--60 pica spaces--for your paper.

4   I bought a 7-room house--3 bedrooms--at 6 1/4 percent today.

Consolidation

5   FOR SALE: 8-room, 3-bath house--4/5 acre at 290 Elm Circle.

20D Growth Index and Skill Building ⑩

DO: Type a 3′ writing on the following ¶s. Determine *gwam* and errors.

DO: Type additional 3′ writings as time permits, trying to improve your speed or control, as appropriate.

All letters are used.

		1′	3′	
			GWAM	

¶1
1.3 SI
5.2 AWL
91% HFW

Just how well are you able to speak and to write? Is   11   4 43
it difficult for you to put your ideas into words that others 23   8 47
can easily understand? If so, you must learn how to use words 36 12 51
with greater ease and control. Choose each one with extreme   48 16 55
care. Control your use of words.   55 18 58

¶2
1.3 SI
5.2 AWL
91% HFW

Some people think that it is essential to use complex   11 22 61
terms to impress others; but it is the right word, not the   23 26 65
size of the word, that is important. Be as concise as possible 35 30 69
in your quest to improve your writing. Use as many words as   48 34 73
are necessary, but as few as you must, to state your thought   60 38 77
in familiar terms.   63 39 79

1′ GWAM | 1 | 2 | 3 | 4 | 5 | 6 | 7 | 8 | 9 | 10 | 11 | 12 |
3′ GWAM | 1 | 2 | 3 | 4 |

58D Problem Typing: Business Letters with Large Envelopes ㉚ *full sheets; Line: 60; date on Line 14*

Prepare two carbon copies and address a large envelope for each of the following letters. Erase and correct any errors you make as you type.

In Problem 1, note the use of *Mrs.* to indicate the dictator's marital status. In Problem 2, note that the listed items are indented 5 spaces from the left margin, are single-spaced with double spacing preceding and following; note, too, that two spaces follow the periods after the numbers. *Be sure to:* set a tabulator stop to indent the date and the closing lines; reset the left margin to type the listed items.

2 carbon

Problem 1

	Words
October 22, 19-- │ Dr. Dorothy Crunk, Chair-	8
man │ Department of Business Studies │ Gate-	16
way Community College │ Cincinnati, OH	23
45218 │ Dear Dr. Crunk: │	28

	Words
We are processing the employment applica-	36
tion of Miss Arlene Spencer, who lists you as	45
one of her references. She completed her	53
training in your department this past June.	62

	Words
Our Office Aides must move frequently from	71
one assignment to another; therefore, a pros-	80
pective aide should possess great adaptability,	89
the ability to adjust immediately not only to	99
new situations but also to new employers and	108
to new co-workers. One of our interviewers	116
wonders whether Miss Spencer would be able	125
to adapt quickly enough.	130

	Words
Do your work-experience records contain any	139
information that would be helpful to us in	148
assessing Miss Spencer's likelihood of success	157
as one of our Office Aides? We shall appre-	166
ciate your giving us this information either	175
on the enclosed form or by telephone.	182

	Words
Sincerely yours, │ (Mrs.) Rhoda L. Lee │	190
Personnel Officer │ lkd │ Enclosure │ cc Mr.	198
William R. Hathaway, Jr.	202/223*

*Includes envelope address.

Problem 2

	Words
October 22, 19-- │ Mrs. Ellen K. Burroughs │	8
9 Franklin Street │ Middletown, OH 45042 │	16
Dear Mrs. Burroughs: │	21

	Words
If you will complete the enclosed work-	28
preference record and return it to us in the	37
postpaid envelope supplied for your conve-	46
nience, we shall place your name on our regis-	55
ter as an Office Aide.	59

	Words
Please fill in the form completely. It provides	69
spaces for you to indicate (among other items	78
of information):	82

	Words
1. The date of your availability for	90
assignment	92
2. Your preference in work location	100
3. Your preference in type of business	108
operation	110

	Words
We are pleased to have you join our growing	119
staff of temporary office assistants. Upon	128
your success rests our own. We shall do	136
whatever we can to assure that mutual	144
success.	146

	Words
Sincerely yours, │ (Mrs.) Rhoda L. Lee │ Per-	154
sonnel Officer │ lkd │ Enclosure	159/172

Problem 3

Type the letter of Problem 2 again, but with the following changes:

	Words
Address: Miss Deborah Chisenhall	8
5687 Cincinnati Pike	12
Dayton, OH 45449	16
Salutation: Dear Miss Chisenhall:	20
Dictator: (Miss) Loraine Dorsey	153
Official Title: Personnel Assistant	157
Reference Line: Use your own initials	160/172

LESSON 59

59A Preparatory Practice ⑦ *each line three times; then 1' writings on Line 4*

Alphabet   David O. Whaley hopes to have a quick jet flight to Brazil next month.
Figures   Dial 926-5718 or 926-5739 to obtain your copy of this 40-page booklet.
Figure-symbol   Won't the B & B (Bixler & Barnes) stock pay 4%, plus a $2.30 dividend?
Fluency   If you wish to write well, use those words that we all can understand.

│ 1 │ 2 │ 3 │ 4 │ 5 │ 6 │ 7 │ 8 │ 9 │ 10 │ 11 │ 12 │ 13 │ 14 │

• Self-Improvement Practice

The following lines of drill material are correlated with the five lessons that constitute Section 3, with two lines of drill provided for each lesson.

The lines designated for a specific lesson emphasize the figures presented up to and including that lesson. *Reach* with the *fingers*.

Lesson 16   The 5 women and 18 men took Flight 158 to New York on May 5.
5 8 1   Did 15 of the 55 boys make a grade of 88 on the June 8 test?

Lesson 17   Each of the 2 men worked 250 hours from March 5 to April 20.
2 0 :   Check these flights: Delta 285 at 8:05; United 120 at 8:12.

Lesson 18   Ken is 36 years and 10 months old, and he weighs 266 pounds.
3 6 /   Buy 3 preferred shares at 38 1/8; 6 common shares at 26 3/8.

Lesson 19   What is the sum of 9 and 94 and 403 and 649 and 138 and 492?
4 9 Shift lock   The overall OLYMPIAN record: WON, 494; TIED, 49; LOST, 199.

Lesson 20   Did Flight 277 arrive at 7:37 p.m., or was it delayed again?
7 - - -   Forty-six boys took the test--a 5-minute writing--on May 17.
| 1 | 2 | 3 | 4 | 5 | 6 | 7 | 8 | 9 | 10 | 11 | 12 |

COMMON PROOFREADER'S MARKS (CORRECTION SYMBOLS)

Study carefully the following proofreader's marks, their meanings, and their applications. They will be encountered in Section 4 and subsequent ones.

CORRECTION   SYMBOL AND ILLUSTRATION

Correction	Symbol	Illustration
Add space	#	We should get underway by noon tomorrow.
All caps	≡≡≡	He requested a copy of Economics by Morganroth.
Cap letter	Cap or ≡	She selected an unusual oriental rug at Clossons.
Close up space	⌒	Letters of good will exert great influence today.
Delete (take out)	ℒ	The morning sessions begin at 9 a.m.
Insert	∧ ∨	"We meet on the 15th of June," she said. (Mondays,)
Insert parentheses	( )	Take these steps: (1) Assemble a 4-carbon pack;
Insert period	⊙	Your interest is appreciated. Every effort . . . .
Lower-case letter	l.c. or /	She received a set of exquisite China as a gift.
Move left	⌐	⌐ Your interest in our new product is very . . . .
Move right	⌐	Your interest in our product is very gratifying . . . .
Paragraph	¶	. . . on your next visit. ¶ Please let me know . . . .
Transpose	tr or ∿	Ask Rita to back order the four last items on the list.
Underline	ital or —	He is an editor for Reader's Digest, or so he says!

58A Preparatory Practice ⑦ *each line three times; then 1' writings on Line 4*

Alphabet   Jenny Nixon left my squad last week and gave back a prize she had won.

Figures   Gary reported on the following rooms: 6, 10, 18, 25, 27, 39, and 140.

Figure-symbol   Was his 4-year lease (May 23 expiration) renewed May 10 at a 5% boost?

Fluency   When the profit statement is in good form, take it to the tax auditor.

     | 1 | 2 | 3 | 4 | 5 | 6 | 7 | 8 | 9 | 10 | 11 | 12 | 13 | 14 |

58B Technique Practice: Response Patterns ⑦ *each line once from the book, twice from dictation*

which is | of these | of course | amount of | number of | some of | part of | on our

it will | have to | for this | that this | at this | on this | to this | this letter

this matter | this time | that this | that it | so that | hope that | it was | if we

there are | it would | for this | that it | in order | will not | as you | thank you

as well | as well as | as soon | as soon as | we will | we will be | thank you for

58C Addressing a Large Envelope and Folding a Letter ⑥

Large envelopes (No. 10) are preferred for letters with enclosures and for letters of two or more pages.

Begin the address 2½" from the top edge and 4" from the left edge of the envelope. This placement meets the POD read-zone requirements for optical scanning, as illustrated below. The Post Office Department directs that *all* addresses be SS, regardless of the number of lines.

DO: Type an envelope from the illustration.

Type addressee notations (Hold for Arrival, Personal, Please Forward, and the like) a triple space below the return address and 3 spaces from left edge of envelope. The notations may be either underlined or typed in all capitals.

Begin mailing notations (AIRMAIL, SPECIAL DELIVERY, REGISTERED, and the like) below the stamp position and at least 3 line spaces above the envelope address. The notations should be typed in all capitals.

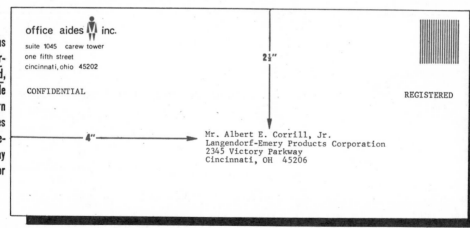

office aides inc.
suite 1045   carew tower
one fifth street
cincinnati, ohio 45202

CONFIDENTIAL

2½"

REGISTERED

4"

Mr. Albert E. Corrill, Jr.
Langendorf-Emery Products Corporation
2345 Victory Parkway
Cincinnati, OH 45206

FOLDING A LETTER FOR A LARGE ENVELOPE

Step 1. With the letter face up on the desk, fold slightly less than one third of the letterhead up toward the top.

Step 2. Fold down the top of the letter to within ½" of the bottom fold.

Step 3. Insert the letter into the envelope with the last crease toward the bottom of the envelope and with the last fold up.

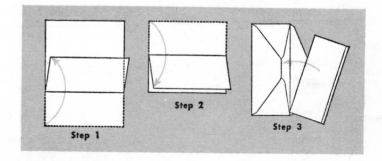

Step 1

Step 2

Step 3

SECTION 4 ▶ SYMBOL LEARNING AND SKILL BUILDING

LESSONS 21–25

Purpose. To learn to type symbols, improve number control, and build higher basic skill. You will also learn to type corrected copy.

Machine Adjustments. Line: 60; SS word and sentence drills, unless otherwise directed; DS and indent ¶s 5 spaces.

Self-Improvement Practice. Select from page 48 material to type that meets your need. Two lines are provided for each lesson.

LESSON 21

21A Preparatory Practice ⑦ *each line twice SS; DS after second typing of line*

Alphabet	Pam questioned why Vic Bortz must make six more jet flights.
Figures	The box is 6 5/8 by 9 1/2 feet and weighs 375 to 400 pounds.
Shift keys	Dr. Clayton moved to Atlantic City, New Jersey, on April 26.
Fluency	Did Keith make the six boys sign the form when he paid them?

| 1 | 2 | 3 | 4 | 5 | 6 | 7 | 8 | 9 | 10 | 11 | 12 |

21B Stroking Technique for ' ! " _ (Underline) ⑧ *each tryout drill twice*

' (Apostrophe). *Nonelectric:* Type ' (shift of **8**) with *right second finger:* k'k 'k 'k
Electric: Type ' (to right of ;) with the *right fourth finger:* ;'; '; ';

! (Exclamation Point). Type ' and backspace; then type a period (!). (If the machine has a key for ! type it with the *left fourth finger*.) Space twice after the exclamation: Try! Don't stop! Keep on!

" (Quotation). *Nonelectric:* Type " (shift of **2**) with *left third finger:* s"s "s "s
Electric: Use *right fourth finger* to type " (shift of '): ;"; "; ";

_ (Underline). *Nonelectric:* Type _ (shift of **6**) with *right first finger:* j_j _j _j
Electric: Use *right fourth finger* to type _ (shift of −): ;_; _; _;

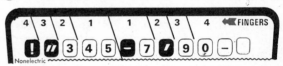
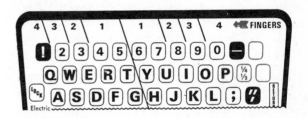

> **To Underline:** Backspace (or move by hand) to first letter of the word; then type the underline once for each letter in the word.

21C Stroking Technique Practice ⑮ *each line three times SS; DS after third typing of line*

Words

1	' (Nonelectric)	k'k 'k 'k It's so. I'm next. It's accuracy that is needed.	12
	' (Electric)	;'; '; '; It's so. I'm next. It's accuracy that is needed.	
2		Try! Don't stop! Keep right on typing! Type with control!	12
3	" (Nonelectric)	"s "s Sue typed "lose" for "loose" and "chose" for "choose."	12
	" (Electric)	"; "; Sue typed "lose" for "loose" and "chose" for "choose."	
4	_ (Nonelectric)	_j _j _j Use a <u>quick</u> stroke. Keep the eyes on the copy now.	12
	_ (Electric)	_; _; _; Use a <u>quick</u> stroke. Keep the eyes on the copy now.	
5	Review	The principal said, "It's right! Stand by your principles!"	12

57D Problem Typing: Business Letters in Modified Block Style ㉓

Problem 1

Line: 60; date on Line 14; standard spacing of 3 blank lines between date and address. After reviewing Style Letter 2, page 99, type the following letter. Erase and correct errors on the original and the file copy.

3-1-73

	Words
October 21, 19--	3

Mr. Gary R. Fischer, Office Manager	10
Wright–Patterson Manufacturing Co.	17
1867 Memorial Parkway	22
Newport, KY 41075	26

Dear Mr. Fischer:	29

Office Aides walk right in and help you out	38
during those rush periods when your work	46
piles up and your workers bog down.	54

Whatever the paperwork bottleneck––order	62
handling, billing, letter or report preparation,	72
data processing––Office Aides, Inc., has a staff	82
of top-flight personnel to help you move the	91
work along with maximum efficiency. And	99
unlike many temporary-employee firms, Office	108
Aides will work wherever it is most conve-	116
nient for you––in your offices, or in <u>ours</u>.	127

Although new to the Cincinnati area, Office	135
Aides, Inc., is well known and widely used in	145
New York, Chicago, Atlanta, and Miami. In	153
Cincinnati we have already supplied temporary	162
office help to such firms as General Plastics	172
Corp., Merry Toy Company, Queen City	179
Printing Company, and Hilton–Jennings.	187

The enclosed brochure describes our services	196
and methods of operation. Get ready now for	205
your next rush season by dialing 271–8811 and	214
discussing your temporary-help needs with	223
Mr. Seybold, one of our work relations coordi-	232
nators. He is well qualified to fit the man	241
(or woman) to the job.	245

Sincerely yours,	249

John D. Morganroth	253
Assistant Sales Manager	257

slr	258

Enclosure	260

Problem 2

Line: 60; date on Line 14; standard spacing of 3 blank lines between date and address. Prepare two cc's, one for Mr. K. L. Stewart. Type the enclosure and carbon copy notations in the form illustrated on page 99.

	Words
October 21, 19--	3

Mr. N. K. Lenz, Office Manager	10
Product Development Corporation	16
1799 Woodburn Street	20
Covington, KY 41014	24

Dear Mr. Lenz:	28

Thank you for calling on us when you needed	36
additional office help recently. We hope you	46
liked Dianne O'Bannon's work as much as she	54
enjoyed working in your Sales Department.	63

Although you have used only our stenographic	72
services so far, we have a number of people	81
qualified in other work areas: machine cal-	89
culation, data processing, accounting, and	98
duplicating. Please give us the opportunity	107
to serve you whenever peak work loads make	116
on-the-premises assistance desirable.	123

The enclosed booklet describes the educational	133
and experience backgrounds of several mem-	141
bers of our traveling work force. These	149
thumbnail summaries are typical of those we	158
have on file for most of our "temporary assis-	167
tants." If we don't have on our regular staff	176
an employee who meets the requirements of	185
the job, we'll tell you so and try to find one	194
who does. You can depend on Office Aides!	203

Sincerely yours,	206

William R. Hathaway, Jr.	211
Work Relations Coordinator	217

slr	218

Problem 3

If time permits, type two 1' writings on the opening lines and two 1' writings on the closing lines of Style Letter 2, page 99. Then type a 5' writing on the entire letter.

21D Skill-Transfer Typing ⑩ *a 1′ writing on each line*

DO: Compare the rates on Sentences 1 and 4, 2 and 5, 3 and 6. The difference in rates may show the "cost" of typing from script.

DO: Type additional 1′ writings on the script sentence for which the widest difference is shown between typing from script and typescript.

SPACING RULE: Space once after an exclamation point used within a sentence. See Line 6.

Words

1	Easy	A light touch is the right touch to use to build good skill.	12
2	Figures	Ken read aloud pages 137, 264, and 389 of the 450-page book.	12
3	Figure-symbol	My 1967-68 report read, "This year's earnings are our best!"	12

| 1 | 2 | 3 | 4 | 5 | 6 | 7 | 8 | 9 | 10 | 11 | 12 |

4	Easy	*The good workman always does what he does as well as he can.*	12
5	Figures	*On June 2, Flight 159 left at 7:20 with 36 men and 48 women.*	12
6	Figure-symbol	*I typed 37 words; then Sue said, "Don't stop!" and I didn't.*	12

21E Skill-Progression Typing ⑩

DO: Type two 1′ writings on each ¶. Try to complete the ¶ before time is called. Determine *gwam*.

Stroking Cue: Make low, quick reach-strokes; keep hands and arms almost motionless.

All letters are used.

3′ GWAM

¶1
1.3 SI
5.2 AWL
90% HFW

Time is important. It is the one constant in daily life, — 4
for all have the same amount of it. The way we use time is — 8
what makes for our unequal accomplishments. — 11

¶2
1.3 SI
5.2 AWL
90% HFW

How time is used can determine the limit of our success, — 14
for time is as important for work as it is for getting the — 18
most enjoyment out of free hours. Time should be prized — 22
highly and used wisely to gain maximum success. — 25

¶3
1.3 SI
5.2 AWL
90% HFW

The chance of having to do our work over is increased — 29
by starting to do it before we have thought through all the — 33
problems involved. Thinking takes time and time is one of — 37
our most valuable commodities, but we will save time if we — 41
will take time to think before we begin our work. — 44

3′ GWAM | 1 | 2 | 3 | 4 |

LESSON 57

57A Preparatory Practice ⑦ *each line three times; then 1' writings on Line 4*

Alphabet   Hal's quick flip to the Bronx end zone went just above Myers' fingers.

Figures   Invoices 4997 and 5023, both dated November 16, are due on December 8.

Figure-symbol   Lenz & O'Brien's Invoice #4956 for $738 (less 2% discount) is now due.

Fluency   May five of the big men work with the foreman for the next eight days?

| 1 ' 2 | 3 | 4 | 5 | 6 | 7 | 8 | 9 | 10 | 11 | 12 | 13 | 14 |

57B Technique Practice: Response Patterns ⑦ *each line once from the book, twice from dictation*

I am | I have | I would | I will | I hope | I can | that I | that we | and we | with you

will be | would be | to us | to make | to do | to me | able to | as to | is to | wish to

up to | and to | as the | about the | have the | you may | you would | as you | is not

for you | from you | with your | on your | and your | we do | we hope | if we | all of

which we | as we | not be | as to | be able | be in | is to | is in | there is | are not

57C Guides for Erasing Original and File Copies ⑬ *full sheet; Line: 65; SS; 3" top margin*

Make 1 carbon copy: original
carbon sheet
file copy sheet

First, study the Guides below. Then erase and correct any errors you make as you type the Guides as shown. Before removing the paper from the typewriter, proofread; then correct any errors not already corrected.

	Words
GUIDES FOR ERASING ORIGINAL AND FILE COPIES	9
TS	

After typing the → first line, reset left margin stop 4 spaces in.

1. Move the carriage to the extreme left or right to prevent   21
    eraser crumbs from falling into the well of the typewriter.   33
    (This step is not necessary on the Selectric.)   43

2. Pull the original sheet forward and place a 5" x 3" card   56
    (or one slightly larger) in front of the first carbon sheet.   68

3. Return the original sheet and make the erasure on it with a   81
    hard (typewriter) eraser. Brush the eraser crumbs away from   93
    the typewriter. An eraser shield is helpful but not essential. 106

4. Remove the protective card (unless more than one carbon copy   120
    is being made, in which case place the card in front of the   132
    second carbon sheet). With a soft (pencil) eraser, erase the 144
    error on the carbon (file) copy.   151

LESSON 22

22A Preparatory Practice ⑦ *each line twice SS; DS after second typing of line*

Alphabet Why not have Judge Burt Kumpf quiz the six local boys today?

Figures I built 7-room houses--28 in all--on 36th Street in 1949-50.

Symbols Shouldn't we <u>show</u> and also <u>tell</u> the "how" and "why" of this?

Fluency The six girls can handle the quantity of forms without help.

 | 1 | 2 | 3 | 4 | 5 | 6 | 7 | 8 | 9 | 10 | 11 | 12 |

22B Sustained Skill Building ⑩

DO: Type a 3′ writing on the ¶s of 21E, page 41 (preceding page). Determine *gwam*. Practice difficult words by typing each one four or five times.

DO: Type a second 3′ writing on the ¶s, trying to increase your speed and maintain your control. Determine *gwam*.

Continuity Cue	Reduce the time interval between strokes. Use a "rippling" (not metronomic) rhythm in typing short and easy words. Type long words with a quick, smooth, and flowing movement from one letter to the next and from one word to the next.

22C Stroking Technique for $ & ( ) [Left and Right Parentheses] ⑧ *each tryout drill twice*

$ (Dollars). Type **$** (shift of **4**) with the *left first finger:* f$f $f $f

& (Ampersand or "and"). Type **&** (shift of **7**) with the *right first finger:* j&j &j &j

([Left Parenthesis]. Type **(** [shift of **9**] with the *right third finger:* l(l (l (l

) [Right Parenthesis]. Type **)** [shift of **0**] with the *right fourth finger:* ;);););

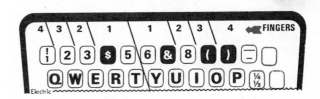

22D Stroking Technique Practice ⑧ *each line twice SS; DS after second typing of line*

1 $ and & A check for $2,375 was sent to Nietz & Johnson on August 14.

2 (and) We sold the short-term (due in 91 days) U.S. Treasury Bills.

3 $ & ( ) North & Owen's note for $1,850 (due 6/4) was paid on May 27.

4 Review We mustn't use "it's" (contraction) for "its" (the pronoun).

5 Consecutive/ direct Fred Hunt hauled many hundred pounds of freight in my truck.

 | 1 | 2 | 3 | 4 | 5 | 6 | 7 | 8 | 9 | 10 | 11 | 12 |

office aides inc

suite 1045 carew tower one fifth street cincinnati, ohio 45202 telephone (513) 271-8811

	Words in Parts	5' GWAM
Begin date at center on Line 14		
Date line October 20, 19--	3	1
3 blank lines (4th line space)		
Miss Janet Wellington	8	2
Republic Supply Company	13	3
2670 Queen City Avenue	17	4
Address Cincinnati, OH 45238	22	5
DS		
Salutation Dear Miss Wellington:	26	6
DS		
The modified block style has some distinctive features, as	12	8
shown by this letter and described in the enclosed pamphlet.	24	10
The date, complimentary close, and name and official title of	37	12
the dictator are begun at the horizontal center of the page.	49	15
These can be placed correctly with one tabulator adjustment.	61	17
Body Special lines (reference, enclosure, and carbon copy notations)	74	20
are placed at the left margin, a double space below the last	86	22
of the closing lines. If the dictator's name is part of the	99	25
closing lines, only the typist's initials are required in the	111	27
reference. If the dictator's initials are used, they precede	123	30
those of the typist and are usually typed in capital letters.	136	32
The modified block style, about which you inquired yesterday,	148	35
is widely used by the clients for whom we prepare letters.	160	37
We think you will like it, too.	167	38
Complimentary close Sincerely yours,	3	39
3 blank lines (4th line space)		
Typed name Randall B. Parkhurst	8	40
Official title Communications Director	12	41
DS		
Reference initials lkd	13	41
DS		
Enclosure notation Enclosure	15	42
DS		
Carbon copy notation cc Mr. John R. Rodgers, Jr.	21	43

STYLE LETTER 2: *Modified Block Style, Block Paragraphs; Mixed Punctuation (Typed in Pica Type)*

Mixed Punctuation. With *mixed punctuation*, as illustrated above, a colon follows the salutation and a comma follows the complimentary close.

Open Punctuation. With *open punctuation*, no punctuation follows the opening and closing lines unless one of them ends with an abbreviation.

22E Skill-Transfer Typing ⑩

1. Type two 1′ writings on each ¶. Determine your *gwam* for the better writing on each ¶.

2. Type a 3′ writing beginning with ¶ 1 and typing as far as you can until time is called. Compare 3′ *gwam* with best 1′ rate on each ¶.

Difficulty controls for "mixed" copy (words and figures) are determined for the words only. Punctuation marks and symbols used with words, such as quotation marks and parentheses, are considered to be a part of the word with which they are typed. See ¶ 2.

All letters are used.

		3′ GWAM
¶1 1.3 SI 5.2 AWL 90% HFW	Most men can do just about anything they think they can,	4
	for belief is magic. If they think they are not equal to	8
	what is expected of them, they won't be able to use the	11
	wonder-working power of faith in themselves to realize the	15
	true success they should have.	17
¶2 1.3 SI 5.2 AWL 90% HFW	Many workers are retired by the time they are 65 or 70	21
	years old. The so-called "golden age" (more age than gold)	25
	will come more quickly than we realize. We must have a	29
	hobby for our present enjoyment and for the days to come	33
	when we may have considerable free time.	35

| 1 | 2 | 3 | 4 |

22F Rough Draft ⑦ *study the correction symbols; then type each drill line once or more*

Rough Draft: Copy corrected with pencil or pen and ink. Some of the most common correction symbols are shown at the right.

Correction Symbols

Cap. or ≡ means capitalize
∧ means insert
ℰ means delete (take out)
[means move to left

means add space
/ or l.c. means lower-case letters
____ means underline

		Words
1	use a light, quick strokes to build the highest typing skill.	12
2	Many # men mentioned the points fred listed for us to discuss.	12
3	l.c. The Principal said, "It's the Principle of (rule) to follow."	12
4	Typing Cue: # keep your eye on the copy; use a quick strokes!	12
5	Bart will read the cards on which the date of the Trade was given shows.	12

55D Building Speed and Control ⓴

1. Type each of the following ¶s as two 1' writings, once for *speed* and once for *control*.

2. Use all three ¶s for two 5' writings. Determine *gwam* and errors for the better writing.

All letters are used.

	1'	5'

¶ 1
1.4 SI
5.4 AWL
85% HFW

Words are the tools we use to communicate. They must be selected | 13 | 3 | 33
wisely and used with care. A short, simple word is generally preferred | 28 | 6 | 36
to a long one. You must not, however, be afraid to use any word that | 42 | 8 | 39
conveys the precise meaning you want to get across. | 52 | 10 | 41

¶ 2
1.4 SI
5.4 AWL
85% HFW

Be quick to realize that a large vocabulary is vital to success- | 13 | 13 | 44
ful writing. The more extensive your store of usable words and word | 27 | 16 | 46
meanings, the more precise your message is likely to be. On the topic | 41 | 19 | 49
of words, be sure you have the right ones at hand. | 51 | 21 | 51

¶ 3
1.4 SI
5.4 AWL
85% HFW

You must try hard to build a good vocabulary. You must read ex- | 13 | 23 | 54
tensively, look up the meanings of unfamiliar words, and actively use | 27 | 26 | 57
those words. In this way you can learn to produce quickly the exact | 41 | 29 | 59
word to get just the effect you seek in your writing. | 51 | 31 | 62

1' GWAM | 1 | 2 | 3 | 4 | 5 | 6 | 7 | 8 | 9 | 10 | 11 | 12 | 13 | 14 |
5' GWAM | 1 | 2 | 3 |

LESSON 56

56A Preparatory Practice ⑦ *each line three times; then 1' writings on Line 4*

Alphabet Daryl Javits was quick to pick a green Mercedes–Benz for his next car.
Figures Fred had 160 at the 3-, 5-, and 7-day workshops on June 8, 14, and 29.
Symbol-shift Is the notation on this memorandum Bob's, Neal's, Chuck's, or R. D.'s?
Fluency The right chance at the right time may make a big profit for the firm.

| 1 | 2 | 3 | 4 | 5 | 6 | 7 | 8 | 9 | 10 | 11 | 12 | 13 | 14 |

56B Building Speed and Control ⓴ *repeat 55D, above*

56C Problem Typing: Business Letters in Modified Block Style ㉓

1. Study Style Letter 2, page 99. Note the placement of the date and the closing lines. Read the brief explanation of *mixed punctuation*.

2. Use a 60-space line; modified block style with block paragraphs; mixed punctuation; date on Line 14.

3. Set a tabulator stop at the horizontal center point to indent to the position for typing the date and the closing lines.

4. When the letter has been typed once, make pencil corrections as needed; then retype the letter, *preparing two carbon copies.*

23A   Preparatory Practice ⑦ *each line twice SS; DS after second typing of line*

Alphabet   Did Peter Wallington quiz Evelyn Jackson about her tax form?

Symbols   "Truth," a man once said, "doesn't hurt unless it <u>ought</u> to!"

Figure-symbol   Hunt & Dwyer's $623.75 check (Check 1489) is dated April 10.

Fluency   The firm holds the usual title to the visual aids they sell.
             | 1 | 2 | 3 | 4 | 5 | 6 | 7 | 8 | 9 | 10 | 11 | 12 |

23B   Stroking Technique for # * % ⑥ *each tryout drill twice*

 # (Number or Pounds). Type # (shift of **3**) with the *left second finger:* d#d #d #d

Note. Before a figure, # is the symbol for *No.*; after a figure, it is the symbol for *pounds*. See Line 1 of 23C, below.

* (Asterisk). *Nonelectric:* Type * (shift of –) with the *right fourth finger:* ;*; *; *; *Electric:* Type * (shift of **8**) with the *right second finger:* k*k *k *k

% (Percent). Type % (shift of **5**) with the *left first finger:* f%f %f %f

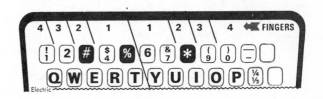

23C   Stroking Technique Practice ⑩ *each line three times SS; DS after third typing of line*

		Words
#	d#d #d #d Ship Order #165 for 437# of Compound #98 on May 2.	12
* (Nonelectric)	*; *; *; My first * refers to page 290, ** to pages 305-307.	12
* (Electric)	*k *k *k My first * refers to page 290, ** to pages 305-307.	
%	f%f %f Will the 6% rate be changed to 5% or possibly 5 1/2%?	12
Review	Smith & Carey's account is $2,957.83 (for 5/30 Order #1460).	12

23D   Rough Draft ⑦ *study the correction symbols; then type each line twice*

Correction Symbols

◠ means close up   *tr or ↻* means transpose   ⌐ means move to right

		Words
1	⌐ Don't space between figures and symbols: #, $, %, /.	12
2	Shift when typing # (no. or lbs.), % (percent), and " (quote).	12
3	Use the * (asterisk) for the footnote to refer to Page 264.³	12
4	Never let the fear element keep you from doing your best.	12
5	Order #1460 from Dieckman and Muncy (dated 3/29) is $1,570.85.	12

SECTION 9 ▶ BUSINESS LETTERS

LESSONS 55–61

Purpose. To learn to type business letters neatly and quickly, to prepare carbon copies, to address envelopes, and to fold letters.

Machine Adjustments. Line: 70, unless otherwise directed; SS drills and problems; DS and indent timed writing ¶s 5 spaces.

Self-Improvement Practice. Type phrases of 55B, below, of 57B, page 100, of 58B, page 102, or the Self-Improvement Practice, page 107.

LESSON 55

55A Preparatory Practice ⑦ *each line three times; then 1' writings on Line 4*

Alphabet   Dr. Robert Wachs received a quaint onyx ring from Jack Pelz of Venice.

Figures   Please turn to page 350 and answer Items 2, 4, 6, 7, 8, 9, 10, and 16.

Symbol-shift   "Have sunglow all winter," she said, "with a Magic Sun Lamp by Solco."

Fluency   It is the wish of the chairman to have all the workmen at the meeting.

| 1 | 2 | 3 | 4 | 5 | 6 | 7 | 8 | 9 | 10 | 11 | 12 | 13 | 14 |

55B Technique Practice: Response Patterns ⑩ *each line once from the book, twice from dictation*

The phrases presented below and in subsequent lessons are among those most often used in business communication. Learn to type them rapidly and accurately.

Technique Cue: Read a phrase with one sweep of the eye and type it as a unit, with no perceptible pause between words. *Space quickly.*

to you | to your | to our | to have | to him | like to | to be | of the | in the | to us
to the | for the | on the | with the | and the | from the | that the | at the | by the
is the | you will | you have | you are | you can | and you | that you | to you | it is
for your | of your | to your | in your | we are | we have | we will | we would | to be
of the | of our | this is | of this | one of | we can | in this | should be | that the
if you | with you | that you | may be | do not | in our | in your | can be | have been

55C Drill on Assembling and Inserting a Carbon Pack ⑬ *full sheet; Line: 65; SS; 3" top margin*

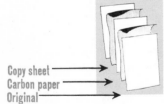

Copy sheet
Carbon paper
Original

1. Read ¶ 1 below and assemble a carbon pack as directed there.

2. Read ¶ 2, then insert the pack as instructed.

3. Type the following material in the form illustrated.

	Words
ASSEMBLY AND INSERTION OF A CARBON PACK	8

TS

After typing the first line, reset left margin stop 4 spaces in.

1. Place the sheet on which the file (or carbon) copy is to be   21
made flat on the desk; then place a sheet of carbon paper,   33
carbon side down, on top of the paper. (If you desire more   48
than one carbon copy, add another plain sheet and another   60
carbon sheet for each copy.) Finally, place the sheet for   72
the original on top of the carbon paper.   80

Use the margin release and backspace 4 times to type "2."

2. Pick up the papers and tap them lightly on the desk (with the   94
glossy side of the carbon paper toward you); then insert the   106
pack into the machine (carbon side toward you as you insert   125
the papers). Roll the pack in far enough for the feed rolls   139
to grip the papers; finally, operate the paper-release lever   151
to release the pressure and eliminate the wrinkles.   161

23E Skill-Comparison Typing ⑳

1. Type a 1' writing on each ¶. Determine *gwam* for each writing. Compare rates.

2. Type two more 1' writings on each of the two ¶s on which you had the lowest *gwam*.

3. Type two 3' writings, starting with ¶ 1 and typing as far as you can until time is called. Determine *gwam* and compare with your best 1' rate.

Return Cue: *Make the return without looking up at the end of the line.*

All letters are used.

		3' GWAM

¶1
1.2 SI
5.0 AWL
96% HFW

Up to now, much of your typing has been from quite easy   4

copy. Many of the words came from the list of common words   8

with two to five letters and just one syllable. This simple   12

copy was used to help you to build a good typing skill.   15

¶2
1.4 SI
5.4 AWL
86% HFW

From now on, try to type such short and simple words as   19

two-letter balanced-hand words by word-recognition response   23

and not by letter response. To do this, you must think the   27

word with real vigor, but not think the individual letter.   31

¶3
1.5 SI
5.8 AWL
76% HFW

This progressive-difficulty copy has a few long and less   35

frequently used words and a few words of many syllables. From   39

your experience in typing these specialized paragraphs, you can   43

learn to vary your stroking pattern for the copy to be typed.   47

3' GWAM | 1 | 2 | 3 | 4 |

LESSON 24

24A Preparatory Practice ⑦ *each line twice SS; DS after second typing of line*

Alphabet   Wilbur Jamieson packed the very large box of quartz mineral.

Figure-symbol   Orr & North's Check #2035 for $648.10 should be for $864.10.

Shift key   Dick Webb and Max King will go with Jim Carr to Zurich soon.

Fluency   In May, the ancient jewels can be seen at the downtown shop.

| 1 | 2 | 3 | 4 | 5 | 6 | 7 | 8 | 9 | 10 | 11 | 12 |

24B Typing for Control ⑩

Type two 3' writings of 23E, above, on the *control level*. Type at a rate that is 4 to 8 words lower than your best 1' rate made when typing the ¶s as 23E.

5 half sheets; 70-space line; DS; 5-space ¶ indention; 1½″ top margin

In Alertness Training you must pay attention to what is typed and to do what you are told to do in the sentence you type. Always type the entire sentence before you follow any directions given in the sentence you are typing.

For example, the second sentence of Alertness Training 1 directs you to type the first sentence again at a speed slower than your first typing. As the third sentence, then, retype the first sentence; then continue to type the paragraph.

1-22-73

1

Type at a speed that is well within your zone of control. Type the first sentence again, but type at a speed that is 8 to 10 words slower than your first typing. Type with quiet, even stroking. Underline the preceding sentence with an unbroken line; then start a new paragraph. Center and type the next sentence in all capital letters on a separate line, with a blank line space before it, and without typing the period. Think as you type.

2

Pay attention to what you type. Move the carriage to the first word of the paragraph, and type over the first sentence. Without changing the margin stops, type the next sentence on one line to begin 5 spaces outside the left margin and with a double space before it. It is the duty of a typist to check each typed page and to correct all errors.

3

Center ACTION TYPING 3 as a heading a triple space above this line, remembering to release the shift lock before typing the figure 3. When typing, underline words that are printed in *italics*, so underline the italicized word in this sentence. Beginning at the left margin a double space below this completed sentence, type the alphabet in all capitals and the figures 1 to 10, with a space after each letter and figure; then remove the paper, reinsert it to type on the reverse side, and type your own return address and current date in correct position for a 60-space line personal letter.

4

Lock the shift key when you type the next sentence in all capital letters. Type with ease. Add an exclamation point to the preceding sentence. Position the carriage and underline the second sentence; then reposition the carriage and continue to type the paragraph. As you type the next sentence, correct the misspelled words. The reply to our questionnaire does not warrant our recommending him for promotion. Remove the paper, reinsert it, and type over the first word of the paragraph.

5

Center and type your name in all capital letters a triple space above this line. Type the following sentence as rapidly as you can type with a sense of ease and control. It is up to me to build my skill in typing to as high a level as possible. Remove the paper, reinsert it, and type over your name centered above the paragraph; then continue to type the remainder of this paragraph. Center and type the current date a double space below this line.

24C Stroking Technique for ½ and ¼ ⑥ *each tryout drill twice*

½ **(Fraction Key).** Type ½ (at right of letter **p**) with the *right fourth finger* and without shifting: ;½; ½; ½;

¼ **(Fraction Key).** Type ¼ (shift of ½) with the *right fourth finger:* ;¼; ¼; ¼;

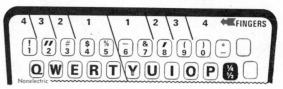

24D Stroking Technique Practice ⑩ *each line three times SS; DS after third typing of line*

		Words
½	Type fractions in the same way: 1/2 and 2/3--not ½ and 2/3.	12
¼	Peter Lopez said the total of 25¼, 36¼, 47¼, and 90¼ is 199.	12
Figure-symbol	Don's 4¼% note (for $750) was paid on May 26 by Check #1839.	12
Symbols	Don't hurry or worry--just type <u>right</u> to learn to typewrite!	12

| 1 | 2 | 3 | 4 | 5 | 6 | 7 | 8 | 9 | 10 | 11 | 12 |

24E Rough Draft ⑦ *each line twice SS; DS after second typing of line*

		Words
1	[l.c. The Half sheets of paper (8½ by 5½ inches) has just have 33 lines.	12
2	Roy--as the would-be leader--is was gift ed with 20-20 hindsight!	12
3	Their Teachers said, cc use a quick strokes; keep eyes on copy!"	12
4	In 1967, Weyth and Pointer stock sold at 25½; and in 1968, at 40¼.	12
5	[Add these words to the list: generally, shipments. handled,	12

24F Skill-Transfer Typing ⑩ *a 1' writing on each sentence*

DO: Compare the rates on Sentences 1 and 4, 2 and 5, 3 and 6. The difference in rates may show the "cost" of typing from rough draft.

DO: Type additional 1' writings on the rough draft sentences for which the widest difference occurs between it and typescript.

			Words
1	Easy	The auditors for their firm can make their report on May 26.	12
2	Figures	On July 25, Flight 480 had 37 women, 18 men, and 9 children.	12
3	Figure-symbol	O'Neil & Long's $750 note (due 3/26) was paid by Check #481.	12

| 1 | 2 | 3 | 4 | 5 | 6 | 7 | 8 | 9 | 10 | 11 | 12 |

			Words
4	Easy	[l.c. An Elements of doubt kept # them from help ing with the Project.	12
5	Figures	Didn't 46 of the 350 boys and of the 89 girls /27) pass the test?	12
6	Figure-symbol	Jim Webb's fare is #234.50 (less 6%--a net cost of $220.43.	12

Problem 2: Memo with Table

Half sheet; 65-space line; block style; SS; begin on Line 7; leave 8 spaces between columns

Add the following headings over the three columns: Year, Winner, NWAM.

			Words
February 28, 19--	SUBJECT: Some Typewriting Champions	(¶ 1)		11
Championship typewriting contests were great sport for typewriter companies during the first half of the 20th century. The highest speeds attained in these one-hour contests are given below.			25
			41
			50

1922	George Hossfield	144	55
1923	Albert Tangora	147	60
1941	Margaret Hamma	149	65

(¶ 2) Winners of other contests (at lower speeds or for shorter periods of time) include: Stella Pejunas, Cortez Peters, Grace Phelan, Norman Saksvig, and Stella Willins.   78 92 98

Problem 3: Letter with Table

Modified block, blocked ¶s; open punctuation; return address on Line 11; 60-space line; center table, leaving 4 spaces between columns

	Words
761 Fairfield Avenue	Bridgeport, Connecticut 06604	February 28,	13
19-- Dr. John B. Sheppard	Educational Services, Inc.	240 Madison	26
Avenue	New York, New York 10016	Dear Dr. Sheppard	36

(¶ 1) The series of typewriting workshops you conducted during the past year proved to be most rewarding and motivating to Connecticut teachers. It was reassuring to see that your skill-building procedures had a dual base: experimental as well as experiential.   49 64 79 88

(¶ 2) Please send the indicated number of copies of the three items you used in demonstrating effective teaching procedures.   101 112

20	Timed Homework Practice Record, T	$20.00	121
25	High-Speed Typewriting Drills	6.25	129
2	Guided Writing Record, T	4.00	136

(¶ 3) The teachers in Trumbull High School were most enthusiastic about being able to give more guided writings without depending on a stopwatch to indicate quarter-minute guides. We plan to make one of the guided writing records available to students for extra practice in one of our small typewriting labs.   149 163 177 192 197

(¶ 4) I know you travel nationally to help teachers improve typewriting instruction, but I hope your schedule will permit you to return to Connecticut soon to demonstrate again that "learning can be fun."   210 223 237

Cordially yours | Howard Prentice   243

Problem 4: Table on Postal Card

Type the table in Problem 2 on a postal card (or on paper cut to that size: 5½″ x 3¼″), using SOME TYPEWRITING CHAMPIONS as the main heading. Leave 4 spaces between columns. DS the items in the table.

do

2-21-73

LESSON 25

25A Preparatory Practice ⑦ *each line twice SS; DS after second typing of line*

Alphabet | Will my box be packed with quick-frozen foods by Jim Vaughn?

Figures | Our address will be 14867 West 35th Street after October 29.

Figure-symbol | Will Mr. Link's $5,000 Policy #23-678 expire on May 6, 1974?

Fluency | Ken paid for the work with his half of the sale of the land.

| 1 | 2 | 3 | 4 | 5 | 6 | 7 | 8 | 9 | 10 | 11 | 12 |

25B Stroking Technique for ¢ (Cent or Cents) and @ (At) ⑥ *each tryout drill twice*

¢ **(Cent or Cents).** *Nonelectric:* Type ¢ (an unshifted character to the right of ;) with the *right fourth finger:* ;¢; ¢; ¢;
Electric: Type ¢ (shift of **6**) with the *right first finger:* j¢j ¢j ¢j

@ **(At).** *Nonelectric:* Type @ (shift of ¢) with the *right fourth finger:* ;@; @; @;
Electric: Type @ (shift of **2**) *with the left third finger:* s@s @s @s

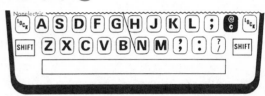

SPACING RULES: 1. Space before and after typing @, which is used in typing bills. **2.** Do not space between ¢ and the figure it follows. | **Note.** These spacing rules apply when the symbols are used in a sentence or in typing bills, but not when used in typing drills, such as the tryout drills.

25C Stroking Technique Practice ⑩ *each line three times SS; DS after third typing of line*

¢ | I paid 98¢ for a pen and 16¢ for a pencil, a total of $1.14.

@ | Eleanor bought 12 7/8 yards @ $6.75 and 9 2/3 yards @ $5.40.

¢ and @ | Use ¢ and @ when typing bills; as, Ship 647 lbs. @ 89¢ a lb.

¢ and @ | Space after @, but not between the figure and ¢, *, #, or $.

| 1 | 2 | 3 | 4 | 5 | 6 | 7 | 8 | 9 | 10 | 11 | 12 |

25D Rough Draft ⑩ *each line three times SS; DS after third typing of line*

Words

1 | ~~Miss~~ *Zelma* Quigley (will) have *some* lunch fix~~c~~ed at Ko[pp]e *for Bryan?* | 12

2 | ~~When is~~ Kent & C[l]ayton's note (plus *of #38,765* 5½% interest) *is* due? ☉ | 12

3 | [Sam Werder said Myna munson s[o]d[d] Five hundred desks *in July.* | 12

4 | [T]he elements of dang[c]er on this [J]ob will make *workmen* ~~them~~ ~~very~~ careful. | 12

5 | The *last* sale of 9 *don* note books @ 18¢ *each* came to $19.44. | 12

LESSON 54

54A Preparatory Practice ⑦ *each line three times; then 1' writings on Lines 2 and 4*

Alphabet | Jane Fox owns a copy of the book Zelma Quade has given to all members.
Figures | On May 5, we added 7 stations: 358, 359, 360, 361, 362, 363, and 364.
Figure-symbol | Send the following items: 3 sets K-217F @ $6.75; 4 prs. M826 @ $9.20.
Fluency | We mailed your statement to the address given on the card you sent us.

| 1 | 2 | 3 | 4 | 5 | 6 | 7 | 8 | 9 | 10 | 11 | 12 | 13 | 14 |

54B Growth Index ⑧ *one 5' writing; determine* gwam *and errors*

All letters are used.

	GWAM	
	1'	5'

¶1
1.4 SI
5.4 AWL
85% HFW

If climbing the ladder to success is vital to you, you possess an advantage over many who have no strong feeling one way or the other. This is just as true in college as it is on the job. Your instructors can guide you, but you must do the work. History is filled to the brim with great men who had harsh strikes against them in health, education, and even intelligence. But one asset they did possess. They wanted to learn; they wanted to win the prize; they expected to reach their goal. Desire and action are effective qualities. Put them to work for you immediately.

	1'	5'
	13	3	49
	27	5	52
	42	8	55
	56	11	57
	70	14	60
	85	17	63
	99	20	66
	113	22	68
	116	23	69

¶2
1.4 SI
5.4 AWL
85% HFW

Do you ever feel that you are in the wrong place as you try to master a difficult problem or succeed in a new job? You usually have these feelings because you have not prepared well enough. The way to eliminate the difficulty is to master every new learning and every new skill that will help you past some hurdle that may lie ahead. Do you think you might want to establish your own business some day? Then learn to analyze; learn to communicate well; learn to make decisions. Improve each of the skills required in your work or study, and you will feel in the right place.

	13	26	72
	27	28	75
	41	31	78
	55	34	80
	69	37	83
	82	40	86
	97	42	89
	111	45	92
	116	46	93

1' GWAM | 1 | 2 | 3 | 4 | 5 | 6 | 7 | 8 | 9 | 10 | 11 | 12 | 13 | 14 |
5' GWAM | 1 | 2 | 3 |

54C Problem Typing Measurement: Tables and Word Division ㉟

Get Ready to Type . . . . 5'
Timed Production . . . . 25'
Proofread . . . . 5'

Type the problem at the right and those on page 95 as directed. Correct errors as you type. Give each problem a quick final check *before you remove it from the typewriter* and correct any errors you have not already corrected.

Problem 1: Word Division

Half sheet; line: 60; DS; 1" top margin; columnar spacing as indicated

Words

PREFERRED POINTS TO DIVIDE WORDS			7
Word	Syllables	Divide	15
advertisement	ad/ver/tise/ment	adver-tise-ment	24
agreements			31
carefully			38
determination	*(Indicate all syl-*	*(Indicate preferred*	48
self-propelled	*lables for all*	*division point or*	57
synonymous	*words.)*	*points for all words.)*	64

KEY | 14 | 6 | 17 | 6 | 16 |

25E Growth Index ⑰

1. Type a 3′ writing. Determine *gwam* and number of errors.
2. Type two 1′ writings on each ¶, typing once for speed and once for accuracy.
3. Type a second 3′ writing on the *control level*. Determine *gwam* and number of errors. Compare your rate and control with the first writing. Be guided by this comparison in your next practice.

All letters are used.

		GWAM	
		1′	3′

¶1 1.3 SI 5.2 AWL 90% HFW

	1′	3′
To the extent that men of good skill and good will want	11	4
to work and can work, jobs must be made available to them; but	24	8
business and industry are not welfare agencies, and workers	36	12
must have both good skill and good will. Most men realize	48	16
that this is so, but not all are adequately prepared for work.	60	20
The need is for far more and far better education for all.	72	24

¶2 1.3 SI 5.2 AWL 90% HFW

	1′	3′
More and better education may not be the final answer to	11	28
the problem of matching men and jobs, for automation has made	24	32
the question of jobs a difficult one. How will workers keep	36	36
their jobs when machines can do the work as well as the workers	48	40
can? This is recognized by the experts as the big problem	61	44
we must face in the years just ahead.	68	47

```
1′ GWAM |  1  |  2  |  3  |  4  |  5  |  6  |  7  |  8  |  9  | 10  | 11  | 12  |
3′ GWAM |       1       |       2       |       3       |       4       |
```

● Self-Improvement Practice   *each line three or more times*

1 *Lesson 21* Tom's father said, "Might won't make right!" He's so right!
2 ' ! " _   Mrs. O'Donovan just won't pay for this book, Technique Cues!

3 *Lesson 22* Was King & Jordan's check (or was it Mr. King's) for $5,200?
4 $ & ( )   Cole & Meade, Inc., gave $750 to the cause (the Boys' Club)!

5 *Lesson 23* The * refers to Item #9, the 6% charge on Ed's $25,000 note.
6 # * %   The 2% discount on Bill #467 (for *** Pads) comes to $38.90.

7 *Lesson 24* The 5¼% rate has been changed to 5½% and will go to 6% soon.
8 ½ ¼   Take full sheets (8½ by 11″) or all half sheets (8½ by 5½″).

9 *Lesson 25* Mark sold a pen @ 89¢, pad @ 27¢, and 24 pencils @ 15¢ each.
10 ¢ @   Note the correct spacing: 24 @ 9¢ each, $2.16; Order #97-A.

```
|  1  |  2  |  3  |  4  |  5  |  6  |  7  |  8  |  9  | 10  | 11  | 12  |
```

Problem 3: Three-Column Tabulation

Full sheet; DS; reading position; 8 spaces between columns

			Words
WESTMINSTER COLLEGE BUILDING FUND			9
Contributions Received in Third Quarter			15

Name	State	Amount	
George W. Anderson	Pennsylvania	$ 1,750.00	24
Edward O. Babcock	Idaho	500.00	30
Myron T. Buffington	Pennsylvania	1,500.00	39
Marilyn O. Crawford	Indiana	2,000.00	47
D. Wesley Dodds	Ohio	500.00	53
Arlene N. Ruskin	Utah	275.00	58
Marjorie McC. Thomas	Ohio	425.75	65
Arthur N. Tomasson	California	15,000.00	74
Alexander R. Trexler	West Virginia	375.00	82
Norton C. Wallingford	Ohio	3,500.00	90
Edward O. Wilson	Pennsylvania	225.00	97
Robert H. Woodside	New York	75.00	104
T. N. Woolson	Maine	50.00	109
Henry Harrington Young	Michigan	100.00	117

PROOFREADING PRACTICE

It takes time to proofread carefully, but it is time well spent, for you will then know by your own proof that your work is right or wrong. Before you can correct your errors, you must find them. Before you can claim competence in proofreading and correcting your errors, you must find ALL your errors and correct them, preferably BEFORE you remove the work from the typewriter.

Double-check the accuracy of your typing. Give special attention to checking the spelling of names and check numbers to see that no inaccuracy gets by you. A misspelled name can irritate the recipient and an inaccurate figure can confuse the records. Demonstrate evidence of your proofreading competence. Recheck all work in today's typing to see if you have corrected all errors.

SECTION ▷5▷ IMPROVING BASIC SKILLS

LESSONS 26–30

Purpose. To improve stroking, response patterns, and use of machine parts.

Machine Adjustments. Line: 60; SS drills, unless otherwise directed; DS and indent ¶s.

Self-Improvement Practice. Selected lines from page 54 until you can demonstrate control.

LESSON 26

26A Preparatory Practice ⑧ *each line three times SS; DS between three-line groups*

Alphabet	Vern Flynn made six quick shots to win the Jets a big prize.
Figures	The 43 men, 67 women, and 125 children sailed today at 8:09.
Figure-symbol	Coe & Lowe's bonus in 1967-8 was $252; in 1969, it was $340.
Fluency	May they pay for the big sign with half the profit due them?

| 1 | 2 | 3 | 4 | 5 | 6 | 7 | 8 | 9 | 10 | 11 | 12 |

26B Technique Practice: Response Patterns ⑮ *each line three times; practice difficult word groups*

Lines 1-2: Type at a controlled pace: read a letter, type it; then read and type the next letter.

Lines 3-4: Try for a "chained" response: read and type a *word* or a *syllable* at a time; then the next.

Lines 5-7: Type short, easy words by word response; longer or more difficult ones letter by letter.

1	Letter-level response	only after you; refer my tax case; my opinion; extra reserve
2		As you are aware, my estate tax case was, in fact, deferred.
3	Word-level response	visit the city; fix the chair; the proxy is; if the chairman
4		It is the duty of men to work; their wish, to make a profit.
5	Combination response	if you care to, when you try it, if only he, she refers also
6		you may see; get the facts; the opinion of; refer the reader
7		He treated the data with care; he gave the facts with vigor.

| 1 | 2 | 3 | 4 | 5 | 6 | 7 | 8 | 9 | 10 | 11 | 12 |

26C Manipulative Parts Drill: Space Bar, Shift Keys, and Shift Lock ⑩

Type each line at least twice for precise control of machine parts.

1	Space bar	we pay for it; plans to send half; many a man offers to work
2		Set your sights for the top; then do your best to get there.
3	Shift-keys	1-I; 5-V; 10-X; 30-XXX; 40-XL; 50-L; 75-LXXV; 100-C; 1,000-M
4		Our guests are: Pam and Don; Sylvia and Harl; Roz and Jack.
5	Shift lock	she is a new CPS; join the AMS; define quixotic and charisma
6		A critique of Bey's book, OMEGA, appears in Literary Review.

| 1 | 2 | 3 | 4 | 5 | 6 | 7 | 8 | 9 | 10 | 11 | 12 |

Modified block; open punctuation; 60-space line; current date on Line 14; correct errors; address envelope

Alertness cue: Your typed lines will not be the same as those in the copy.

WESTMINSTER COLLEGE

Office of Vice-President
for Development

(814) 555-1212
New Wilmington, PA 16142

	Words
December 6, 19--	3

Mr. Edward O. Babcock, Esq. | 8
3176 State Street, W. | 12
Boise, Idaho 88703 | 16

Dear Mr. Babcock | 20

Idaho doesn't seem so far away now that we have received | 31
your letter with your check for $500 as your "investment in | 42
our youth" program. We thank you for your generous gift, and | 52
Even more, we thank you for your continued interest in and | 60
concern for Westminster College and its continued growth. | 72

Last year we had gifts from two other alumni who reside in | 84
Boise Idaho, but we have not had any response to our letters | 95
this year asking for their continued support. The names | 106
of these alumni and the amount each gave are listed below: | 118
 # Mrs. Leonora Moore Judd $ 500 | 124
    Edward Kimmon   1,000 | 128
Will you be good enough |
I hope it is not asking too much of you to try to contact | 137
Mrs. Judd and Mr. Kimmon to see if you can get them to make | 149
a contribution to the College again this year. We very much | 159
want to add their names to the honor roll where your name | 171
heads the list for Idaho and nearby states. | 180

Again, thanks you for your check and good wishes. Thanks you, too, | 193
for any help you can give us in contacting Mrs. Judd and | 204
Mr. Kimmon. | 207

Sincerely yours | 210

Student Chairman
Vice-President for Development | 213
All caps → Annual Alumni Fund | 217

26D Skill-Comparison Typing ⑰

1. Type a 1' writing on each ¶; compare *gwam*.

2. Type one or more 1' writings on the slower ¶, trying to exceed the rate on the faster ¶.

3. When your rate on one ¶ exceeds that on the other, switch to the slower ¶ for additional practice.

4. Type a 3' writing on both ¶s; determine *gwam*.

Right margin 72

All letters are used.

		GWAM		
		1'	3'	
¶1 1.2 SI 5.0 AWL 95% HFW	Life has never been a mere one-way street. Instead, it	11	4	33
	requires both give and take, earn as well as yearn. This is	23	8	37
	just as true today as it was yesterday, and as it will be to-	36	12	41
	morrow. We should all give our fair share.	44	15	44
¶2 1.4 SI 5.4 AWL 85% HFW	What is the size of an equitable share? The real answer	56	19	48
	must come from your evaluation of giving and taking, of earn-	68	23	52
	ing and yearning, of capability as well as need. Will you	80	27	56
	give, or just make an excuse for taking?	88	29	58

1' GWAM | 1 | 2 | 3 | 4 | 5 | 6 | 7 | 8 | 9 | 10 | 11 | 12 |
3' GWAM | 1 | 2 | 3 | 4 |

LESSON 27

27A Preparatory Practice ⑧ *each line three times SS; DS between three-line groups*

Alphabet Quick approval by Rex Evans might "sew it up" for Don Jantz.

Figures Type these figures: 28, 46, 39, 57, 208, 840, 196, and 375.

Figure-symbol Can you make 10% profit on #3849 @ $6.72 a dozen (56¢ each)?

Fluency The eight men who work on the dock come in during the night.

| 1 | 2 | 3 | 4 | 5 | 6 | 7 | 8 | 9 | 10 | 11 | 12 |

27B Typing from Dictation ⑦ *once with the book open; once with the book closed*

Do not type the color dividers

also city busy duty body visit panel title vigor civic angle

of the |is the |by the |and the |to the |to them |for the |for them

to 59 the 573 fix 482 work 2948 held 6393 spend 20373 social

00 22 88 44 99 33 77 55 66 11 50 121 391 846 390 551 205 691

27C Skill-Comparison Typing ⑰

1. Type ¶ 1 of 26D, above, as a 1' writing to establish a base rate.

2. Type two 1' guided writings on ¶ 1 for speed (base rate plus 6-8 *gwam*); then two slightly slower writings for precise control.

3. Repeat Steps 1 and 2 for ¶ 2 of 26D, above.

4. Type a 3' writing on both ¶s combined. Determine *gwam* and errors.

5. Compare the 3' *gwam* with that typed in Lesson 26.

Full sheet; DS; 65-space line; 5-space ¶ indention; 2" top margin; correct errors

Alertness cue: Your typed lines will not be the same as those in the copy.

	Words
[all caps] To Our Partners in Education *[triple-space]*	6
¶ A Colleges such as Westminster ^now faces two major	16
problems: ~~in common with~~ better prepared and more highly motivated	26
students ~~, and~~ as well as the "knowledge explosion." We	37
have too many students ^for our present facilities. We need more classrooms,	52
dormitories, laboratories, professors, library	61
books, and space to meet the needs of our	70
students and those "knocking at our doors."	79
Alumni News quotes our President as	88
saying, that ¶ Ours is a college of distinction	96
SS and indent quoted ¶ in spite of our many needs. We maintain	104
the high educational ideals and standards	112
set by the distinguished men ^and women who studied	123
at ~~this college~~ .Westminster before the present deluge of	131
students. We now need their help. ~~They~~ Let's	140
~~must be our partners in education~~ tell them so.	143
They ~~will~~ won't fail us in this time of need.	151
¶ The honor roll for this year's partners in	160
education goes to the printer soon. Space	168
has been reserved on it for your name.	176
Let us put it there! Send your check	184
or pledge NOW.	187

27D   Manipulative Parts Drill: Tabulator and Backspacer ⑱ *three or more times SS*

Tabulating Cue: *Reach* to the tab bar or key; tab and type without pausing.

Backspacing Cue: *Reach* with the little finger to backspace; move back quickly and type.

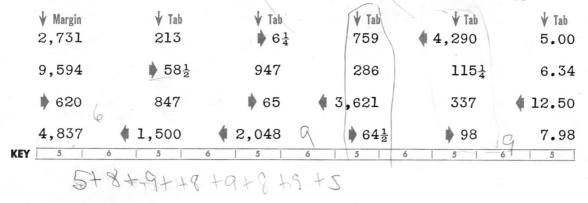

↓ Margin	↓ Tab	↓ Tab	↓ Tab	↓ Tab	↓ Tab	1' GWAM
2,731	213	▶ 6¼	759	◀ 4,290	5.00	6
9,594	▶ 58½	947	286	115¼	6.34	12
▶ 620	847	▶ 65	◀ 3,621	337	◀ 12.50	19
4,837	◀ 1,500	◀ 2,048	▶ 64½	▶ 98	7.98	26

KEY   5   6   5   6   5   6   5   6   5   6   5

LESSON 28

28A   Preparatory Practice ⑧ *each line three times SS; DS between three-line groups*

Alphabet	Janice kept two quiet prize lynx she got from Bev in Dallas.
Figures/shift keys	Use area codes: Waco, 817; Hays, 913; Enid, 405; Mesa, 602.
Figure-symbol	That check, #4639, for $1,582.40 is dated February 21, 1970.
Fluency	Go to the city for the auto signs and pay the firm for them.

| 1 | 2 | 3 | 4 | 5 | 6 | 7 | 8 | 9 | 10 | 11 | 12 |

28B   Technique Practice: Stroking ⑧ *each line three times SS; DS between three-line groups*

Double letters	Russ will see that the staff accounts for all food supplies.
Consecutive/direct	June ordered a gross of tax receipts from a Fort Myers firm.
Adjacent keys	We saw column upon column of troops poised for quick action.
First/third rows	Many a man never quite wins the big prize of complete peace.

| 1 | 2 | 3 | 4 | 5 | 6 | 7 | 8 | 9 | 10 | 11 | 12 |

28C   Typing from Dictation ⑥ *once with the book open; once with the book closed*

it is, to do, of us, by me, or go, if he, is so, do an, I am
by 46; do 39; for 495; when 2736; girls 58412; height 638574
if we, go in, is my, go up, is in, for you, she was, and are

Do not type the color dividers

Jack & Jill's|1720 Elm|at 9:30 a.m.|lend at 6½%|get 5# @ 48¢

| 1 | 2 | 3 | 4 | 5 | 6 | 7 | 8 | 9 | 10 | 11 | 12 |

28D   Manipulative Parts Drill: Tabulator and Backspacer ⑫

DO: Repeat the drill of 27D, above, typing it only twice. Work for improved control of machine parts.

DO: Type a 1' writing on the drill. Determine *gwam*.
GOAL: Approximately ⅓ of your straight-copy rate.

53A   Preparatory Practice ⑧ *each line three times; 1' writings on Line 4*

Alphabet   Mr. Brown was dazzled by the quick jumps of the five or six young men.

Figure-symbol   Does the 10% discount on Bedford & Hunt's Invoice #469 come to $23.58?

One-hand words   The union referred only a few of my cases to the referee for decision.

Fluency   They did not include in the report the profits due the firm in August.
                  | 1 | 2 | 3 | 4 | 5 | 6 | 7 | 8 | 9 | 10 | 11 | 12 | 13 | 14 |

53B   Building Control ⑫ *line: 70; ¶ indention: 5; DS*

1. Type a 1-, a 3-, and a 5-minute writing on the *control level*. Pace your typing at a rate you can control with a high degree of accuracy.

2. After each writing, determine an appropriate goal for the next writing—fewer words and greater accuracy or more words with the same accuracy—and type to achieve that goal.

All letters are used.

1.4 SI
5.4 AWL
85% HFW

	GWAM		
	3'	5'	

Learning the "time cost" of correcting errors in typing is best done by making a check of the time you require to erase and correct an error on an original and carbon copy. When this was done with some typists, it was found that the most proficient required twenty-six seconds; most required about forty-five seconds; and some required a complete minute to erase and correct one error on an original and carbon copy. The assumption can be made, then, that it will take you about thirty seconds to make each correction. If you type a three-minute writing at forty-eight words a minute but make and correct two errors, your actual typing time will be just two minutes. You must realize the high price you pay for the errors you make, and then you must learn to type with a high degree of accuracy. You will type more when you type with control even though you seem to be typing at a slower speed. Type as fast as you can but as slow as you must to type with accuracy.

	3'	5'	
	4	3	42
	9	5	44
	14	8	47
	18	11	50
	23	14	53
	27	16	55
	32	19	58
	37	22	61
	41	25	64
	46	28	67
	51	31	70
	56	33	72
	61	36	75
	65	39	78

3' GWAM | 1 | 2 | 3 | 4 | 5 |
5' GWAM | 1 | 2 | 3 |

28E Skill-Comparison Typing ⓖ *as directed in 26D, page 50*

All letters are used.

		GWAM	
		1'	3'

¶1
1.3 SI
5.2 AWL
90% HFW

How can office workers keep their jobs if machines can | 11 | 4 | 36

do the work better than the workers do? This is one of the | 23 | 8 | 40

most perplexing questions of this new age of automation. A | 35 | 12 | 44

partial answer to it may lie in the area of more as well as | 47 | 16 | 48

improved training. | 51 | 17 | 49

¶2
1.5 SI
5.6 AWL
80% HFW

Change is inevitable. It encompasses our work as much | 62 | 21 | 52

as it affects other facets of our lives. We must therefore | 74 | 25 | 56

prepare for change instead of let it overtake us. If your | 85 | 28 | 60

job is being jeopardized, prepare for a prized one. | 96 | 32 | 64

```
1' GWAM | 1 | 2 | 3 | 4 | 5 | 6 | 7 | 8 | 9 | 10 | 11 | 12 |
3' GWAM |      1      |      2      |      3      |      4      |
```

LESSON 29

29A Preparatory Practice ⑧ *each line three times SS; DS between three-line groups*

Alphabet   Jack Heintz now plans a daily quota of six very big mallard.

Figures   You may call my residence, 571-2639, or my office, 281-4600.

Figure-symbol In a call-in campaign, 13,480 (57%) said "No" on Issue #926.

Fluency   If they sign the union form, may they then see the chairman?

```
| 1 | 2 | 3 | 4 | 5 | 6 | 7 | 8 | 9 | 10 | 11 | 12 |
```

29B Manipulative Parts Drill: Tabulator and Return ⑦ *at least twice*

Center + 10 ↓

Tab ---→Reach the finger to   Return

the tabulator bar or key.------Tab------→Depress it quickly,   Return

then move back to home position.-----→Reach to the return

lever or key quickly, too.

29C Skill-Comparison Typing ⓖ

1. Type ¶ 1 of 28E, above, as a 1' writing to establish a base rate.

2. Type two 1' guided writings on ¶ 1 for speed (base rate plus 6-8 *gwam*); then two writings at a slightly slower rate for precise control.

3. Repeat Steps 1 and 2 for ¶ 2 of 28E, above.

4. Type a 3' writing on both ¶s combined. Determine *gwam* and errors.

5. Compare the 3' *gwam* with that in Lesson 28.

52C Problem Typing ⃝20

Problem 1: Two-Column Tabulation

Full sheet; DS; 8 spaces between columns; reading position; correct errors

		Words
RANK OF VOCATIONAL TRAITS		5
DS		
OF		6
DS		
OUTSTANDINGLY SUCCESSFUL SECRETARIES		13
TS		
Accuracy	1	15
Responsibleness	2	19
Dependability	3	22
Intelligence	3	25
Courtesy	5	27
Initiative	5	30
Judgment	5	32
Personal Pleasantness	9	37
Personal Appearance	9	41

Problem 2: Composing and Typing

Modified block; open punctuation; your return address; current date

Compose and type a letter to your instructor to say that you found a reference to the 1924 study typed as Problem 1 and that the study is now out of print. Tabulate the first four traits and their ranking and indicate your amazement that "Honesty" is not among these.

Add a final paragraph stating your opinion as to the probable reason "Honesty" was not ranked among the first four traits of outstandingly successful secretaries.

Type your name in signature position; then make pencil corrections as needed, and retype the letter in acceptable form.

Problem 3: Letter with Enclosure

Letterhead (or full sheet); 60-space line; modified block; open punctuation; current date

If a letterhead is used, type the date on Line 16. If plain paper is used, type Westminster College on Line 14; New Wilmington, Pa. 16142 on Line 15; and the current date on Line 16.

```
     still, send your check for this year's contribution and help
Westminster maintain its role as a college of distinction.

                    Sincerely yours


                    Student Chairman
                    ANNUAL ALUMNI FUND

Enclosure
```

	Words
Mr. Anton J. Gabbert | 237 Radcliffe St. |	11
Bristol, Pa. 19007 | Dear Mr. Gabbert | (¶ 1)	18
As Student Chairman of Westminster College	27
Alumni Fund, I hope to interest you in join-	36
ing other distinguished alumni in an "invest-	45
ment in youth." You can do this through your	54
contribution to the Annual Alumni Fund.	62
(¶ 2) The enclosed copy of part of an editorial	70
from the Alumni News tells something of our	81
needs and our hopes. Please read it; then	89
send in your pledge of support for your col-	99
lege. Better still, send your check for this	108
year's contribution and help Westminster	116
maintain its role as a college of distinction.	126
Sincerely yours | (Operate return 4 times) Stu-	130
dent Chairman | ANNUAL ALUMNI FUND |	136
Enclosure	138

52D Technique Practice ⃝12 *each line twice without error*

Left shift	Henry and I are going to Maryland in May, but Paul is going to Norway.
Right shift	Dick West left for Greece, but Clay Spillman went to France with Carl.
Both shifts	Were Paul and Robert asked to imitate Leslie's typewriting techniques?
Both shifts	"Get SPEED and ACCURACY," Mr. Ward said, "for real typewriting power."
Both shifts	John and Frank spent April in Mexico City and June and July in Brazil.

| 1 | 2 | 3 | 4 | 5 | 6 | 7 | 8 | 9 | 10 | 11 | 12 | 13 | 14 |

29D Skill-Transfer Typing ⓴ *three 1' writings on each ¶; determine* gwam

To determine percents of transfer: Divide your straight-copy rate into your statistical rate, your script rate, and your rough-draft rate.

Your statistical rate should approximate 65-75% of your straight-copy rate; your script rate, 75-85%; and your rough-draft rate, 70-80%.

	1' GWAM
¶1 1.4 SI 5.4 AWL 85% HFW	
The purposes of business letters are many and varied.	11
Letters are used to seek or inform, to direct or explain, to	23
gain or retain goodwill, to name only a few functions. Their	36
value is great; the cost is vital, too.	43

¶2   *39*
1.4 SI
5.4 AWL
85% HFW

A 1967 study revealed that an average first-class letter	11
cost $2.49 as compared to only $1.83 in 1960--an increase of	24
over 36%. The cost stood at just $1.17 apiece through 1953.	36

1' GWAM | 1 | 2 | 3 | 4 | 5 | 6 | 7 | 8 | 9 | 10 | 11 | 12 |

¶3
1.4 SI
5.4 AWL
85% HFW

More than twenty billion pieces of mail are dictated each — 12
year in American business offices. Based on the cost of just — 24
a few years ago, you can see with great ease that the size of — 36
our annual letter budget is fantastic. — 44

¶4
1.4 SI
5.4 AWL
85% HFW

¶ The ~~largest element~~ *biggest factor* in lettle cost is labor. # *Reduce* ~~Lower~~ the — 12
[cost of this *human* factor--increase *the* production of the ~~O~~ne — 24
who dictates and *the one who* makes notes and types-- and you ~~immediately~~ — 36
reduce ~~the greatest~~ *a major* cost of writing letters. — 44

LESSON 30

30A Preparatory Practice ⑧ *each line three times SS; DS between three-line groups*

Alphabet   When Ziggy Bux joined my squad, five players took more care.

Figures   Add ZIP to your letters: 15213, 90024, 45227, 85026, 33116.

Figure-symbol   Purchase 275 units @ 30¢ ($82.50) and 140 units @ 65¢ ($91).

Fluency   If a man is paid a high fee, he may work with improved zest.
   | 1 | 2 | 3 | 4 | 5 | 6 | 7 | 8 | 9 | 10 | 11 | 12 |

30B Typing from Dictation ⑦ *once with the book open; once with the book closed*

if it is; and to do; by the way; do the work; lend me a hand

sow 20#; paid 6%; make $73; 8:15 p.m.; 4/6 or 2/3; a #9 sock

we may; if you were; try to get; they are in; she was at the

Do not type the color dividers   10% 475# $89.50 #66|7:15 p.m.|2' x 6"|30# @ 12¢|Kelso & Cole

Problem 2: Rough-Draft Tabulation

Half sheet; DS; 12 spaces between columns; center the copy both vertically and horizontally

Center heading (DIFFERENTIATED ~~ED~~ING VOICE ^TONE QUALITIES | 7

Telephone Tips TS | 10

Good		Bad	14
Pleasant		Expressionless	18
[Friendliness ~~ness~~		*Mechanical* ~~Robot-like~~ to	22
Cap ≡ cordial		Indifferen~~ce~~t	26
Cheerfulness ~~ness~~		Impat~~e~~ient	30
Interesting ~~ed~~		Inattentive	35

Problem 3

Retype Problem 2, correcting all errors as you type.

51D Building Speed and Control (10) *line: 70; ¶ indention: 5; DS*

1. Type three 1' writings: first, for control; second, for speed; and third, for control. Control writings: circle errors; note *gwam*.

2. Type two 2' writings: first, for speed; next for control. Determine errors and *gwam* for the control writing. Compare with 1' control writing.

All letters are used.

	2' GWAM
1.5 SI 5.6 AWL 80% HFW	

Always try to put first things first in every job you decide to do, | 7 44

and you can win the prize you seek. This is especially important if you | 14 51

have the goal of improving your skill in typewriting. Many things go | 21 58

into developing expertness at the typewriter, but first is the use of | 28 65

right techniques, including the efficient use of all the operative parts | 35 73

of the typewriter. | 37 74

2' GWAM | 1 | 2 | 3 | 4 | 5 | 6 | 7 |

LESSON 52

52A Preparatory Practice (8) *each line three times; 1' writings on Line 4*

Alphabet   J. B. Deckers, from the next floor, gave away grapes on the quiz show.

Figures   The population of Houston in 1950 was 596,163; in 1960 it was 938,219.

Long words   Today, car buyers are knowledgeable about performance characteristics.

Fluency   How well did the eight boys do the problems you assigned for homework?

| 1 | 2 | 3 | 4 | 5 | 6 | 7 | 8 | 9 | 10 | 11 | 12 | 13 | 14 |

52B Building Speed and Control (10) *type 51D, above, as directed*

30C Growth Index ⑩ *type a 3' writing; practice words or word groups that caused hesitation or error; type another 3' writing; determine* gwam *on the better writing*

All letters are used.

		GWAM	
		1'	3'

¶1
1.4 SI
5.4 AWL
85% HFW

There is an old saying which suggests: Take care of the ... 11 | 4 | 40
pennies and the dollars will take care of themselves. This ... 23 | 8 | 44
is very good advice in handling money, and it can be applied ... 36 | 12 | 48
quite directly to other phases of life, also. ... 45 | 15 | 51

¶2
1.4 SI
5.4 AWL
85% HFW

For instance, if you learn to accept or conquer each of ... 56 | 19 | 55
your little frustrations as they occur every day, you will ... 68 | 23 | 59
develop the ability to face personal crises if and when they ... 80 | 27 | 63
arise. You will also learn to maintain a clear head and not ... 92 | 31 | 67
be panicked by the size of the next major problem that might ... 104 | 35 | 71
block your progress. ... 108 | 36 | 72

1' GWAM | 1 | 2 | 3 | 4 | 5 | 6 | 7 | 8 | 9 | 10 | 11 | 12 |
3' GWAM | 1 | 2 | 3 | 4 |

30D Skill Building ㉕

DO: Type the two ¶s of 30C, above, without being timed. Try to increase control and reduce errors.

DO: Type a 1' guided speed writing on each ¶ of 30C, with your instructor calling the guide.

DO: If time permits, type the four ¶s of 29D, page 53, without timing. Try for improved control.

● Self-Improvement Practice

Space bar   The man who plans for success is already well on his way up.

Shift keys   He shifts to type: @ (at), * (asterisk), and & (ampersand).

Shift lock   He knows what the abbreviations PBX, AMS, CPA, and ZIP mean.

Tabulator   56021 [5] 8742 [5] 2973 [5] 9954 [5] 2835 [5] 2146 [5] 82470

Center + 8 ↓

Tabulator and return   Tab --------------------------------→ Return without spacing   Return
at the end of the line.

Backspacer   The words to and too are still too frequently misused today!

Short words   to do so is he by she and the for with work lend forms their

Long words   fantastic progress themselves frustrations maintain chairman

| 1 | 2 | 3 | 4 | 5 | 6 | 7 | 8 | 9 | 10 | 11 | 12 |

51A Preparatory Practice ⑧ *each line three times; 1' writings on Line 4*

Alphabet   Dr. Foxburgh and Mr. Jackson quit Paris and are in Vevey, Switzerland.

Figure-symbol   Order #590-C read, "Ship 30 doz. #621 ✳✳ Star Brand at $4.78 a dozen."

Drill on sw   The Swede swore he saw the swords swung swiftly at the Swiss swimmers.

Fluency   The chairman of the Endowment Fund said a big check had been received.
                  | 1 | 2 | 3 | 4 | 5 | 6 | 7 | 8 | 9 | 10 | 11 | 12 | 13 | 14 |

51B Drill on Typing Columnar Headings ⑫

To Determine Center of Column: Method 1. (1) Read and add the numbers on the scale at the left and right edges of the column; (2) divide the total by 2 for the center point.

Note. This method is not new to you, for you used it to determine the center of special-size paper (35B, page 60).

Method 2. From point at which column begins, space forward once for each two letters, figures, or spaces in the longest line (the line that requires the most strokes to type). Disregard a leftover stroke.

To Type a Columnar Heading: From center of column, backspace once for each two letters or spaces in the heading. Disregard a leftover stroke. Begin to type where the backspacing ends.

Drill 1. Draw vertical pencil lines approximately 4" apart and 2" long. Use Method 1 (at left) to determine center; then center and type between the lines the following heading:

TYPING COLUMNAR HEADINGS

Drill 2. Use Method 2; 10 spaces between columns.

Name	Birthday
George Washington	February 22, 1732

Drill 3. Repeat Drill 1 with vertical lines 3 inches apart; Drill 2 with 6 spaces between columns.

51C Problem Typing ⑳

Problem 1: Tabulation with Columnar Headings

Half sheet; SS; 8 spaces between columns

Center the problem vertically; center the headings and the columns horizontally.

In Column 2, type the words of Column 1 but show all syllables; in Column 3, type the same words, but show the preferred point or points of division.

Check your syllabication and word division; then retype the problem to include any corrections you have made.

			Words
WORD DIVISION			3
Syllable Identification and Preferred Divisions	DS		12
		TS	
Word	Syllables	Divide	21
		DS	
alignment	a/lign/ment	align-ment	27
comparable			35
correction			42
contractual			51
crucible			57
feasible			63
mystical			69
possible			75
syllable			82
expressing			89
expression			96
expressive			103

KEY | 11 | 8 | 14 | 8 | 13 |

Purpose. To apply basic skill to typing simple communications, and to improve basic techniques.

Machine Adjustments. 70-space line; SS drill lines; DS when directed to do so.

Self-Improvement Practice. Type selected lines from page 65 and repeat as time permits.

LESSON 31

31A Preparatory Practice ⑧ *each line three times SS; DS after third typing of line*

Alphabet	A new gold plaque may be awarded at the next Schuylkill Jazz Festival.
Figures	You may contact Evelyn and Pat by calling either 631–9460 or 257–8273.
Figure-symbol	The 2% discount on Todd's Bill #963 (for $1,450.87) amounts to $29.02.
Fluency	If these girls handle the work right, Mr. Clayborne may make a profit.

| 1 ' 2 | 3 | 4 | 5 | 6 | 7 | 8 | 9 | 10 | 11 | 12 | 13 | 14 |

31B Technique Practice: Stroking ⑮ *each line three times; then 1' writings on Line 5*

First-row keys	Have Benny, Mac, and Zora Nixon been on vacation in Brazil and Panama?
Home-row keys	Gladys Skaggs was glad she had some of Hal Hall's fad jewelry to wear.
Third-row keys	We try to treat the young workers as we treat the top men of our firm.
Figures	The typed line of 8 1/2 inches has 85 pica spaces or 102 elite spaces.
Fluency	The busy city authorities have to handle many civic problems promptly.

| 1 ' 2 | 3 | 4 | 5 | 6 | 7 | 8 | 9 | 10 | 11 | 12 | 13 | 14 |

31C Problem Typing: Informational Memorandums ⑳

Problem 1: Memorandum on the Block Style

Half sheet; line: 60; 1½″ top margin; block style; SS

Type the following memorandum. Use current date. Circle errors.

Note. Three words (15 strokes) are counted for the date.

L.M. 30   R.M. 35

			Words
Down 9 spaces; type date on	1½″ (9 line spaces) top margin		
Line 10	*Current date*	Operate return mechanism	3
11		4 times (3 blank line spaces)	
12			
13			
14	SUBJECT: The Block Style	3 balance	8
15		DS	
16	This memorandum is typed in the block style. Note that all		20
17	lines begin flush with the left margin, with double spacing		32
18	(one blank line space) between paragraphs.		41
19			
20	The use of the block style for typing letters, memorandums,		53
21	and other personal or office communications is common today		65
22	and will probably grow in favor as its value is recognized.		77
23	Since lines begin at the left margin, the date and subject,		89
24	when used, are typed to begin at this point.		98

Problem 1: Rough Draft of Manuscript

Full sheet; line: 65; 5-space ¶ indention; DS; 1½″ top margin; SS and indent enumerated items 5 spaces from each margin; SS table; 4 spaces between columns; correct errors

	Words

Abbreviating in Business Correspondence — 8

"When in doubt, write it out" once was an admonition to students of — 22

shorthand that applied equally to other business writers, too. There is — 35

evidence, however, that "long shorthand" is not very efficient and that ab- — 50

breviating is no longer taboo in business communication. Modern — 63

business practice is based on the concept of efficiency, and the judicious — 78

use of abbreviations adds to efficiency without offending the — 91

equally important human relation aspect of business correspondence. — 105

Here are some basic principles of abbreviating: — 115

1. Use only those abbreviations that are commonly known. — 127
2. Spell out all words that would be conspicuous if — 137
   abbreviated in formal typewritten text. — 146
3. Use abbreviations in informal writing and also in tables, — 159
   footnotes, records, and technical writing. — 168

Listed below are some types of abbreviations that are commonly — 181

used in both personal and business correspondence: — 191

Personnel Titles	Doctor	Dr.	197
Company names	Incorporated	Inc.	203
Street names	Boulevard	Blvd.	209
Department names	Department	Dept.	215
Association names	Delta Pi Epsilon	DPE	222
State names	California	Calif.	229

Problem 2: Three-Column Table

Half sheet; SS; 12 spaces between columns; center the heading and the columns horizontally; center the problem vertically

	Words

SOME STATE NAMES, THEIR REGULAR ABBREVIATIONS, — 9
AND TWO-LETTER ZIP CODE ABBREVIATIONS — 17

			Words
Arizona	Ariz.	AZ	20
California	Calif.	CA	24
Colorado	Colo.	CO	28
Illinois	Ill.	IL	31
Indiana	Ind.	IN	34
Massachusetts	Mass.	MA	39
Michigan	Mich.	MI	43
Mississippi	Miss.	MS	47
New York	N.Y.	NY	50

Problem 2: Memorandum on Typing Paper

Half sheet; line: 60; block style; SS

Type on the control level with a 1½″ top margin. Circle errors. Retype if time permits.

REMEMBER to leave 3 blank lines below the date and to DS before and after paragraphs.

		Words
Line 10	*Current date*	3
11		
12		
13		
14	SUBJECT: Center Point	8
15		
16	Most typing paper is 8½ inches wide and 11 inches long with	20
17	66 lines to the page; a half sheet (8½ by 5½ inches) has 33	32
18	lines. A line has 102 elite or 85 pica spaces.	41
19		
20	The exact horizontal center of the paper is at 51 for elite	53
21	or 42½ for pica type. Unless otherwise directed, use 50 for	66
22	the elite center (instead of 51) and 42 for the pica center	78
23	(instead of 42½).	81

31D   Skill-Transfer Typing ⑦ *each line as two 1' writings, or each typed four times; line: 60*

	Words
A majority of the women questioned the chairman's authority.	12
This paper, 8½ inches wide, has 85 pica or 102 elite spaces.	12
An 11-inch sheet is 66 lines long; half of the sheet, 33 lines	12

LESSON 32

32A   Preparatory Practice ⑧ *each line three times*

Alphabet	When is J. C. Paxton required to move his zoology lab from Room K-261?
Figures	On April 18, Elizabeth moved to Apartment 36-A, 2450 West 79th Street.
Figure-symbol	Is Frohm & Kelly's $12,750 note (with 5½% interest) due on January 19?
Fluency	The author is skeptical of the authenticity of those formal documents.

| 1 | 2 | 3 | 4 | 5 | 6 | 7 | 8 | 9 | 10 | 11 | 12 | 13 | 14 |

32B   Technique Practice: Response Patterns ⑮ *each line three times; then 1' writings on Line 5*

Stroke	The executive expects the expert to explain his action to the auditor.
Combination	Six of the states do not have the same wage and tax laws that we have.
Stroke	Flight 476 left Rome at 8:15 a.m. and arrived in New York at 3:29 p.m.
Combination	Nine seniors pointed to the easy quiz questions to support their case.
Word-recognition	The aid the men got from us did much to help them get their work done.

| 1 | 2 | 3 | 4 | 5 | 6 | 7 | 8 | 9 | 10 | 11 | 12 | 13 | 14 |

32C   Problem Typing: Memorandums ⑳

Problem 1: Type Problem 2 of 31C, above, as directed. Review learning elements. Circle errors.

49D Skill-Comparison Typing ⑫ *Line: 70; 5-space ¶ indention; DS*

1. Type easy ¶ 1 as a 1′ control writing to determine your base *gwam*.
2. Type two 1′ writings of ¶ 2 on the *exploration level*, trying to reach your base rate. **Note.** The 1′ rate will be twice the 2′ rate shown in Column 1 at the right.
3. Type a 2′ writing on the *control level.*
4. Type a 3′ writing on the *control level.*
5. Circle errors on the 2′ and 3′ writings and compare the *gwam*.

All letters are used.

	GWAM	
	2′	3′

¶ 1
1.3 SI
5.2 AWL
90% HFW

The typewriter has changed the place of women in the world, for it opened the doors of the business office to them. They now fill many jobs that used to be for men only. That the need for women in business is recognized is shown by the many ads for competent women workers that are found in the daily papers.

2′	3′	
6	4	46
14	9	50
21	14	55
28	19	60
31	21	62

¶ 2
1.6 SI
5.8 AWL
75% HFW

Numerous positions are available in the local offices of diversified companies. Duties such as typing, taking shorthand, and filing are very common. Those who apply for jobs with these companies must be aware of the skills that a job requires, as they will be expected to use them as well as related skills.

2′	3′	
38	25	66
44	29	71
51	34	76
58	39	80
62	41	83

2′ GWAM | 1 | 2 | 3 | 4 | 5 | 6 | 7 |
3′ GWAM | 1 | 2 | 3 | 4 | 5 |

LESSON 50

50A Preparatory Practice ⑧ *each line three times; 1′ writings on Line 4*

Alphabet For the chemical test, J. K. Pew may request a large-size box and vat.
Figure-symbol Is the up-to-date report on Bill #6753–48 on <u>Profits</u> due May 19 or 20?
One-hand words A few dead trees were scattered among the great grove of orange trees.
Fluency The auditor said the profit due you should have been paid before this.

| 1 | 2 | 3 | 4 | 5 | 6 | 7 | 8 | 9 | 10 | 11 | 12 | 13 | 14 |

50B Skill-Comparison Typing ⑫ *type 49D, above, as directed*

50C Skill-Transfer Typing ⑩ *line: 60; SS; each line for two 1′ writings; compare gwam*

		Words
Straight copy	The six girls who are in our office do their work with ease.	12
Figure-symbol	Order #836 comes to $197.50 and is to be shipped by July 24.	12
Script	The new chairman may not want you to sign the amendment now.	12
Rough draft	lc. Will Rodney handle the problems of form for your the firm today.	12

Problem 2: Memorandum on Centering Information

Half sheet; line: 60; block style; SS

Type current date on Line 10; subject on Line 14. Circle errors. Retype if time permits.

Note. Paragraph headings are emphasized by capitalizing important words and by underlining.

	Words
Current date	3
SUBJECT: Horizontal Centering	9
<u>Get Ready to Center</u>. Move both margin stops to the ends of	25
the scale. Clear the tabulator stops; move the carriage or	37
carrier to the center of the paper. Set a tabulator stop.	49
<u>Steps for Centering</u>. Tabulate to the center of the paper.	65
From this center point, backspace once for each two letters	77
(or letter and space) in the line. If the line has one odd	89
or leftover letter, disregard it and start typing where the	101
backspacing ends.	104

32D Drill on Typing Outside the Margins (7) *right margin: center + 30*

1. Depress the margin release or margin bypass **(25)** and backspace 5 spaces into left margin.
2. Type the 71-space sentence, below, three times, typing until the carriage locks (ignore the ringing of the bell); then depress the margin release (bypass) and complete the typing.

Set right margin stop 3 or more spaces beyond the line ending you want.

LESSON 33

33A Preparatory Practice (8) *each line three times*

Alphabet	Was Len Burke amazed by the very excellent report given by Jeff Quinn?
Figures	My 174-page research report has 28 tables, 6 graphs, and 53 footnotes.
Figure-symbol	Was the rate on Dodd & Boyd's note of $5,000 (date 2/8/69) 6½% or 7%?
Fluency	Try to improve the quality without reducing the quantity of your work.

| 1 | 2 | 3 | 4 | 5 | 6 | 7 | 8 | 9 | 10 | 11 | 12 | 13 | 14 |

125-72

33B Problem Typing: Horizontal Centering (20)

Problem 1

1. Get ready to center. (See ¶ 1 of Problem 2, above.)
2. Study HOW TO CENTER, below.
3. Center and type each line at the right.

HOW TO CENTER: From center of paper, backspace *once* for each *two* letters, figures, spaces, or punctuation marks in the line. Do not backspace for a leftover stroke. Start to type where the backspacing ends.

Half sheet; DS; 1½" (9 line) top margin

	Words
FREE TUTORING SERVICE *10*	5
TS	
Honors Society *7*	7
offers *3*	9
Free Tutoring to Freshmen and Sophomores *20*	17
Mondays and Thursdays, 3:45 p.m. *16*	24
Rooms 206 and 208, Royce Hall *14*	30
First Session on Monday, October 10 *7*	37

Problem 1: Memorandum with Tabulated Items

Words

Full sheet; DS; 2" top margin; 65-space line; 5-space ¶ indention; SS tabulated lines; decide spacing between columns

THE ZIP CODE SYSTEM   4

DS

The Zoning Improvement Plan   10

TS

ZIP Code divides the country into delivery units, each desig-   22
nated by a five-digit number. The first digit represents one of   35
ten geographic areas; the second digit, a specific portion of a   48
geographic area; the third digit, one of the 553 sectional center   61
areas for sorting mail; and the last two digits, today's delivery   74
zone numbers. Here are some examples of the ZIP Code numbers and   87
the new two-letter state abbreviations recommended for use with   100
the ZIP numbers: 104

Reset margin
stop

Deerfield	MA	01342	107
Jamestown	KS	66948	111
Las Cruces	NM	88001	115
McGregor	TX	76657	119
Marble City	OK	74945	123
Forest Hill	MD	21050	127

Type the ZIP Code number on the line with the city and the   139
state name or abbreviation with two spaces between them. The ZIP   152
Code number should be included in the letter address as well as   165
in the envelope address.   170

Problem 2: Letter with Tabulated Items

Words

Full sheet; 60-space line; tab stop at center; return address on Line 16; modified block style (see page 71); decide on the spacing between tabulated items

(Your return address; current date) Miss Eloise Leffingwell | 20
President, Alpha Chapter | Delta Pi Epsilon | New York University | 32
New York, New York 10003 | Dear Miss Leffingwell | At a recent meeting   44
of business teachers, I talked with three | members of other DPE   57
chapters who now live in nearby cities. | Each of these teachers   70
expressed an interest in transferring | their DPE membership to   82
Alpha Chapter. Their names, chapters, | and chapter numbers are   94
given below: | 97

Roger N. Fitzhugh	Beta	561	103
Lera B. Jackson	Gamma	389	108
Estelle Norabach	Gamma	72	113

What is the procedure for transferring membership from one | 125
DPE chapter to another? I shall be glad to get this informa- | 137
tion to these DPE members and to invite them to our next Alpha | 149
Chapter meeting if you wish me to do so. | Sincerely | *Your name*   164

Problem 2: Centered Lines

Half sheet; DS; 1″ top margin;
center each line horizontally

	Words
HORIZONTAL CENTERING	4
TS	
Move Margin Stops to Ends of Scale	11
Clear Tab Stop Settings	16
Set Tab Stop at Center	21
From Center, Backspace "Once for Two"	28
Disregard Leftover Stroke	33
Begin to Type at Point Backspacing Ends	41
Type the Line	44
Tabulate to Center	48
Center and Type Each Remaining Line	55

Problem 3: Centered Lines

Half sheet; DS; 1½″ top margin;
center each line horizontally

	Words
Dinner Dance	3
TS	
Benefit of Scholarship Funds	8
LEADERSHIP CLUB	11
Music by Alphonse Garcia and Orchestra	19
Saturday, 19 November, 19--	25
Sussex House	27
Twelve Dollars, a Couple	32

Problem 4: Centered Lines

Retype Problem 3, but in all capital letters.

33C Building Control ⑧ *one 1′ and two 2′ writings on the control level; circle errors*

70-space line;
5-space ¶ in-
dention; DS

1.4 SI
5.4 AWL
85% HFW

All letters are used.

When typing, think the word, or think the sequence of letters if the word is long or unusual. Adjust your speed to the kind of material you are to type. Emphasize an even and flowing motion, and type without pausing between one word and the next.

	G W A M	
	1′	2′
	13	6	31
	27	14	38
	42	21	46
	50	25	50

1′ GWAM | 1 | 2 | 3 | 4 | 5 | 6 | 7 | 8 | 9 | 10 | 11 | 12 | 13 | 14 |
2′ GWAM | 1 | 2 | 3 | 4 | 5 | 6 | 7 |

33D Setting the Margin Stops ⑦

60-space line; 5-space
¶ indention; DS

1. Set the margin stops for an exact 60-space line (left: center — 30; right, center + 30).
2. Type the sentence, below, at a slow rate; stop as soon as the bell rings. Instead of typing the remainder of the sentence, type the figures 123 (etc.) until the machine locks. The last figure typed is the number of spaces the bell on your typewriter rings before the carriage locks.
3. Subtract 3 from the number of bell cue spaces (Step 2) and move the right stop to the right that far: center + 30 + 3 to 7 or more.

4. Type the sentence again. If the bell rings as you are typing a word, complete it, make the return, and continue to type. If the machine locks as you are typing a word, depress the margin release (margin bypass) and complete the word.

If the bell rings on the space between words, make the return at once or type the next word before making the return if it is a short word. This is often desirable because of your typing momentum.

When the carriage locks, depress the margin release and type on.

33E Listening for the Bell ⑦

Type the ¶ of 33C, above, as two 1′ and one 2′ writings on the *control level*. Listen for the ringing of the bell to warn of the line ending. Your typed lines will not be the same as the lines appearing in the ¶ in 33C.

48D Drill on Drawing Lines at the Typewriter ⑮

To Draw Pencil Lines: Place the pencil point on the type bar guide (36) above the ribbon, in the cardholder (12) notch, or against the aligning scale (33). Hold the pencil firmly against the paper.

Horizontal Line. Place the pencil in position, depress the carriage-release lever, and draw the carriage across to make the line of whatever length is desired.

Centering on Lines. To determine the center of a line, (1) read and add the numbers on the cylinder scale at the beginning and end of the line; (2) divide by 2. The resulting number is the center of the line.

Vertical Line. Operate the automatic line finder or ratchet release (6). Place the pencil in position, and turn the cylinder (platen) forward (away from you) for the length of line desired. Return the automatic line finder to its normal position.

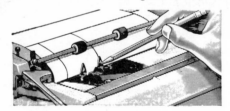

Drills on Drawing Horizontal Lines

1. Type the following sentence:

   They played quite a good game.

2. Draw a pencil line under the sentence, leaving a little space between the down-stem letters and the line. Note the relationship of the line to the typed letters.

3. Draw an approximate 4″ pencil line; then center and type the sentence of Drill 1 correctly placed on the line. Be sure the letters with down stems do not cut through the line.

4. Type a 3″ underline; remove the paper; reinsert it; align; then center and type the sentence of Drill 1 correctly placed on the line.

Drills on Drawing Vertical Lines

5. Draw two vertical pencil lines about 2″ long and about 4″ apart. (Return the finder to normal position.) Near the top of the space between the lines, center and type the following heading:

   DRAWING VERTICAL LINES

6. Draw a pencil line under the heading just typed.

7. Draw two vertical pencil lines about 2″ long and 3″ apart. (Return the line finder to normal position.) Near the top of the space between the lines, center and type your name; then DS and center and type the current date.

8. Repeat Drills 4, 5, and 6.

LESSON 49

49A Preparatory Practice ⑧ *each line three times; 1′ writings on Line 4*

Alphabet   Zora and John Voight played a number of quiet games with Chuck Baxter.

Figures   Your Certificates 36285A and 47190C bear the date of January 20, 1969.

Figure-symbol   Didn't Mr. Lee wire, "Ship 6 cars of 4/4 C&B Oak on West's Order #96"?

Fluency   The civic group may ask for a formal audit of the records in February.

        | 1 | 2 | 3 | 4 | 5 | 6 | 7 | 8 | 9 | 10 | 11 | 12 | 13 | 14 |

Note. Remove the paper; then reinsert it, gauge the line and letter, and type over the first and last word of the last line typed.

49B Drill on Drawing Lines at the Typewriter ⑩

Repeat Steps 3, 4, and 5 of 48D, above. Appraise the accuracy of your centered lines and of the placement of the typing on the horizontal lines.

34A Preparatory Practice ⑧ *each line three times*

Alphabet | Jean and Gladys quickly won several prizes at the Foxburgh track meet.
Figures | Flight 590 left for Paris with 34 girls, 16 boys, and 28 men on May 7.
Figure-symbol | My letter read, "Wire best price on 9 cars 4/4 C & B Oak f.o.b. Erie."
Fluency | It will pay you to take the needed time to learn to control your mind.

| 1 | 2 | 3 | 4 | 5 | 6 | 7 | 8 | 9 | 10 | 11 | 12 | 13 | 14 |

34B Building Control ⑫ *two 1' and two 3' writings on* control level; *circle errors*

70-space line; 5-space ¶ indention; DS

The ringing of the bell is a signal that you will have just a few more strokes to type before the machine will lock. Listen for it, and it will tell you, even without your looking up from the textbook, when to make the return. Acquire the habit of paying attention to the bell, and you will realize an immediate gain in your typing power.

1' GWAM | 1 | 2 | 3 | 4 | 5 | 6 | 7 | 8 | 9 | 10 | 11 | 12 | 13 | 14 |
3' GWAM | | 1 | | 2 | | 3 | | 4 | | 5 |

GWAM	
1'	3'
13	4	27
27	9	32
42	14	37
56	19	41
68	23	45

34C Problem Typing: Announcements ⑳

Problem 1: Announcement with Centered Line

Half sheet; 60-space line; block style; 1½" top margin

	Words
October 26, 19---	3

3 blank line spaces

The first in our exciting series of Fall FORUMS is to be on	15
Wednesday, November 6, at 8:15 p.m. in Science Hall. The	27
subject will be	30
"Radioactive Isotopes"	35
The speaker, Dr. Anton Szechenyi, of the Nuclear Science	46
Service, Inc., will discuss some biological and biomedical	58
applications of isotopes to the space program.	67

Problem 2: Centered Announcement

Half sheet; DS; 1½" top margin; center each line

	Words
SCIENCE FORUM	3
Lecture on Radioactive Isotopes	10
By Dr. Anton Szechenyi	14
of the	16
Nuclear Science Service, Inc.	22
in Science Hall	25
Wednesday, November 6, 8:15 p.m.	31

Problem 3: Alertness Training

Type Problem 2 again as directed, except that you will type it in capitals. (To type in capitals, depress the shift lock.)

Alertness cue: Don't let the figures trip you!

The textbook may not always warn you by an "alertness cue" that there is a problem in the material to be typed. It is your responsibility to see that all your work is correct in form, content, and meaning. This is why alertness training is important.

34D Listening for the Bell ⑩ *two 3' writings on the* control level; *circle errors*

60-space line; 5-space ¶ indention; DS

Type 34B, above. Your typed lines will not be the same as those in the ¶. If typing a word when the bell rings, complete it; if the machine locks, depress the margin release (margin bypass) and complete the word.

LESSON 48

48A Preparatory Practice ⑧ *each line three times; 1' writings on Line 4*

Alphabet   Will Judge Alexander Vonrique permit the seizure of your bank records?

Figure-symbol   On May 17, we shipped Lukin & Decker 6 cars of #923Y valued at $5,840.

Shift keys   Edward Kuhn and George Lyon flew to Italy, Greece, and Spain on May 2.

Fluency   Ken may find that some elements of their problems are hard to isolate.

| 1 | 2 | 3 | 4 | 5 | 6 | 7 | 8 | 9 | 10 | 11 | 12 | 13 | 14 |

48B Errorless Typing ⑦ *each line twice without error or three times with not more than 1 error to a line*

	GWAM		
	Words	15"	12"
If you have lots of pluck, you won't need to depend on luck.	12	48	60
Appreciation of their work is of first importance to the workers.	13	52	65
A man must learn to control himself before he tries to control others.	14	56	70

| 1 | 2 | 3 | 4 | 5 | 6 | 7 | 8 | 9 | 10 | 11 | 12 | 13 | 14 |

48C Problem Typing ⑳

Problem 1

Full sheet; DS; determine space between columns

Center the problem in reading position; center the headings horizontally.

Type Column 1 as shown; in Column 2, type the words of Column 1 with the diagonal to indicate all syllables; in Column 3, type the words of Column 1 with the hyphen to indicate the preferred point of division. Check the divisions in Column 3 with a dictionary or your instructor. (Do not type the numbers beside Column 1 words.)

Tabulating cue: Tabulate from column to column.

	SYLLABLE IDENTIFICATION AND WORD DIVISIONS			Words
	Application of Guides, Pages 80-81			15
1	educated	ed/u/cat/ed	edu-cated	22
2	paragraph			28
3	graduation			36
4	dependable			43
5	physically			50
6	mechanical			58
7	impartially			66
8	impression			73
9	condition			80
10	expelling			86
11	progressing			94
12	progression			102
13	imply			106
14	abounds			111
15	wouldn't			117
16	strangely			123
17	greedy			127

KEY	11	7	14	8	13

Problem 2: Composing and Typing

Half sheets; line: 60; SS

Compose and type a brief explanation of why each of the last five words of Column 1, Problem 1, (13-17) should not be divided. Type the ¶s in block form similar to Problem 1, page 80, numbering each ¶ (1 to 5). Check your explanations with pages 80 and 81. Make pencil corrections as needed; then retype.

LESSON 35

35A Preparatory Practice ⑧ *each line three times*

Alphabet   Were quite big loans applied for by J. H. McVay and Baxter K. Ziegler?

Figures   A half sheet is 8½ by 5½ inches and has 33 lines (6 lines to an inch).

Figure-symbol   Items marked 26-A, 345-X, and 789* sell at 10% discount until April 7.

Fluency   Nancy and Henry worked on the problem with their usual vigor and zeal.

| 1 | 2 | 3 | 4 | 5 | 6 | 7 | 8 | 9 | 10 | 11 | 12 | 13 | 14 |

35B Problem Typing: Report on Centering ⑳

Problem 1

Full-size sheet; 70-space line; 5-space ¶ indention; DS; 3" (18-space) top margin

Words

CENTERING ON SPECIAL-SIZE PAPER   6

To center a line on special-size paper or card, first determine   19

the center of the paper (or card). To do this, add the numbers from at   33

the scale at the Left and Right edges of the paper; divide by 2.   46

The resulting number will be the center of the paper (or card).   59

When you are and type lines   To center on special-size paper (or card), follow the rules summarized below.   81 / 84

Center each line DS
Insert the paper
Add scale numbers at left and right edges of paper   94
Divide sum by 2 for center   100
Follow steps for getting ready to center   108
Back space from center "once for two"   115

Center the line and type   120

Problem 2: Centering on Special-Size Paper

1. Insert a half sheet (5½" by 8½") with the *long edge at the left*. Use DS; 2" top margin.
2. Determine the center and set tab stop.
3. Center horizontally and type only the main heading and centered lines of the body of Problem 1, above.

Problem 3: Centering on Special-Size Paper

1. Fold the half sheet used in Problem 2 from bottom to top.
2. Insert the folded sheet, creased edge at left.
3. Use a 1½" top margin.
4. Center and type the heading of Problem 1.

35C Listening for the Bell ⑩

Full-size sheet; 60-space line; 5-space ¶ indention; DS; 3" top margin

Type Problem 1 of 35B, above, with a 60-space line. Listen for the bell to warn of the line ending. Your typed lines of the ¶s will not be the same as those of the problem, but it will not be necessary for you to divide any word when typing with the shorter (60-space) line. The centered lines can be typed without changing the margin stops. Type at less than your top speed and listen for the bell.

Problem 2

Full sheet; line: 60; SS

Center the problem vertically in reading position; center the headings horizontally.

After typing the first line of ¶ 1, reset the left margin stop 4 spaces to the right. Backspace into left margin to type the numbers 2, 3, 4, and 5.

Note. Study Problems 1 and 2 so that you will know how to divide words when it is necessary for you to do so.

WORD DIVISION — 3

"Do Not" and "Avoid" ~~Rules~~ *Guides* — 8

TS

1. To avoid dividing *a* words, *& you may have* a line ~~may be~~ approximately — 21
five ~~5~~ strokes longer or shorter than the desired ending. — 33

2. Avoid dividing *after* a two-letter syllable at the beginning of a — 47
word. *Try to divide elsewhere in the word.* — 56

3. Avoid dividing initials, proper names, numbers, or abbre- — 69
viations. *Initials or a given name may be separated* — 80
from a surname when necessary. — 86

4. Do not divide a word of five or fewer letters. — 98

5. Do not *l.c.* ~~D~~ivide from the remainder of the word: — 109
l.c. A. A one-letter syllable at the beginning or end of a — 120
word; as, against, steady. — 126
l.c. B. A syllable without a vowel; as, shouldn't. — 136
c. A two-letter syllable coming at the end of a word; — 147
as, strongly. — 150

47D Aligning and Typing Over Words ⑫ *line: 60; SS*

Locate the variable line spacer (3) and the aligning scale (33).

1. Type the sentence below but do not make the return:

Use the alignment scale to align your copy.

2. Move the carriage (or element) so a word with the letter "i" is above the scale. Note that a white line points to the center of the letter "i" in the word.

3. Study the relation of the top of the scale to the bottom of the letters with down stems.

It is important for you to get an eye picture of the exact relation of the typed line to the top of the scale so you will be able to adjust the paper correctly to type over a word with exactness.

4. Remove the paper; reinsert it. Gauge the line so the bottoms of the letters are in correct relation to the top of the aligning scale. Operate the variable line spacer (3) if necessary to move the paper forward or backward. Operate the paper release (16) to move the paper to the left or right if necessary when centering the letter "i" over one of the white lines on the scale.

5. Check the accuracy of your alignment by setting the ribbon control (21) for stencil position and typing over one of the letters. If necessary, make further alignment adjustments. *Return the ribbon control to typing position.*

6. Type over the words with the letter "i" in the sentence, moving the paper forward or backward, to the left or right, as necessary for correct alignment.

7. Type the following sentence; remove the paper; then reinsert it; gauge the line and letter; and type over the first and final words.

It is wise for this firm to dismiss the men.

8. Repeat the entire drill if time permits.

35D Special Characters ⑫ *each line three or more times*

' Minutes, Feet (apostrophe)
" Seconds, Inches, Ditto (quotation mark)
× Times, By (lower-case x with a space before and after)
– Minus (hyphen with space before and after)

+ Plus (diagonal; backspace; hyphen)
÷ Divided by (hyphen; backspace; colon)
= Equals (hyphen; backspace; roll platen forward slightly; hold it in position; type hyphen; return platen to line position)

1   The 2' speed range, typed with the 15" call of the guide, is 30 to 46.

2   A rug 15'6" x 18'9" will be just right for a room that is 20'6" x 25'.

3   His problem is 27 x 89 – 364 ÷ 2. What is the sum of 157 + 509 – 263?

4   Ed said 5 x 90 – 62 + 136 ÷ 2 = 262 and 7 x 284 – 965 + 301 ÷ 2 = 662.

5   If 32 x 564 – 897 + 109 equals 17,260, what would 57 + 509 – 63 equal?

| 1 | 2 | 3 | 4 | 5 | 6 | 7 | 8 | 9 | 10 | 11 | 12 | 13 | 14 |

LESSON 36

36A Preparatory Practice ⑧ *each line three times*

Alphabet   Did Frank expect to solve the jigsaw puzzle more quickly than Bob Lee?

Figures   Move 90 to 100 chairs to Rooms 236-8 for the 4:15 lecture on the 27th.

Special symbols   Check this problem: 20 x 367 – 541 + 891 ÷ 2 = 3,845. Is that right?

Fluency   You can speed up your typing by thinking the word rather than letters.

| 1 | 2 | 3 | 4 | 5 | 6 | 7 | 8 | 9 | 10 | 11 | 12 | 13 | 14 |

36B Centering on Typed Lines ⑦ *DS; follow steps of 35B, page 60*

1. Type a 5½" line with the underline.
2. Type a 3" line with the underline.
3. Center and type your name on the 5½" line.
4. Center and type the date on the 3" line.

36C Problem Typing: Memorandum and Postal Cards ⑳ *half sheet; 2 postal cards*

Problem 1: Memorandum with Subject Line

Half sheet; 50-space line; 1½" top margin; block style; SS

October 29, 19—

SUBJECT: Typing Postal Cards

A postal card is 5½ by 3¼ inches and has a total of 19 lines. Since both top and bottom margins require 2 or 3 lines each, there will be just 12 to 15 lines for typing.

Each line has 55 pica or 66 elite spaces, but the left margin will take 3 or 4 spaces and the right margin 2 or 3 spaces. The writing line, then, is limited to 48 to 50 pica or 59 to 61 elite spaces.

Words
3

3 space for Left margin 9
3 space for 19
29
Right margin 39
44
54
64
74
83

LESSON 47

47A Preparatory Practice (8) *each line three times; 1' writings on Line 4*

Alphabet   Won't Judge Robb have to quiz Mr. Kruptman and five or six local boys?

Figures   Don Parker moved from 2479 East 135th Street to 2628 West 60th Street.

Fractions   Can John Webb add these fractions: 2/3, 3/4, 4/5, 5/6, 7/8, and 9/10?

Fluency   The authority of those in power should be used for the benefit of all.

| 1 | 2 | 3 | 4 | 5 | 6 | 7 | 8 | 9 | 10 | 11 | 12 | 13 | 14 |

47B Technique Practice: Stroking (10) *each line three times*

Home-row keys   Hal Skaggs had a bad fall as he made a gallant dash to raise the flag.

First-row keys   Anna Mae McVay became excited when Calvin Bixmont raced over the line.

Third-row keys   Is it true that you were the ones who raised the issue of party lines?

Adjacent keys   As we were saying, it is our opinion that power belongs to the people.

Direct reach   Myrtle looked for a place to hide the junk Fred Hunt left in the yard.

| 1 | 2 | 3 | 4 | 5 | 6 | 7 | 8 | 9 | 10 | 11 | 12 | 13 | 14 |

47C Problem Typing: Guides for Word Division (20)

Problem 1

Full sheet; line: 60; SS

Center the problem vertically in reading position; center the heading horizontally.

After typing the first line of ¶ 1, reset the left margin stop 4 spaces to the right. Backspace into left margin to type the numbers 2, 3, and 4.

Alertness cue: Don't let the hyphen in the heading trip you.

WORD-DIVISION GUIDES

TS

     Words 4

1. Type a hyphen at the end of the line to indicate the division. Try to put enough of the word on the line to suggest what the completed word will be. Type the remainder of the word on the succeeding line.   17 28 39 47

2. Divide after a one-letter syllable in a word (as, separate) unless the word ends with <u>able</u>, <u>ible</u>, or <u>ical</u>—the two-syllable endings you must keep as a unit (as, deplor-able). If 2 one-letter syllables come together, divide between the vowels (as, continu-ation).   59 73 85 96 104

3. When dividing words ending in <u>cial</u>, <u>tial</u>, <u>cion</u>, <u>sion</u>, or <u>tion</u>, keep the endings as a unit (as, expres-sion).   119 131

4. When the final consonant in a word is doubled in adding a suffix, divide between the double letters (as, compel-ling); but when a syllable is added to a word that ends in double letters, divide after the double letters (as, will-ing, dismiss-ing).   144 155 167 178 182

Problem 2: Message Typed on a Postal Card

1. Use 2 postal cards (or paper cut to size of a 5½-by 3¼-inch card).

2. Insert card; determine center; then set stop for a 48-space line.

3. Type the date on Line 3; then type the postal card message given below.

Note. The salutation and complimentary close are omitted because of limited space for the message.

4. Remove the typed card; turn it message side down; then insert the second card; and type the same message.

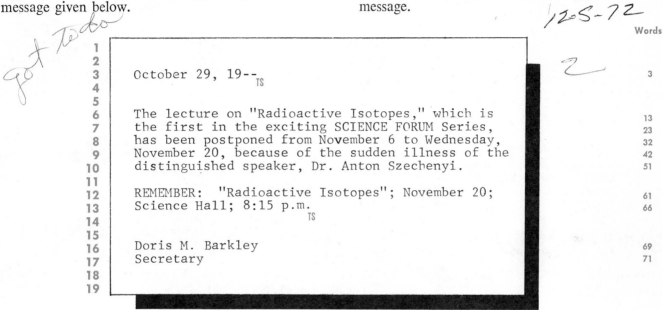

		Words
October 29, 19-- TS		3
The lecture on "Radioactive Isotopes," which is		13
the first in the exciting SCIENCE FORUM Series,		23
has been postponed from November 6 to Wednesday,		32
November 20, because of the sudden illness of the		42
distinguished speaker, Dr. Anton Szechenyi.		51
REMEMBER: "Radioactive Isotopes"; November 20;		61
Science Hall; 8:15 p.m. TS		66
Doris M. Barkley		69
Secretary		71

Problem 3: Addressing Postal Cards

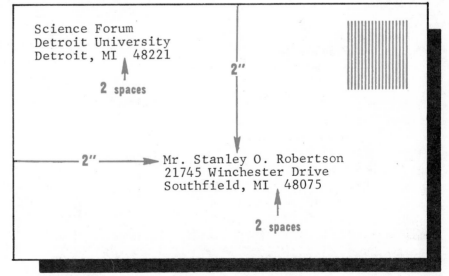

LEARN:

1. SS and block both the return and the postal card addresses.

2. The new state abbreviations are two capital letters typed without a period or space between. For automatic sorting into destination bins by the Optical Character Reader, the ZIP Code *must* be used. (See the Reference Guide, page viii, for a complete list of the new two-letter state abbreviations.) It is still permissible, however, to spell the state name in full or to use standard abbreviations.

3. Type the return address in the upper left corner of the card on the address side, beginning on Line 2 from the top edge and 3 spaces from the left edge.

4. Type the address about 2″ from the top edge of the card and begin it 2 inches from the left

edge. Have 1 or 2 spaces between the state abbreviation and the ZIP Code.

DO: 1. Insert the first card typed as Problem 2, above, and type the address side of the card as shown.

2. Insert the second card typed as Problem 2, above. Address the card to:

Miss Elfreda Trimble
1609 Pontchartrain Blvd.
Detroit, Mich.   48203

46C Drill on Spacing Main and Secondary Headings ⑫

LEARN: Double-space between main and secondary headings, if both are used; triple-space between last line of heading (whether main or secondary) and first line of columns (or columnar headings).

Type the drill at right with 12 spaces between columns; set margin and tab stops as directed on page 77; center the headings horizontally.

			Words
Main heading → TELEPHONE AREA CODE NUMBERS DS			5
Secondary heading → Ten Major Cities			9
TS			
New York	New York	212	13
Chicago	Illinois	312	17
Los Angeles	California	213	23

KEY | 11 | 12 | 10 | 12 | 3 |

46D Problem Typing: Three-Column Tabulations ⑳

Problem 1

Half sheet; SS; 12 spaces between columns

Center the problem vertically (page 64), the headings horizontally (page 57), and the columns horizontally (page 77).

Tabulating cue: Tabulate from column to column.

			Words
TELEPHONE AREA CODE NUMBERS DS			6
Ten Major Cities			9
TS			
New York	New York	212	13
Chicago	Illinois	312	18
Los Angeles	California	213	23
Philadelphia	Pennsylvania	215	29
Detroit	Michigan	313	33
Houston	Texas	713	37
Baltimore	Maryland	301	41
Cleveland	Ohio	216	45
Dallas	Texas	214	49
Washington	D.C.	202	52

KEY | 12 | 12 | 12 | 12 | 3 |

Problem 2

Half sheet; SS; 8 spaces between columns

Center the problem in exact vertical center and the headings horizontally.

Type Column 1 as shown; in Column 2, type the words of Column 1 with the diagonal (/) to indicate all syllables; in Column 3, type the words of Column 1 with the hyphen (–) to indicate the preferred point of division. (See Guides, pages 67 and 80).

			Words
SYLLABLE IDENTIFICATION AND WORD DIVISION			8
Application of Page 67 Guides			16
anoints	a/noints	anoints	19
beginner	be/gin/ner	begin-ner	25
doubted			30
dropped			35
equalled			40
ideas			44
children			50
controlled			57
described			63
destined			69
knowledge			75
manuscript			83
possessed			89
separates			96
transferred			103
transcripts			111

KEY | 11 | 8 | 12 | 8 | 12 |

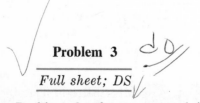

Problem 3

Full sheet; DS

Type Problem 2, above, centered in reading position. (See page 64.)

36D Special Characters ⑩ *each line three or more times*

/ Insert (Type / between words at point inserted material is to go; then roll platen backward (toward you) and type inserted matter. Return platen to line position.)

! Exclamation (see page 40).
Pounds (see page 44).
° Degree (Roll platen backward a half space; hold in position; type small o.)

                   of the   very

1 Have most/students tried quite hard to learn to type/well?

2 Paul said, "The box weighs 310#." I exclaimed, "Never. It couldn't."

3 The boiling point of water is 212° F. and the freezing point is 32° F.

4 Morris said this problem is correct: 936 x 7 − 458 + 170 ÷ 2 = 3,132.

5 The problem is 27 x 89 − 364 ÷ 2. What is 157 x 409 − 263 + 238 ÷ 12?

| 1 | 2 | 3 | 4 | 5 | 6 | 7 | 8 | 9 | 10 | 11 | 12 | 13 | 14 |

36E Errorless Typing ⑤ *each line once without error or three times with not more than 1 error a line*

All of us will have problems to be solved at some period in our lives.

Each day's work calls for the application of preceding days' learning.

Since I can't escape problems in life, I must learn how to solve them.

| 1 | 2 | 3 | 4 | 5 | 6 | 7 | 8 | 9 | 10 | 11 | 12 | 13 | 14 |

LESSON 37

37A Preparatory Practice ⑧ *each line three times*

Alphabet   May Jack provide a few extra quiz questions or problems for the girls?

Figures   In 1965, Lynn & Beard had 84 salesmen; in 1967, 230; and in 1968, 491.

Figure-symbol   Does 30 x 156 − 374 + 928 ÷ 4 = 1,308½? Does 40 x 516 + 273 = 20,913?

Fluency   The duties of the chairman have been taken over by Elvis until August.

| 1 | 2 | 3 | 4 | 5 | 6 | 7 | 8 | 9 | 10 | 11 | 12 | 13 | 14 |

37B Technique Practice: Manipulative Parts ⑩ *each drill three times*

                             Center ⟶

Tabulator and return   Depress the tab bar (or flick your electric key) to move from column to column.

Margin release   Use the margin release (or margin bypass) to type outside the margins.

Shift lock   To assure the fastest service, we use the National ZIP Code Directory.

Hyphen and dash The editor-in-chief--if that's his new title--used an up-to-date list.

Centered line   Backspace-from-Center Method

| 1 | 2 | 3 | 4 | 5 | 6 | 7 | 8 | 9 | 10 | 11 | 12 | 13 | 14 |

Problem 2: Three-Column Tabulation

Half sheet; SS; 8 spaces between columns

Center the problem vertically (page 64), the heading horizontally (page 57), and the columns horizontally (page 77).

Technique cue: Tabulate from column to column without looking up from the copy. Reach to the tab bar or key without moving the hand out of typing position.

Single

	WORDS FREQUENTLY MISSPELLED		Words
	TS		6
accessible	accidentally	accommodate	13
announced	appearance	athletic	19
believable	benefited	consensus	25
definitely	disappointed	dissatisfaction	33
eligible	existent	extraordinary	40
governor	gauge	guarantee	45
independent	inoculate	insistence	51
judgment	justifiable	knowledgeable	58
laid	liaison	likelihood	63
maintenance	manageable	miscellaneous	70
occasionally	occurrence	personal	77
permissible	personnel	pertinence	83
precede	principle	privilege	89
procedure	prominence	questionnaire	96
recommend	referring	resistance	102
singular	smooth	soluble	107
transferred	truly	various	112
vicinity	withhold	zoology	117

KEY   12   8   12   8   15

45D   Building Speed and Control ⑩   *two 1' writings for speed; two 1' writings for control*
one 2' writing for speed; one 2' writing for control

All letters are used.

	GWAM		
	1'	2'	

1.4 SI
5.4 AWL
85% HFW

As tabulating is an extension of centering, which you have been   13   6 | 46

doing for quite some time, it is not new to you. When you were typing   27   13 | 53

words or figures in columns at different times, you were told how many   41   21 | 60

spaces to leave between the columns. From now on, you will use guides   55   28 | 67

for the horizontal placement of columns but must often use judgment as   69   35 | 74

to how many spaces should be left between them.   79   40 | 79

1' GWAM | 1 | 2 | 3 | 4 | 5 | 6 | 7 | 8 | 9 | 10 | 11 | 12 | 13 | 14 |
2' GWAM | 1 | 2 | 3 | 4 | 5 | 6 | 7 |

LESSON 46

46A   Preparatory Practice ⑧   *each line three times; 1' writings on Line 4*

Alphabet   Our unexpected freezing weather may have killed John Quinley's shrubs.

Figure   Paul typed page 27 on May 9, page 34 on May 10, and page 56 on May 18.

Figure-symbol   "All the world's a stage" is from Act II, Line 139, of As You Like It.

Fluency   The total endowment is not big enough to meet the needs of the school.

| 1 | 2 | 3 | 4 | 5 | 6 | 7 | 8 | 9 | 10 | 11 | 12 | 13 | 14 |

46B   Building Speed and Control ⑩

Type 45D, above, as directed except you will determine *gwam* and errors for the 2' *control writing.*

Problem 1

Type the problem once on a half sheet, SS, in exact center; and once on a full-size sheet, DS, in reading position. Center the problem vertically (see Basic Rule at right); and center each line horizontally.

REVIEW OF CENTERING ELEMENTS *4*
TS

Block Style *5*
Spaces in Horizontal Inch *12*
Center of Paper *7*
Lines in Vertical Inch *11*
Basic Rule for Horizontal Centering *17*
Centering on Special-Size Paper *13*
Setting Margin Stops *10*
Postal Cards *6*
Backspace-from-Center Vertical Centering *20*
Special Characters *9*
Bell Cue *4*

Vertical Centering: Backspace-from-Center Method

BASIC RULE. From vertical center of paper, roll platen (cylinder) back once for each two lines, two blank line spaces, or line and blank line space. Ignore leftover line.

Steps in Vertical Centering

1. To insert paper to vertical center, start spacing down from *top edge of paper*:
   a. *Half sheet*: Down 6 TS — 1 SS (to Line 17).
   b. *Full sheet*: Down 11 TS + 1 SS (to Line 34).

2. From vertical center:
   a. *Half sheet*, SS or DS: Follow Basic Rule (back 1 for 2).
   b. *Full sheet*, SS or DS: Follow Basic Rule (back 1 for 2); then back 2 SS for *reading position*.*

REMEMBER: TS (2 blank line spaces) after main heading.

NOTE: The mathematical method of vertical centering is taught on page x.

*About 2 line spaces above actual vertical center.

---

got to do

Problem 2: Postal Card with Centered Heading

12-8-22

48-space line; block style

	Words
ATTENTION CLUB TENNIS PLAYERS	6
TS	
The Mixed Doubles Tennis Match now scheduled for	16
May 18 will be rescheduled for May 25 because of	26
conflicts in area sports activities.	33
DS	
All entries should be in not later than May 21.	43
Call 621–4630 to be entered in the match.	52
TS	
Loren T. Parker, Chairman	57
Athletic Club Tennis Committee	63

Problem 3: Announcement

Half sheet; 60-space line; current date on Line 8; block style

Type Problem 2 as an announcement with 3 blank line spaces between the date and the centered heading. It will not be necessary for you to divide any words when typing the problem with the 60-space line, but your lines will not be the same as those shown in Problem 2. Let the bell indicate the line ending.

Purpose. To build skill in tabulating; to learn the principles of word division; and to improve typing speed and control.

Machine Adjustments. Line: 70. Drills: SS. Timed writings: DS, 5-space ¶ indention. Problems: as directed.

Self-Improvement Practice. Type the Alertness Training paragraphs as directed in Self-Improvement Practice, page 96.

LESSON 45

45A   Preparatory Practice (8) *each line three times; then 1' writings on Line 4*

Alphabet
Figures
Figure-symbol
Fluency

Maude Parker will visit the Chicago zoo before joining Alexis Quigley.
On May 28, 158 boys and 347 girls took a history test on pages 69-102.
Add the 4% sales tax of $7.22 (on $180.56) to Webb & Orr's Bill #8390.
Ruth did not blame her neighbor for being skeptical about the visitor.

| 1 | 2 | 3 | 4 | 5 | 6 | 7 | 8 | 9 | 10 | 11 | 12 | 13 | 14 |

45B   Tabulating Drills (12)

Drill 1. Arrange the following 4 words in 2 columns with 12 spaces between columns. (Follow Guides 1, 2, and 3 at right.)

accommodate   bookkeeping
controlled   definite

Drill 2. Arrange the 3 groups of figures in 3 columns with 8 spaces between columns. (Follow Guides 2 and 3.) **Note.** Space forward or backspace to align figures at the right.

432,165   78,234   9,061
82,560   4,397   16,203

Preparing to Tabulate

1. Preparatory Steps
a. Move margin stops to extreme ends of scale.
b. Clear all tab stop settings.
c. Move carriage to center of paper.
d. Decide spacing between columns—preferably an even number of spaces (4, 6, 8, 10, etc.).
2. Setting Left Margin Stop

From center of paper, backspace 1 space for each 2 letters, figures, symbols, and spaces in longest line of each column and for each 2 spaces left between columns. *Set the left margin stop at this point.* **Note.** Carry forward to the intercolumn the extra space that may occur at the end of the longest line of a column; to the next column the extra space that may occur in an intercolumn. If an extra space occurs at the end of the longest line of the final column, drop it.
3. Setting Tab Stops

From left margin, space forward once for each letter, figure, symbol, and space in longest line in the first column and for each space to be left between first and second columns. *Set tab stop at this point for second column.* Follow similar procedure for additional columns. TABULATE FROM COLUMN TO COLUMN.

45C   Problem Typing (20)

Problem 1: Two-Column Tabulation

Half sheet; SS; 10 spaces between columns

Center the problem vertically (page 64), the heading horizontally (page 57), and the columns horizontally (Guides 2 and 3, above).

WORD STUDY		Words
	TS	2
already	all right	6
bathroom	bank draft	10
bondholders	bona fide	14
cupful	de facto	17
northeast	dining room	22
percent	inasmuch as	26
postman	post office	30
wastebasket	price list	34

KEY | 11 | 10 | 11 |

37D   Growth Index ⑫   one 3' writing and one 5' writing on the control level; circle errors

70-space line; 5-space ¶ indention; DS

All letters are used.

	GWAM 1'	3'	5'

¶ 1
1.4 SI
5.4 AWL
85% HFW

When you type, concentrate on what you are typing and how you are   13   4   3
to type it. If you find this difficult to do while people around you   27   9   5
are talking and moving about, block out the noise by becoming involved   41   14   8
in what you are doing and nothing can distract you. Realize the need   55   18   11
for and the importance of concentration and think of how you can focus   70   23   14
your undivided attention on what you are typing no matter what is going   84   28   17
on around you.   87   29   18

¶ 2
1.4 SI
5.4 AWL
85% HFW

Concentration cannot be given to you as a gift by a teacher,   12   33   20
parent, or friend. You must decide, on your own, whether learning to   26   38   23
type well is to become one of your major goals. Once this decision   40   42   25
has been reached, the next step is to address yourself to the problem   54   47   28
of concentrating on one single goal at a time until eventually you   67   51   31
are able to utilize the power that is latent within you.   78   55   33

1' GWAM | 1 | 2 | 3 | 4 | 5 | 6 | 7 | 8 | 9 | 10 | 11 | 12 | 13 | 14 |
3' GWAM | 1 | 2 | 3 | 4 | 5 |
5' GWAM | 1 | 2 | 3 |

● **Self-Improvement Practice**   *each line three or more times*

All letters, figures, and symbols are used in the sentences.

		Words in Line	GWAM 20"	15"	12"
1	Lead a boy to college where they try to make him think.	11	33	44	55
2	With faith enough and work enough, we can do about anything.	12	36	48	60
3	We may not be born great, but we can try to work up to greatness.	13	39	52	65
4	A good many of the workers of this world need to have a faith lifting.	14	42	56	70
5	Use ⁂ for a footnote, and use ¢ and @ in typing a bill.	11	33	44	55
6	He wrote, "Sam's Policy 765432, due in 1980, is for $2,500."	12	36	48	60
7	Check #453 (dated July 29) is for $167.80, but Paul owes $176.80.	13	39	52	65
8	Lane & Roth gave a 2% discount on Bill #345 (dated May 6) for $789.10.	14	42	56	70
9	Do some distance thinking--far ahead of where you are!	11	33	44	55
10	A man may be down, but he's never out until he gives up.	12	36	48	60
11	The next goal to be realized: a gain of a word or two each week.	13	39	52	65
12	James has quite as much zeal for his work as he has for his pay check.	14	42	56	70
13	The year's high for Manox was $89\frac{1}{2}$; it sold at 82 today.	11	33	44	55
14	Be uniform in typing fractions: 1/2 and 1/4--not 1/2 and ¼.	12	36	48	60
15	If 109 x 6 - 57 + 83 = 680, what will 902 x 3 - 754 + 183 ÷ 2 be?	13	39	52	65
16	I say the following problem is right: 360 x 4 - 854 + 710 ÷ 12 = 108.	14	42	56	70

44D Problem Typing ㉒ *2' to get ready; 20' to type, with errors erased and corrected*

Problem 1: Modified Block Letter

60-space line; return address on Line 14; address envelope; fold and insert letter

	Words
1368 Forest Green Drive | Ogden, Utah	7
84403 | October 30, 19–– | Mrs. Rubye Man-	15
ville | Emerson College | 1121 Washington	22
Blvd. | Ogden, Utah 84404 | Dear Mrs. Man-	30
ville | (¶ 1) You asked me to let you know	37
the nature of the interview and | tests I took	46
yesterday at the Briggs Chemical Company. |	55
(¶ 2) The employment test included English,	62
spelling, arithmetic, | and typewriting. I think	72
I did well on these tests; but I | was nervous	81
when taking the typewriting test and made	89
some | errors, I am sorry to report. |	96
(¶ 3) In the interview, I was asked about my	104
club activities, my | hobbies, and my com-	112
munity involvements. Attitudes, I was | told,	121
are considered as important as aptitudes; and	130
the job | interview is used to evaluate the	139
applicant's attitudes as | the tests are used to	148
evaluate her skill competence. |	155
(¶ 4) I shall let you know the results of my	162
interview if I get a | call from the Company.	171

	Words
I thank you for all the help you have | given	180
me, and it has been more than you probably	189
know. | Sincerely yours | Lorna Jane Crawford	197/225

Problem 2: Alertness Training—Personal Letter Without Addresses

60-space line; date on Line 20

	Words
October 30, 19–– | Dear Kathie | (¶ 1) Let me	7
tell you about my job interview and tests at	16
Briggs | Chemical Company yesterday. | (¶)	23
(For ¶ 2, type ¶ 3 of Problem 1.)	82
(For ¶ 3, type only the first sentence of ¶ 2.)	93
(¶ 4) I shall let you know the results of my	105
interview if I get a | call from the Company. |	114
Yours | (*Signature in ink: Lorna Jane*)	117

Problem 3: Alertness Training

Type the letter of Problem 1, addressing it to Mr. R. N. Heilman \| 1062 Elberta Drive \| Ogden, Utah 84404. Add an appropriate salutation.

(192 words)

● Self-Improvement Practice *each line at least three times*

1	Balanced-hand	Six of their girls may go on the right lane by the lake if they do go.
2	One-hand	Bart Kimmon was aggravated after only a few union cases were referred.
3	Combination	The staff at the car lot wanted him to make a trade after ten minutes.
4	Adjacent-key	The guides were in columns as we went over the trails after the lions.
5	Double letters	Bill and Ann will soon see the bookkeeping committee from Mississippi.
6	Number-symbol	Call 701 771-4084 or 701 771-4085 at 2:30 p.m. about Shipment #29-468.
7	Special symbols	Frank is sure this problem is correct: 369 x 7 + 125 – 840 ÷ 4 = 467.
8	Degree symbol	It was 82° in Miami, 4° below zero in Missoula, and 36° in Pittsburgh.
9	Number-symbol	Approximately 10% of the #139 machines were priced incorrectly at $89.
10	Combination	He must often make a choice between the easy wrong and the hard right.
11	Balanced-hand	The auditor for the firm of Burns & Mantleman can make a report today.

| 1 | 2 | 3 | 4 | 5 | 6 | 7 | 8 | 9 | 10 | 11 | 12 | 13 | 14 |

SECTION 7 ▶ PERSONAL COMMUNICATIONS AND COMPOSING

LESSONS 38–44

Purpose. To learn to type personal notes and letters, to address envelopes, and to compose at the typewriter (think and type).

Machine Adjustments. Line: 70 spaces, unless otherwise directed; SS drills and problems; DS and indent timed writing ¶s 5 spaces.

Self-Improvement Practice. Type selected lines from page 76, or type each line as directed and as time permits.

LESSON 38

38A Preparatory Practice ⑧ *each line three times; Line 4 for 1' writings as time permits*

Alphabet	Jack will be quite vexed when Troy Gilman buzzes the fine new airport.
Figures	18 24 539 670 100 4,281 3,596 1,700 2,344 12,485 96,703 82,314 610,597
Figure-symbol	Check #803 for $914.56 (dated February 27) was mailed to Dodge & Sons.
Fluency	The eight girls may want a ride to the game if the bus is not on time.

| 1 | 2 | 3 | 4 | 5 | 6 | 7 | 8 | 9 | 10 | 11 | 12 | 13 | 14 |

38B Building Speed and Control ⑫

1. Type each ¶ of 37D, page 65, as a 1' *exploration-level* writing. Speed up the stroking for these writings.

2. Type the ¶s as a 5' *control-level* writing. Reduce the speed of stroking for this writing.

38C Problem Typing: Personal Note in Block Style ⑳

2 half sheets; line: 50; block style; SS

1. Type the following note as illustrated. Circle your errors.

2. Type the note a second time, but address it to Elsie. Circle your errors.

Line			Words
7	Date	October 18, 19––	3
8		*Operate return 4 times*	
9			
10			
11	Salutation	Dear Frank	6
12			
13		The Homecoming Queen and her court will be chosen	16
14	Body	by the student body on November 16 in an election	26
15		to be held in Student Center from 8 a.m. to 4 p.m.	36
16			
17		The Student Government Committee asked me to get	46
18		some students to supervise the polls on election	56
19		day. I hope you will be willing to help do this.	66
20		We need you very much. Call me at 621–3078 to let	76
21		me know we can count on you.	82
22			
23	Complimentary	Sincerely yours	85
24	close	*Operate return 4 times*	
25			
26			
27	Writer's name	*Your name*	89
28			
29			

LESSON 44

44A Preparatory Practice ⑧ *each line three times; Line 4 for 1' writings*

Alphabet   Dwight Mystroni lives in a quiet area just six blocks from Jasper Zoo.

Figures   The show was at 1946 E. 37th Street on April 25 and began at 8:30 p.m.

Figure-symbol   Mr. Smith (of Idaho) sold Items #29, #41, and #39* to Jim for $572.69.

Fluency   Lena paid cash for the yams, but I gave them a check for the six hams.

| 1 | 2 | 3 | 4 | 5 | 6 | 7 | 8 | 9 | 10 | 11 | 12 | 13 | 14 |

44B Word-Division Drill ⑩ *half sheets; line: 70; DS; 10 spaces between columns; 1½" top margin*

1. Center WORD DIVISION as the main heading.
2. Type the hyphen (–) to show all acceptable word divisions in typewritten work, as in Line 1.
3. Refer to 39B, page 67, and to the dictionary to check your divisions.
4. Retype the drill.

					Words
Tabulate from column to column	didn't	con-cluded	per-formed	pro-fes-sion	11
	abroad	centrally	supposed	transcribed	19
	lighted	compelled	transmits	performance	28
	across	specially	transcend	conditioned	37
	upon	schedule	troubled	referring	44

KEY | 7 | 10 | 10 | 10 | 10 | 10 | 13 |

44C Growth Index ⑩ *5' control writing; determine gwam and errors; 1' control writings on each ¶ as time permits*

All letters are used.

GWAM
1' | 5'

¶ 1
1.4 SI
5.4 AWL
85% HFW

Our economic system is one in which individuals have the right to   13 | 3 | 42
produce goods and services to be sold to the public at a profit to the   27 | 5 | 45
producer. Since there are laws that govern the operation of a business,   42 | 8 | 48
our "free enterprise" system is subject to those laws and thus is "free"   57 | 11 | 51
just to the extent that the laws allow.   64 | 13 | 53

¶ 2
1.4 SI
5.4 AWL
85% HFW

Under our economic system the customer can choose from many prod-   14 | 16 | 55
ucts and services what he wants to buy. The producer may set the price of   28 | 18 | 58
the product; but if it is too high, the customer will not buy it and so,   42 | 21 | 61
in effect, he controls the price that business can charge for its   56 | 24 | 64
product. The business that does not win customers, fails.   67 | 26 | 66

¶ 3
1.4 SI
5.4 AWL
85% HFW

A business of any size is often owned by many people. They buy   13 | 29 | 69
stock in the hope of earning a profit. If the business prospers, they   27 | 32 | 71
get quarterly dividends, as a rule; and the remainder of the profits   41 | 34 | 74
may be used to expand plant, create new jobs, pay interest on bank   54 | 37 | 77
loans, pay taxes, labor, and other costs of operating a business.   67 | 40 | 80

1' GWAM | 1 | 2 | 3 | 4 | 5 | 6 | 7 | 8 | 9 | 10 | 11 | 12 | 13 | 14 |
5' GWAM | 1   2   3 |

38D Composing and Typing: Sentence Completion (10) *line: 50; 5-space ¶ indention; DS*

1. Type the sentences in ¶ form and fill in the needed information. The line endings will not be the same as those in the copy. Ignore any typing errors you make.

(¶ 1) My name is (*your name*). My home is in (*city or town and state*). My home address is (*street number and name or P.O. Box, city, state, and ZIP Code*). I am a student at (*name of your school*), in (*city and state*). I am now living at (*street address, dormitory, or other*).

2. When you have completed the typing, remove the paper, make pencil corrections, and retype the material on a half sheet with an appropriate top margin.

(¶ 2) The name of the typewriter I use is (*type the name*) and the title of my textbook is (*underline the title or type it in all CAPS*). I type at approximately (*state rate in figures*) gwam. My greatest difficulty seems to be (*too many errors, not enough speed, poor techniques, etc.*).

LESSON 39

39A Preparatory Practice (8) *each line three times; 1' writings on Line 4*

Alphabet — Rex Quig watched jet airplanes flying above the haze in the amber sky.

Figures — We are to study Section 2, pages 95-180, and Section 5, pages 274-360.

Figure-symbol — I sold 1 punch @ $4.50; 72 pencils @ 8¢ each; and 37 rulers @ 9¢ each.

Fluency — Many of the new problems are to be solved when we come to the meeting.

| 1 | 2 | 3 | 4 | 5 | 6 | 7 | 8 | 9 | 10 | 11 | 12 | 13 | 14 |

39B Problem Typing: Memorandum; Personal Note (20)

Problem 1: Memorandum on Word Division

Half sheets; line: 60; SS; 1½" top margin

Type the main heading centered horizontally. After typing the first line, reset the left margin stop 4 spaces to the right. To type the numbers for ¶s 2 and 3, move the carriage (or carrier element) outside the left margin. (See 32D, page 57.) Circle errors; then retype the problem.

	Words
GUIDES FOR WORD DIVISION	5

Reset margin

1. Divide a word between syllables only. (Do not divide a word of five or fewer letters). — 17 / 24

Use margin release; then backspace

2. When a syllable is added to a word that ends in double letters, divide after the double letters (as, express-ing); but if the final consonant is doubled in adding a suffix, divide between the double letters (quit-ting). — 36 / 47 / 58 / 69

3. Do not divide from the remainder of the word (a) a one-letter syllable at the beginning or end of a word, or (b) a syllable without a vowel (as, couldn't), or (c) a two-letter syllable at the end of a word (neat-ly). — 82 / 93 / 104 / 114

LESSON 43

43A   Preparatory Practice ⑤   *each line three times; Line 4 for 1' writings*

Alphabet   H. J. Wexler amazed Cal by reporting so quickly on my five test items.

Figures   On May 9, the 15 girls typed 203 letters, 46 reports, and 78 invoices.

Figure-symbol   Dexter & Marcy's check for $967.20 (Check #1035) was cashed on June 4.

Fluency   It did not take Sue more than six hours to do the work for Mr. Worley.
| 1 | 2 | 3 | 4 | 5 | 6 | 7 | 8 | 9 | 10 | 11 | 12 | 13 | 14 |

43B   Determining the Cost of an Error ⑩

1. Type the ¶s of 42C, page 73, as a 3' *control* writing. Hold your speed to a rate you can maintain with good control. Determine *gwam* and errors.

2. Type the ¶s again for 3', but erase and correct each error as you type. Determine your corrected *wam* and compare with the first writing.

43C   Problem Typing ㉜

Problem Typing Review

Problems 1 and 2

Make pencil notations of the problems and page numbers listed below. Place the notation sheet beside the typewriter. Type each problem once only and, as you type, correct any errors you make. Before removing the typed problem, proofread it and correct any errors you find.

> Problem 1, page 67, centered on full sheet in reading position. (See 37C, page 64.)

> Problem 1, page 70, as directed

do these 11-20-72 Monday

Problem 3: Modified Block Letter

60-space line; return address on Line 16

Erase and correct errors. Address an envelope; fold and insert the letter into the envelope.

	Words
7701 Harrison Place | Gary, Indiana 46410 |	8
October 26, 19-- | Miss Elizabeth Turner |	16
North High School | 2319 Stringtown Road |	24
Evansville, Indiana 47711 | Dear Miss Tur-	32
ner | (¶1) When I studied English with you,	39
there must have been times | that you de-	47
spaired of my learning anything except by	56
rote | memory. I learned more than you	63
realized, for what you are | as well as what	72
you taught, influenced me greatly. |	79

	Words
(¶2) My courses here at the University are	86
often challenging and | sometimes exciting. I	95
think I am doing well this first year | in the	104
"academic halls of learning." For this, I	113
thank my | high school teachers, and I thank	122
you most of all. | Sincerely yours | Nancy	130
McDonald	131/160

Problem 4: Modified Block Letter

Use the return address, date, signature, and directions for Problem 3, except that you will begin the return address on Line 18. Listen for the ringing of the bell to indicate the line endings.

	Words
Miss Mary Alice Knox | 921 Southland Blvd.,	20
E. | Louisville, Kentucky 40214 | Dear Mary	28
Alice | (¶1) My "thank you" letter to your	35
mother was sent by airmail the day after I	44
got back from my weekend with you. The	52
delay in writing you has been caused by a cold	61
I developed two days after I got back here.	70
I am still blowing and wheezing, but I'll live,	80
I am sure! (¶2) I shall long remember this	88
visit to your home. It was most delightful,	97
and I am grateful to all of you for giving me	106
such a happy time. (¶3) Exams are coming	113
up, and I have much to do to get ready for	122
them. I shall write a longer letter soon. In	132
the meantime, my grateful thanks to all of	140
you for a wonderful weekend. Sincerely	151/176

Problem 2: Personal Note

Type the note given at the right, double spacing between single-spaced ¶s. See 38C, page 66, for form.

The | in the copy indicates the end of the 60-space line, or other special line. Do not type it; but when you come to it, make the return without looking up and keep on typing. The title of a book may be typed in all CAPS or underlined. (See ¶ 1.)

Half sheet; line: 60; block style; SS; date on Line 7; reset margin stops in 5 spaces to type quoted ¶ 2; then reset at original margins

	Words
October 20, 19——	*(Operate return 4 times)* Dear Tom	*(¶ 1)* Let	6
me answer your question about freedom of speech on the	campus	18
by quoting from the College Handbook:		30
(¶ 2) The College wants speakers invited to the campus		39
for an open forum to express their ideas freely.		59
(¶ 3) The purpose of an institution of higher learning must		60
always	be the free exchange of ideas. The College adheres to		73
this	purpose at all times.	Sincerely yours	*(Operate return 4*	81
times) E. M. Brownfield		85

39C Skill-Transfer Typing ⑫ *line: 70; ¶ indention: 5; DS*

1. Type a 1' *exploration-level* writing on each ¶. Try to maintain the same speed on the more difficult second and third ¶s (figures and rough-draft copy).

Do this by forcing your fingering speed.
2. Type a 5' *control-level* writing on all ¶s. Determine *gwam* and errors.

All letters are used.

		GWAM	
		1'	5'
¶ 1 1.4 SI 5.4 AWL 85% HFW	Too many young people make the big mistake of postponing the very	13	3 | 30
	difficult decision of the choice of a career. Much thought should be	27	5 | 33
	given to this matter long before college work is begun, yet a final	41	8 | 36
	decision need not always be made by this time, of course.	52	10 | 38
¶ 2 1.4 SI 5.4 AWL 85% HFW	By 1964, career guidance was given to a few kindergarten classes	13	13 | 41
	and in Grades 1, 2, and 3 to children 5 to 7 or 8 years old, but many	27	16 | 43
	schools wait to give this guidance until children are about 10 years old.	42	19 | 46
¶ 3 1.4 SI 5.4 AWL 85% HFW	Guidance experts say that students should all plan to have a programs of study	13	21 | 49
	to equip them for the jobs of the next generations. They will	27	24 | 52
	work more zealously, also, if they enjoy their work and are able to do	41	27 | 54
	it very well.	44	28 | 55

1' GWAM	1 | 2 | 3 | 4 | 5 | 6 | 7 | 8 | 9 | 10 | 11 | 12 | 13 | 14 |
5' GWAM	| 1 | 2 | 3 |

39D Composing and Typing ⑩ *half sheets; line: 60; SS; 1" top margin; date: October 20, 19—*

1. Compose and type a short note to Frank to express your pleasure that he has accepted your invitation to supervise the polls on election day. (See 38C, page 66.)

2. Compose and type a short note to Elsie to express your regret that she cannot accept your invitation to supervise the polls on election day.

Problem 3: Folding and Inserting Letters into Small Envelopes

Study the directions and illustrations for folding and inserting letters into a small envelope; then fold and insert into their addressed envelopes the letters typed as Problems 1 and 2, page 72.

FOLDING A LETTER FOR A SMALL ENVELOPE

Step 1. With the letter face up on the desk, fold from the bottom up to ½ inch of the top.

Step 2. Fold right third to left.

Step 3. Folding from left to right, fold left third to ½″ of last crease.

Step 4. Insert last creased edge first.

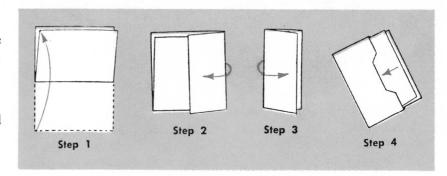

Step 1   Step 2   Step 3   Step 4

42C   Guided Writing for Control ⑩

1. Type two 1′*control* writings. Determine average *gwam*. Divide by 2 for ½′ goals. Identify six ½′ goals for a 3′ writing.

2. Type a 3′ *control* writing. Your instructor will call the ½′ guides. Determine your *gwam* and errors.

All letters are used.

		3′ GWAM

1.4 SI
5.4 AWL
85% HFW

A good deal of time must be given to the actual process of securing   5

one's very first full-time position. Some make the mistake of accepting   9

the first job that is offered. Others see the importance of using an   14

approach that will get the jobs that are best for them. Use all the   19

extra aids you have to find out which jobs are open for which you might   23

qualify. We do hear about jobs from our relatives, friends, and other   28

citizens. The services of the public and private employment agencies   33

can also be of immense aid.   35

3′ GWAM | 1 | 2 | 3 | 4 | 5 |

42D   Drill on Erasing ⑫

Type the sentences as shown, omitting the numbers. Study the guides for erasing given at the right. Erase and correct each error in your typescript.

1 Turn paper froward ro vackward.

2 Ersae lightly; vrush eraser dirt awah.

3 don't dampen eth eraser.

4 Erase thoroughyl; retype the wrod lightyl.

GUIDES FOR ERASING

1. Lift the paper bail.
2. Turn the paper forward if the error is on the upper two thirds of the page or backward if it is on the lower third.
3. Use a plastic shield and a hard eraser.
4. Move the carriage to the left or right as far as you can to keep dirt out of mechanism.
5. Erase lightly—don't "scrub" the error. Brush eraser particles away from page.
6. Return the paper to writing position and type.

LESSON 40

40A Preparatory Practice ⑧ *each line three times; 1' writings on Line 4*

Alphabet   Pat Ford and Sam Oxford will solve the big jigsaw puzzle very quickly.

Figures   24 63 17 80 95 821 624 731 805 1,000 9,376 472,116 2,047,890 6,337,425

Figure-symbol   Bowen's Check #978 is for $211.27 for Invoice #161 ($234.75 less 10%).

Fluency   Some of the other men thought that Sue would be right for the new job.
| 1 | 2 | 3 | 4 | 5 | 6 | 7 | 8 | 9 | 10 | 11 | 12 | 13 | 14 |

40B Word-Division Drill ⑫ *half sheets; line: 70; DS; 10 spaces between columns; 1½" top margin*

1. Type the hyphen (–) to show all acceptable word divisions in typewritten work, as in Line 1.

2. Check your work.

3. Retype the drill, correcting any errors you made.

WORD DIVISION

TS

				Words
				3
couldn't	cen-tered	care-fully	com-mis-sion	11
enough	children	completed	compelling	20
finger	mortgage	knowledge	connection	28
aligned	numbered	preferred	controlling	37
hyphen	students	problems	professing	45
only	transfer	thousands	preferring	52

Tabulate from column to column

KEY | 8 | 10 | 9 | 10 | 10 | 10 | 13 |

40C Problem Typing: Personal Notes ⑳

Problem 1: Note with Centered Line

Half sheet; line: 60; 1" top margin; block style; SS

	Words
October 21, 19--	(*Operate return 4 times*)	3
Dear Larry	(¶ 1) Phi Eta Sigma has sched-	10
uled an open meeting for 12:15 next	Thurs-	19
day. The speaker is to be Professor O'Connor,	28
who will	talk on		32
DS	
"Business Cycles in the U.S."	38
DS	
(¶ 2) Professor O'Connor is always interest-	45
ing and informative.	I hope you can go with	54
me to the meeting. We may get some	use-	62
ful information for our midterm paper. Can	71
you join me?	(*DS*) Yours	(*Operate return 4*	75
times) *your name*	79

Problem 2: Note on Special-Size Paper

Half sheet with long edge at the left; line: 40; date on Line 14; block style; SS (Refer to 35B, p. 60, for centering on special-size paper)

	Words
October 21, 19--	Dear Dick	(¶ 1) The foot-	7
ball game of the season will be	played in	16
Kent on the 30th. I have four	good seats and	25
want you to come for the	weekend. Several	33
choice parties are to	be given, any one of	42
which we'll enjoy.	(¶ 2) Fly over late Friday	50
or early Saturday	morning. Just let me know	59
your arrival	time and flight number so I can	68
meet you.	Yours	*your name*	76

Problem 3: Alertness Training

Insert a half sheet with long edge at the left. Line: 40; date on Line 14. Retype Problem 1.

40D Skill-Transfer Typing ⑩

Type two 1' writings of each ¶ of 39C, page 68, the first on the *exploration* and the second on the *control* level. Compare the *gwam* and errors of the *exploration* and *control* writings.

41D Drill on X-ing Out Words ⑤

When composing and typing a first draft, you may ignore misstrokes that do not make the word unreadable and may x-out unwanted words. To x-out words, strike the x and m alternately with the first or second finger of each hand unless you use an electric machine with a repeat x key.

1. Type: The job interview was my undoing.

2. X-out the last two words of the sentence; then space forward and complete the sentence to read:

The job interview was difficult for me.

41E Composing and Typing ⑩ *full sheet; line: 60; 5-space ¶ indention; DS; 2½″ top margin*

Assume you are living A.D. 3000 and know nothing about our present civilization. You find a 1-cent piece of 1968 coinage. After studying the coin, type a description of what the coin tells you about our civilization; then make needed corrections and retype the composition with appropriate top margin.

LESSON 42

42A Preparatory Practice ⑧ *each line three times; 1' writings on Line 4*

Alphabet   Clay Jenkins will have the money required for our next big cash prize.

Figures   The serial number of his 1968 typewriter is either 2503740 or 2053740.

Figure-symbol   McNeil's Invoice #4296 (our Order #750B dated 10/18) comes to $942.30.

Fluency   The title to the land is now in the hands of the chairman of the firm.

   | 1 | 2 | 3 | 4 | 5 | 6 | 7 | 8 | 9 | 10 | 11 | 12 | 13 | 14 |

42B Problem Typing: Modified Block Letters ⑳

Problem 1: Letter with Line Endings Indicated

Full sheet; line: 60; tab stop at center; return address on Line 16. Address an envelope. Place typed letter under flap of addressed envelope, address side up.

	Words
842 Hibiscus Drive | Tampa, Florida 33617 |	8
October 24, 19-- | (*Operate return 4 times*)	12
Mr. Raymond Lawrence | 920 Pinetree Road |	19
Orlando, Florida 32804 | Dear Ray (¶ 1)	26
I'm no golf pro, I must confess, but I must	35
be better than | I thought because I've sur-	43
vived the Qualifying Round for the | Men's	51
Club Championship. Next comes the big	59
Tournament. |	62

(¶ 2) The whole Tournament will be played   69
week after next, but I \| shall play just one   78
match on Thursday of that week, with the \| 86
semifinals following on Friday and the finals   95
on Saturday. \| 98

(¶ 3) Can you come for a visit with me from   105
Thursday to Monday of \| Tournament Week?   113
Win or lose, after the Tournament ends on \| 121
Saturday, we'll celebrate with a party at our   131
house. I hope \| you can come for the long   139
weekend. \| 141

(¶ 4) Write or telephone to say when you'll   148
arrive--or just come \| on, but in time for   156
the match on Thursday. \| Yours \| (*Operate re-*   162
turn 4 times) Alvin Morgan   165/188

Problem 2: Alertness Training

Type the letter of Problem 1 with the following changes: (1) Begin the return address on Line 18; (2) address the letter to Mr. Lee Flaherty \| 962 Flamingo Drive \| Miami, Florida   32803 \| (3) add an appropriate salutation; (4) omit the final ¶; and (5) address an envelope.   97/119

41A   Preparatory Practice ⑧ *each line three times; 1' writings on Line 4*

Alphabet	Dick will make a quick flight to La Paz, Bolivia, next July or August.
Figures	Get ready for the April 16 test by studying pages 258-307 and 489-502.
Figure-symbol	Leman & Ward's Catalog 70 lists Item #482 at $960 (less 10% for cash).
Fluency	It is well for us to aim high so we can reach somewhere near the mark.

| 1 | 2 | 3 | 4 | 5 | 6 | 7 | 8 | 9 | 10 | 11 | 12 | 13 | 14 |

41B   Errorless Typing ⑫ *each line twice without error or three times with not more than 1 error to a line*

1	One-hand	We are aware that the union monopoly case is exaggerated by the staff.
2	Fluency	A man should want work enough to do and strength enough to do it well.
3	Shift keys	Jean, Alvin, and Carl saw the "Late Midnight Show" on TV Station QJEO.

| 1 | 2 | 3 | 4 | 5 | 6 | 7 | 8 | 9 | 10 | 11 | 12 | 13 | 14 |

41C   Problem Typing: Modified Block Letters ⑳

Problem 1: Style Letter 1, Page 71

Full sheet; line: 60; tab stop at center; return address on Line 14

Type the letter shown on page 71; tabulate to the center point to type the return address and the closing lines.

Problem 2: Speedup in Typing Letters

Type a 1' writing on each of the following parts of Style Letter 1, page 71; then retype the letter:

1. Return address, date, and letter address

2. Salutation and ¶ 1

3. Last ¶ and closing lines

Problem 3: Addressing Small Envelopes

Study the directions and the illustration at the right; then address an envelope for the letter typed as Problem 1.

1. **Return Address.** Type in block style, single spaced, the writer's name, street number and name (or box number), city, state, and ZIP Code in the upper left corner of the envelope. Begin on the second line from the top and 3 spaces from the left edge of the envelope.

2. **Envelope Address.** Begin about 2 inches (on Line 11 or 12) from the top and 2½ inches from the left edge of the envelope. Type the address in block style with single spacing, no matter how many or how few lines are used. *Type the city, state name or abbreviation, and ZIP Code on the last line of the address.*

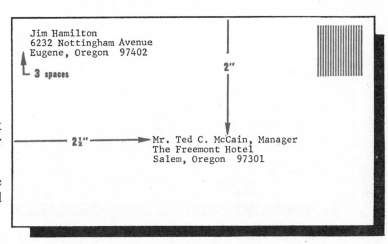

Modified Block

14 line

	Words in Parts	Total Words
	4	4
	9	9
	12	12

Tabulate to center to type return address and date

6232 Nottingham Avenue
Eugene, Oregon 97402
October 23, 19-- *Operate return 4 times*

	17	17
	21	21
	25	25

Address

Mr. Ted C. McCain, Manager
The Freemont Hotel
Salem, Oregon 97301
DS

Salutation

Dear Mr. McCain
DS

| | 3 | 29 |

Thank you for an interesting summer of work at the Freemont.
My assignment in the dining room brought me into contact with
people under many different conditions, some happy and some
difficult. I gained much from my experiences, not the least
of which is an added awareness of the complexity of human
relationships.

	16	41
	28	53
	40	65
	52	77
	64	89
	67	92

Body

It is possible that I may apply for a part-time job later in
the semester. This will depend on the amount of study time
that will be required for my college courses. If I should
apply for a job, may I use your name as a reference?

	12	104
	24	116
	36	128
	46	138

Your offer of work for next summer is sincerely appreciated.
If I do not attend the summer session, I shall be happy to
return to the Freemont where I had so many interesting and
worthwhile experiences this past summer. I shall let you
know my plans very soon. In the meantime, thank you again
for a pleasant summer and all good wishes to you personally.

	12	151
	24	163
	36	174
	48	186
	59	198
	71	210

Tabulate to center to type complimentary close

Sincerely yours *Operate return 4 times*

Jim Hamilton

| | 75 | 213 |

Tabulate to center to type writer's name

Jim Hamilton

| | 77 | 215 |

In the modified block style, the return address, date, complimentary close, and writer's name are typed at the horizontal center of the paper; the inside address, salutation, and lines of the paragraphs are begun at the left margin.

When open punctuation is used, marks of punctuation are omitted after the opening and closing lines unless an abbreviation ends the line.

STYLE LETTER 1: *Personal Letter in Modified Block Style (Typed in Pica Type)*

REFERENCE GUIDE

TYPEWRITER OPERATIVE PARTS

Typewriters have similar operative parts, the names of which vary somewhat from typewriter to typewriter even when the function is the same. These similar operative parts are identified in the four segments of a typewriter given below and on page ii. Each segment is a composite and not an exact segment of any one typewriter. For this reason, the exact location of a part identified in the segment may be slightly different from that on your typewriter; but the differences are, for the most part, few and slight.

Extra parts that are peculiar to the typewriter you operate can be identified by reference to the instructional booklet distributed by the manufacturer of the typewriter. This booklet can be very helpful to you because all its content is directed to the operation of one specific make of machine.

In using the illustrations, follow the line from the number to the part location. Know the function of each part, as explained in the textbook, and learn to operate it with maximum efficiency.

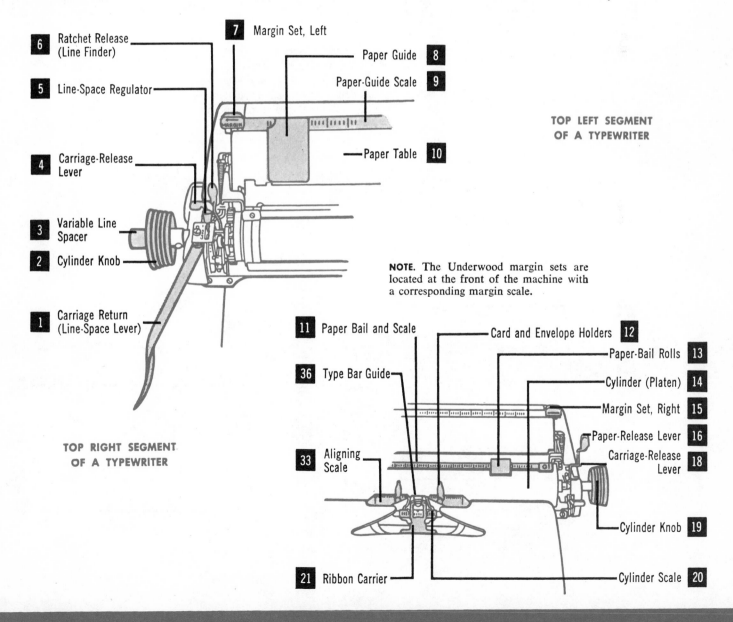

6 Ratchet Release (Line Finder)

7 Margin Set, Left

5 Line-Space Regulator

8 Paper Guide

9 Paper-Guide Scale

4 Carriage-Release Lever

10 Paper Table

3 Variable Line Spacer

2 Cylinder Knob

1 Carriage Return (Line-Space Lever)

TOP LEFT SEGMENT OF A TYPEWRITER

NOTE. The Underwood margin sets are located at the front of the machine with a corresponding margin scale.

11 Paper Bail and Scale

12 Card and Envelope Holders

13 Paper-Bail Rolls

36 Type Bar Guide

14 Cylinder (Platen)

15 Margin Set, Right

16 Paper-Release Lever

18 Carriage-Release Lever

33 Aligning Scale

19 Cylinder Knob

21 Ribbon Carrier

20 Cylinder Scale

TOP RIGHT SEGMENT OF A TYPEWRITER

LOWER SEGMENT OF A MANUAL TYPEWRITER

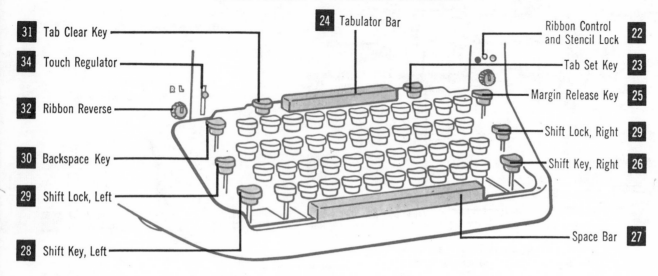

31 Tab Clear Key

34 Touch Regulator

32 Ribbon Reverse

30 Backspace Key

29 Shift Lock, Left

28 Shift Key, Left

24 Tabulator Bar

22 Ribbon Control and Stencil Lock

23 Tab Set Key

25 Margin Release Key

29 Shift Lock, Right

26 Shift Key, Right

27 Space Bar

LOWER SEGMENT OF AN ELECTRIC TYPEWRITER

> ### CHECK YOUR TYPEWRITER TO SEE IF:
> **1.** The position is different for: ¢ @ * _ (underline)
> **2.** These keys have "repeat" action: *backspace, space bar, carriage return, hyphen-underline*
> **3.** Extra keys are used: **+ = ! 1**

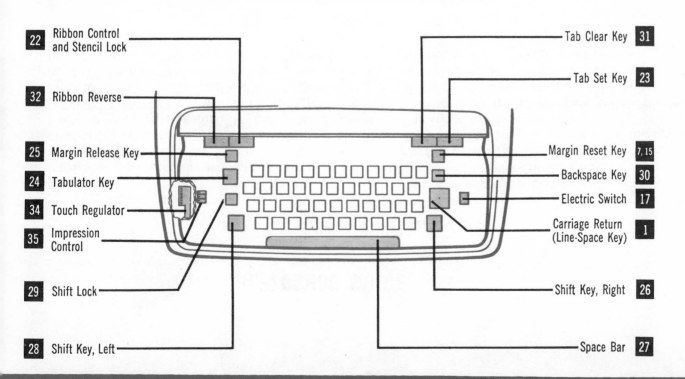

22 Ribbon Control and Stencil Lock

32 Ribbon Reverse

25 Margin Release Key

24 Tabulator Key

34 Touch Regulator

35 Impression Control

29 Shift Lock

28 Shift Key, Left

31 Tab Clear Key

23 Tab Set Key

7, 15 Margin Reset Key

30 Backspace Key

17 Electric Switch

1 Carriage Return (Line-Space Key)

26 Shift Key, Right

27 Space Bar

PAPER GUIDE AND CENTERING POINT

Typewriters are of three types in regard to setting the paper guide and arriving at the center point.

Type 1: ROYAL, OLYMPIA, AND SMITH-CORONA "SECRETARIAL 250" ELECTRIC

Set the paper guide on 0 on the paper-guide scale. When 8½" by 11" paper is inserted with the left edge against the guide, the centering point will be 42 for pica and 51 (or 50 for convenience) for elite machines.

Type 2: IBM MODEL D, AND REMINGTON

The fixed centering point is 0 for both pica and elite machines. Marks on the paper-guide scale aid the typist in setting the paper guide to center paper correctly.

Type 3: SMITH-CORONA NON-ELECTRIC, R. C. ALLEN, IBM SELECTRIC, AND UNDERWOOD

A variety of marks appear on the paper table or copy-guide scale to aid the typist in setting the paper-guide scale for automatic centering of 8½" by 11" paper. Marks on the paper-bail scale indicate the center point of the paper.

If no marks appear on the paper-bail scale to indicate the center point of the paper, insert the paper after the paper guide has been set. Add the carriage scale reading on the left edge of the paper to the reading at the right edge. Divide this sum by 2 to arrive at the center point.

STANDARD DIRECTIONS APPLYING TO ALL TYPEWRITERS

On every typewriter, there is at least one scale, usually the cylinder scale (20), that reads from 0 at the left to 85 or more at the right, depending on the width of the carriage and style of type—either pica or elite. The spaces on this scale are matched to the spacing mechanism on the typewriter.

To simplify direction giving, your instructor may ask you to insert paper into your machine so that the left edge corresponds to 0 on the carriage scale. The center point on 8½" by 11" paper will then be 42 on the carriage scale for a pica machine or 51 (or 50 for convenience) on an elite machine.

If this procedure is adopted, adjust the paper guide to the left edge of your paper after it is inserted with the left edge at 0 on the carriage scale. Note the position of the paper guide. Move it to this point at the beginning of each class period.

SETTING THE MARGIN STOPS

PLANNING THE MARGIN STOPS (7, 15)

To center typed material horizontally, set stops for the left and right margins. Typewriters differ in their mechanical adjustments and the bell rings at different points on different typewriters; but the carriage locks at the point where the right margin stop is set. After the bell rings, there will be from 6 to 11 or more spaces before the carriage locks, some machines allowing more but none fewer than 6 spaces.

Test out your typewriter and determine the number of spaces the bell rings before the carriage locks. Take this into consideration when setting the right margin stop. Since the ringing of the bell is a cue to return the carriage, set the right stop 3 to 7 spaces beyond the desired line ending so the ringing will come at approximately 3 spaces before the point at which you want the line to end.

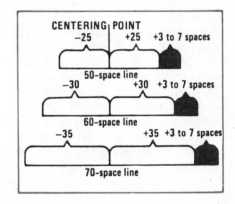

MECHANICS OF SETTING MARGIN STOPS

IBM "MODEL D" AND UNDERWOOD ELECTRIC

To Set Left Margin Stop: Move the carriage to the left margin stop by depressing the return key. Depress and hold down the margin reset key as you move the carriage to the desired new margin position; then release the margin reset key.

To Set Right Margin Stop: Move the carriage until it is against the right margin stop. Depress and hold down the margin reset key as you move the carriage to the desired new margin position; then release the margin reset key.

IBM "SELECTRIC"

To Set Left and Right Margin Stops: Push in on the appropriate stop and slide it to the correct position on the margin scale; release the stop. Use the space bar to move the carrier out of the way when setting a margin stop to the right of the carrier's present location.

(*Continued on page iv*)

SETTING MARGIN STOPS (Continued)

OLYMPIA AND UNDERWOOD NONELECTRIC

To Set Left and Right Margin Stops: Move the left and right margin stops to the desired position on the front scale for the Underwood typewriter and on the scale in back of the cylinder for the Olympia.

The Underwood typewriter has margin indicators (solid geometric shapes) on the front scale to indicate balanced margin set positions. The Olympia has an easy-to-see red line, on the upright plastic guide, to indicate exact position of setting.

REMINGTON ELECTRIC AND NONELECTRIC

To Set Left and Right Margin Stops: Move the left margin stop to the desired position to begin the line of writing. Move the stop for the right margin to the desired position to set the right margin stop.

ROYAL ELECTRIC AND NONELECTRIC

To Set the Left Margin Stop: Pull forward the left margin lever, move the carriage to the desired point, and release the lever. Set the right margin the same way, using the right margin lever.

SMITH-CORONA ELECTRIC

To Set Left and Right Margin Stops: Depress the left carriage-release button and the left margin button and move the carriage to the desired location for the left margin stop; release the two buttons simultaneously.

Use a similar operation to set the stop for the right margin.

SMITH-CORONA NONELECTRIC AND R. C. ALLEN

To Set the Left Margin Stop: Move the carriage to the desired point and touch the left margin button or key.

Set the right margin stop the same way, using the right margin button or key.

Another Method: While holding down the button or key, move the carriage to the point desired; then release the button or key.

KNOW YOUR TYPEWRITER

Your machine may have timesaving features not included in this discussion of operating parts. Learn these features from a study of the manufacturer's pamphlet which describes and illustrates the operating parts of the typewriter you are using. You can get this pamphlet without cost from the manufacturer of your typewriter. The pamphlet will have many ideas for your operative improvement.

CHANGING TYPEWRITER RIBBONS

Techniques for changing ribbons vary from machine to machine. The steps that follow are basic to all machines:

1. Wind the ribbon on one spool, usually the right one.

2. Raise and lock the ribbon carrier as follows: Depress the shift lock. Set the ribbon control for typing on the lower portion of the ribbon. Depress and lock any two central keys, such as *y* and *t*.

3. Remove the ribbon from the carrier. Remove both spools.

4. Hook the new ribbon on the empty spool and wind several inches of new ribbon on it. Be sure the ribbon winds and unwinds in the proper direction.

5. Place both spools on their holders. Thread the ribbon through the ribbon carrier.

6. Release the shift lock. Return the ribbon indicator to type on the upper portion of the ribbon. Unlock the two keys.

7. Clean the keys if necessary to make your work clear and sharp.

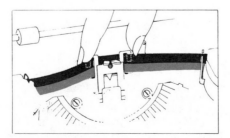

Ribbon Threaded Through the Ribbon-Carrier Mechanism

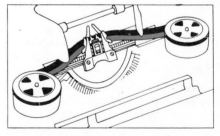

Nonelectric (Underwood)

Path of the Ribbon as It Winds and Unwinds on the Two Spools

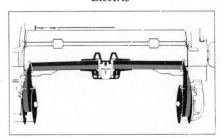

Electric

IBM Ribbon

Letter 1 (top left)

office aides inc

suite 1045 carew tower one fifth street cincinnati,ohio 45202 telephone (513) 271-8811

October 20, 19--

Republic Supply Company
2670 Queen City Avenue
Cincinnati, OH 45238

Attention Miss Janet Wellington

Gentlemen:

The modified block style has some distinctive features, as shown by this letter and described in the enclosed pamphlet.

The date, complimentary close, and name and official title of the dictator are begun at the horizontal center of the page. These can be placed correctly with one tabulator adjustment.

Special lines (reference, enclosure, and carbon copy notations) are placed at the left margin, a double space below the last of the closing lines. If the dictator's name is part of the closing lines, only the typist's initials are required in the reference. If the dictator's initials are used, they precede those of the typist and are usually typed in capital letters.

The modified block style, about which you inquired yesterday, is widely used by the clients for whom we prepare letters. We think you will like it, too.

                              Sincerely yours,

                              Randall B. Parkhurst

                              Randall B. Parkhurst
                              Communications Director

lkd

Enclosure

cc Mr. John R. Rodgers, Jr.

Modified Block, Blocked ¶s, Mixed

Letter 2 (top right)

PD Consultants in Business Practices
PERRY & DERRICK, INC.
111 Lincoln Park / Newark, New Jersey 07102 / Telephone 201-227-0453

                              February 15, 19--

AIRMAIL

Miss Evelyn Terry, Office Manager
Standard Steel Equipment Company
270 - 53d Street
Brooklyn, NY 11232

Dear Miss Terry

          The booklet you requested about letter format is enclosed. The format features described are those adopted by this company. This letter follows them.

          The first line of each paragraph is indented five spaces. The date, complimentary close, company name, and the dictator's name are started at the center point of the paper. We use open punctuation. In this style, punctuation marks are omitted after the date, address, salutation, and closing lines unless an abbreviation is used, in which case the period is typed as part of the abbreviation.

          Although we do not usually show the company name in the closing lines, we have done so here to illustrate for you the correct handling of it. Since the dictator's name is typed in the closing lines, only the typist's initials are used in the reference notation.

          Special mailing notations are typed in all capital letters at the left margin, a double space below the date.

          After you have had an opportunity to examine your copy of Styling Business Letters, I shall appreciate your sending us your impressions of it.

                              Sincerely yours

                              PERRY & DERRICK, INC.

                              Richard S. Perry

                              Richard S. Perry, Manager

mev

Enclosure

Modified Block, Indented ¶s, Open

Letter 3 (bottom left)

BUSINESS WRITING, INCORPORATED

Communications *Consultants*

2203 CEDAR DRIVE, E. / HICKSVILLE, NEW YORK 11804 / 212-869-2560

February 12, 19--

Miss Margaret Lamson
62200 Beacon Hill Road
Waterbury, CT 06716

Dear Miss Lamson

SUBJECT: Letter Writing Manual

Thank you for your letter of February 5 requesting a copy of our Letter Writing Manual. I regret that this manual is not yet in printed form. The mimeographed copies currently available are restricted to use in our offices.

We have adopted the block form illustrated in this letter. You will observe that machine adjustments are simpler, resulting in a saving of much time by the typist. The date, address, salutation, and closing lines all begin at the left margin. Paragraphs are blocked also. The form is used in many business offices.

You should get a copy of our Letter Writing Manual in a few weeks. There is no charge for the manual. We hope you will find it useful. Please write me again if I can send you any additional information.

Sincerely yours

S. James Whitmore

S. James Whitmore
President

rsk

Block, Open

Letter 4 (bottom right)

BUSINESS WRITING, INCORPORATED

Communications  *Consultants*

2203 CEDAR DRIVE, E. / HICKSVILLE, NEW YORK 11804 / 212-869-2560

October 5, 19--

Mr. S. W. Jackson, Manager
North American Cement Corp.
39501 Bartlett Avenue
Boston, MA 02129

AMS SIMPLIFIED STYLE

This letter is typed in the timesaving simplified style recommended by the Administrative Management Society. To type a letter in the AMS style, follow these steps:

1. Use block format with blocked paragraphs.

2. Omit the salutation and complimentary close.

3. Include a subject heading and type it in ALL CAPS a triple space below the address; triple-space from the subject line to the first line of the body.

4. Type enumerated items at the left margin; indent unnumbered listed items five spaces.

5. Type the writer's name and title in ALL CAPS at least four line spaces below the letter body.

6. Type the reference initials (typist's only) a double space below the writer's name.

Correspondents in your company will like the AMS simplified letter style not only for the "eye appeal" it gives letters but also because it reduces letter-writing costs.

S. James Whitmore

S. JAMES WHITMORE - PRESIDENT

akb

AMS Simplified

ADDRESSING ENVELOPES

Address Placement and Spacing. Block the address lines; use single spacing. Type the city and state names and ZIP Code in that sequence on the bottom line.

For a small envelope, start the address lines 2″ from the top and 2½″ from the left edge.

For a large envelope, start the address lines 2½″ from the top and 4″ from the left edge.

State Abbreviations. When the ZIP Code is known, use the 2-letter abbreviation (page viii) in all caps, without a period. Type the ZIP Code 2 spaces after the abbreviation. If the ZIP Code is not known, type the state name in full or use the standard abbreviation.

Notations. Type postal directions, such as AIRMAIL and SPECIAL DELIVERY, below the space required for the stamp. Type HOLD FOR ARRIVAL, PERSONAL, PLEASE FORWARD, etc., a triple space below the return address and 3 spaces from the left edge.

Return Address. Type the return address on the second line from the top and 3 spaces from the left edge.

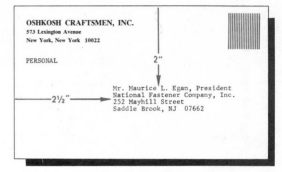

OSHKOSH CRAFTSMEN, INC.
573 Lexington Avenue
New York, New York 10022

PERSONAL   2″

2½″ → Mr. Maurice L. Egan, President
        National Fastener Company, Inc.
        252 Mayhill Street
        Saddle Brook, NJ 07662

Small Envelope

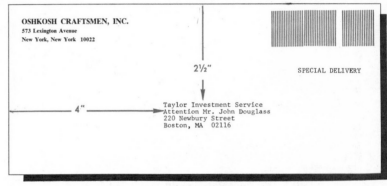

OSHKOSH CRAFTSMEN, INC.
573 Lexington Avenue
New York, New York 10022

2½″

SPECIAL DELIVERY

4″ → Taylor Investment Service
       Attention Mr. John Douglass
       220 Newbury Street
       Boston, MA 02116

Large Envelope

FOLDING-AND-INSERTING PROCEDURE FOR ENVELOPES

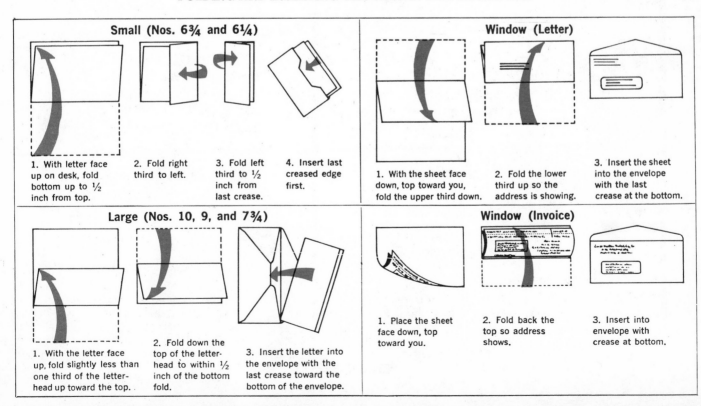

Small (Nos. 6¾ and 6¼)

1. With letter face up on desk, fold bottom up to ½ inch from top.

2. Fold right third to left.

3. Fold left third to ½ inch from last crease.

4. Insert last creased edge first.

Window (Letter)

1. With the sheet face down, top toward you, fold the upper third down.

2. Fold the lower third up so the address is showing.

3. Insert the sheet into the envelope with the last crease at the bottom.

Large (Nos. 10, 9, and 7¾)

1. With the letter face up, fold slightly less than one third of the letterhead up toward the top.

2. Fold down the top of the letterhead to within ½ inch of the bottom fold.

3. Insert the letter into the envelope with the last crease toward the bottom of the envelope.

Window (Invoice)

1. Place the sheet face down, top toward you.

2. Fold back the top so address shows.

3. Insert into envelope with crease at bottom.

Margins and Date Placement. Some offices use standard side margins for all letters. Others vary the side margins according to letter length, as is the case in the following guide:

5-Stroke Words in Letter Body	Side Margins	Date Line
Up to 100	2″	20
101 – 300	1½″	18–12*
Over 300	1″	12

*Date line is moved up 2 line spaces for each additional 50 words.

The horizontal placement of the date depends on the style of letter, design of the letterhead, or a combination of these factors.

Block and AMS Simplified Styles: Type the date at the left margin.

Modified Block Style: Begin date at center point or type it even with right margin.

Address. Type the first line of the address on the fourth line space below the date. Type an official title, when used, on either the first or second line, whichever gives better balance.

Attention Line. Type an attention line, when used, on the second line below the letter address and a double space above the salutation. Type it at the left margin (preferred), or center it.

Subject Line. Type a subject line on the second line below the salutation. In block or AMS Simplified styles, type the subject line even with the left margin. In other styles, type it even with the left margin, at paragraph point, or centered.

Type the word *Subject* in all capitals or with only the first letter capitalized, or omit it (as in the AMS Simplified style).

Company Name in Closing. When the company name is included in the closing, type it in all caps on the second line below the complimentary close.

Typewritten Name and Official Title. Type the name of the writer of a letter and his official title on the 4th line space below the complimentary close, or on the 4th line space below the company name when it is used. Type the writer's name and his official title on the same line, or type the title below the writer's name.

Enclosure Notation. Type an enclosure notation (*Enc.* or *Enclosure*) on the second line space below the reference initials.

Two-Page Letters. Include at least two lines of a paragraph at the bottom of the first page and at least two lines at the top of the second page of a two-page letter. Do the same for any letter of more than one page.

Begin the heading on continuation pages an inch from the top edge of the sheet. You may use either the block or horizontal form. Leave 2 or 3 blank lines between the heading and the first line of the resumed letter; use the same side margins as for the first page.

Second-Page Headings

```
Mr. A. C. Dow          Block
Page 2                 Form
May 6, 19--
```

Horizontal Form

```
Mr. A. C. Dow     2     May 6, 19--
```

GUIDES FOR WORD DIVISION

Divide—

1. Words between syllables only.

2. Hyphenated words and compounds at hyphens only.

3. Words so that *cial*, *tial*, *cion*, *sion*, or *tion* are retained as a unit.

4. A word of three or more syllables at a one-letter syllable. Type the one-letter syllable on the first line unless it is part of such terminations as *ible*, *able*, or *ical*, in which case carry it to the second line. If two one-letter syllables come together, divide between them.

5. A word in which the final consonant is doubled when a suffix is added between the double letters, as *control-ling*.

6. A word that ends in double letters after the double letters when a suffix is added, as *will-ing*.

Do not—

7. Divide a word of five or fewer letters.

8. Separate a one-letter syllable at the beginning or end of a word.

9. Separate a two-letter syllable at the end of a word.

10. Divide the last word on a page.

11. Separate a syllable without a vowel from the rest of a word, as *would-n't*.

Avoid if possible—

12. Separating a two-letter syllable at the beginning of a word.

13. Dividing words at the ends of more than two successive lines.

14. Dividing abbreviations, numbers, and proper names; but a surname may be separated from the initials or given name, when necessary.

TWO-LETTER ABBREVIATIONS FOR STATE, DISTRICT, AND TERRITORY NAMES

These two-letter abbreviations, recommended by the U.S. Post Office Department, should be used for business addresses for which ZIP Codes are known and used.

Alabama	AL	Illinois	IL	North Carolina	NC

Alabama . . . . . . AL
Alaska . . . . . . AK
Arizona . . . . . AZ
Arkansas . . . . . AR
California . . . . . CA
Canal Zone . . . . CZ
Colorado . . . . . CO
Connecticut . . . . CT
Delaware . . . . . DE
District of Columbia . . DC
Florida . . . . . FL
Georgia . . . . . GA
Guam . . . . . GU
Hawaii . . . . . HI
Idaho . . . . . . ID

Illinois IL
Indiana . . . . . . IN
Iowa . . . . . . IA
Kansas . . . . . . KS
Kentucky . . . . . KY
Louisiana . . . . . LA
Maine . . . . . . ME
Maryland . . . . . MD
Massachusetts . . MA
Michigan . . . . . MI
Minnesota . . . . . MN
Mississippi . . . . . MS
Missouri . . . . . MO
Montana . . . . . MT
Nebraska . . . . . NE
Nevada . . . . . NV
New Hampshire . . . NH
New Jersey . . . . NJ
New Mexico . . . . NM
New York . . . . . NY

North Carolina . . . . NC
North Dakota . . . . . ND
Ohio . . . . . . OH
Oklahoma . . . . . OK
Oregon . . . . . . OR
Pennsylvania . . . . PA
Puerto Rico . . . . PR
Rhode Island . . . . RI
South Carolina . . . SC
South Dakota . . . . SD
Tennessee . . . . . TN
Texas . . . . . . TX
Utah . . . . . . UT
Vermont . . . . . VT
Virgin Islands . . . VI
Virginia . . . . . VA
Washington . . . . WA
West Virginia . . . . WV
Wisconsin . . . . . WI
Wyoming . . . . . WY

ASSEMBLING A CARBON PACK

METHOD 1 (Desk Assembly)

1. Place the sheet ("second" or "file copy sheet") on which the carbon copy is to be made flat on the desk; then place a carbon sheet, *carbon (glossy) side down*, on top of the sheet. Add the original sheet (letterhead or plain sheet) on top of the carbon sheet.

    Note. For each carbon copy desired, add one set (the "second" or "file copy sheet" and a carbon sheet).

2. Pick up the carbon pack and turn it so the second sheets and the glossy sides of the carbon sheets face you.

3. Straighten the pack by tapping the top of the sheets gently on the desk.

4. Insert the pack by holding it firmly in one hand while turning the cylinder slowly with the other.

METHOD 2 (Machine Assembly)

1. Assemble paper for insertion into the typewriter (original sheet on top; second sheets beneath).

2. Insert paper, turning the cylinder until the sheets are gripped slightly by the feed rolls; then lay all but the last sheet over the top of the machine.

Deck Assembly of a Carbon Pack

3. Place carbon sheets between the sheets of paper with the *glossy side toward you*. Flip each sheet back as you add each carbon.

4. Roll the pack into typing position.

REMOVING THE CARBON SHEETS

Because carbon sheets do not extend to the top edge of the paper in the machine assembly of a carbon pack, the sheets can be easily removed by pulling them out all at one time as you hold the left top edge of the paper.

GUIDES FOR INSERTING A CARBON PACK

1. *To keep sheets straight when feeding*, place pack under an envelope flap or in the fold of a plain sheet of paper.

2. *To "start" the carbon pack:*
    (a) Release the paper-release lever,
    (b) Feed the pack around the cylinder until sheets appear at the front; then
    (c) Reset the paper-release lever.
    (d) After the pack is inserted, remove the envelope or paper fold.

3. *To avoid wrinkling*, release and reset the paper-release lever after the pack has been partially inserted.

Machine Assembly of a Carbon Pack

SUMMARY OF MANUSCRIPT FORM

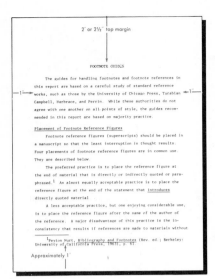

First Page, Topbound

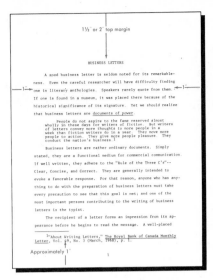

First Page, Unbound

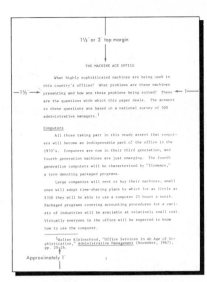

First Page, Leftbound

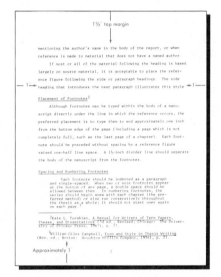

Second Page, Topbound

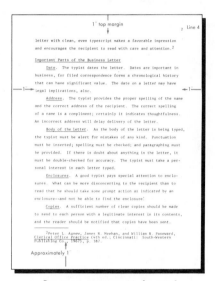

Second Page, Unbound

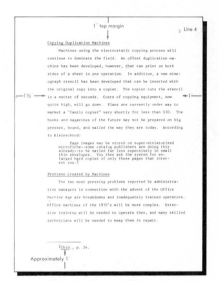

Second Page, Leftbound

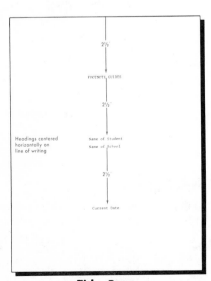

Title Page

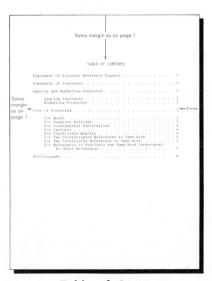

Table of Contents

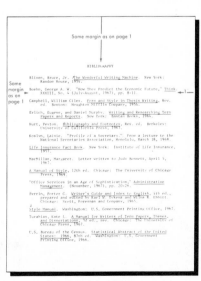

Bibliography

CORRECTION SYMBOLS (PROOFREADERS' MARKS)

Sometimes typed or printed copy may be corrected with proofreaders' marks. The typist must be able to interpret correctly these marks in retyping the corrected copy or *rough draft* as it may be called. The most commonly used proofreaders' marks are shown below.

‖	Align type
Cap or ≡	Capitalize
⌒	Close up
(delete mark)	Delete
ds	Double-space
=/	Hyphen
∧	Insert
∨	Insert apostrophe
⊙	Insert colon
∧	Insert comma

⊙	Insert period
?/	Insert question mark
∨∨ ∨∨	Insert quotation marks
; or ;/	Insert semicolon
# or #	Insert space
#⟶	Insert space between lines
Stet	Let it stand (ignore correction)
(box)	Move to left
(box)	Move to right

no ¶ [	No new paragraph
¶	Paragraph
ss	Single-space
#	Space
SP	Spell out
===	Straighten line
∿ or tr	Transpose
ts	Triple-space
___	Underline
l.c.	Use lower case

CENTERING SUMMARY

HORIZONTAL CENTERING

From the center, backspace once for each two letters, figures, spaces, and punctuation marks in the heading or line to be centered. (In backspacing, disregard an odd or leftover stroke.) Start typing where the backspacing ends.

HORIZONTAL CENTERING—SPREAD HEADINGS

1. From the center, backspace once for each letter except the last one in the heading and once for each space between words.
2. In typing the heading, space once after each letter or character and three times between words.

VERTICAL CENTERING
BACKSPACE-FROM-CENTER METHOD

1. Move the paper to vertical center: 34th line space for a full sheet; 17th line space for a half sheet.

2. Roll the platen back once for each two lines (including blank lines). Ignore an odd or leftover line. Start typing where the spacing ends.
3. For reading position on a full sheet, roll the platen back 2 additional line spaces.

VERTICAL CENTERING
MATHEMATICAL METHOD

1. Count lines and blank line spaces in problem.
2. Subtract lines used from lines on sheet.
3. Divide by 2 to get top and bottom margins. If a fraction results, disregard it.
4. For reading position, subtract 2 from the top margin.
5. Space down from top edge of paper 1 more than the number of lines to be left in top margin.

TABULATION SUMMARY

VERTICAL PLACEMENT

For vertical placement of tables, use either the backspace-from-center or the mathematical method explained on page x.

Spacing after Headings. Leave one blank line between a main and a secondary heading. Leave two blank lines after a secondary heading. If a secondary heading is not used, leave two blank lines after a main heading.

Leave one blank line between a columnar heading and its column.

HORIZONTAL PLACEMENT OF TABULATIONS

Columns. Note the longest item in each column. (If a columnar heading is the longest item, count it as such unless judgment indicates otherwise.) Decide the number of spaces to leave between columns, preferably an even number.

Backspace from the center of the paper once for every two spaces in the longest item in each column and once for every two spaces between all the columns. At the point where you finish backspacing, set the left margin stop for the first column.

From the left margin, space forward once for every stroke in the longest item of the first column and once for each space between the first and second columns. Set the first tab stop. Follow this same procedure for setting tab stops for the remaining columns.

Columnar Headings. Center the columnar headings over the columns.

When a heading has been counted as the longest item in a column, it will usually be necessary to reset the tab stop in order to center the column under the heading.

There are several methods of centering columnar headings over a column, but probably the easiest way is to add the first and last strokes in the column. Divide this sum by 2 to get the center point of the column. Columnar headings are usually underlined.

HORIZONTAL RULINGS

Horizontal lines are often used in a tabulated report to set off columnar headings. A double line is usually placed above columnar headings and a single line below them. A single line is also placed under the last line of the report. These lines can be the exact width of the report, or they can extend several spaces on each side of it.

To type rulings the exact width of the table, first determine the placement of columns. When you set the tab stop for the last column continue spacing forward one space for each stroke in the longest item in that column. Immediately after stroking for the last stroke in this item, move the right margin stop so that the typewriter will lock at this point. Rulings can then be typed across the page until the carriage locks.

Placement of Double Lines. After typing the secondary heading, double-space; type the first of the double lines; then operate the variable line

spacer; move the cylinder forward slightly; type the second line. Double-space between this line and the columnar headings.

Placement of Single Lines. After typing the columnar headings, single-space; type a single line; then double-space to the first columnar entries. Single-space after typing the last columnar entries and type a single line.

Source Note (If Used). Double-space from the single line; type the source note at the left margin or indent 3 to 5 spaces.

TABULATOR STOPS FOR UNEVEN COLUMNS

Uneven Columns. When columns contain amounts of figures of uneven length, set the tab stop at a point that will take care of the greatest number of entries. After tabulating, backspace for longer items or space forward for shorter ones.

Dollar Signs. In a money column, type a dollar sign before the first amount in the column and before the total (if one is shown). Place the dollar sign before the first amount and the total, typed so that it will be one space to the left of the longest amount in the column (usually the total).

Totals. To make them easier to read, totals are usually separated by a double space from the column. Type the total line immediately under the last amount in the column. Do not space before typing the total line.

DRAWING RULED LINES

To Draw Horizontal Lines: Place the pencil point through the cardholder (or on the type bar guide above the ribbon); depress the carriage-release lever to draw the carriage across the line.

To Draw Vertical Lines: Operate the line finder. Place the pencil point or pen through the cardholder (or on the type bar guide above the ribbon). Roll the platen up the page until you have a line of the desired length. Remove the pen or pencil and reset the line finder.

HOW TO ERASE AND CORRECT ERRORS

Using an Eraser Shield

1. Depress margin-release key and move carriage to extreme left or right to prevent eraser crumbs from falling into the typing mechanism.
2. To avoid disturbing the paper alignment of the type, turn the cylinder forward if the erasure is to be made on the upper two thirds of the paper; backward, on the lower third of the paper.
3. To erase on the original sheet, lift the paper bail out of the way, and place a 5″ x 3″ card *in front of* the first carbon sheet. Use an eraser shield to protect the writing that is not to be erased. Brush the eraser crumbs away from the typewriter.
4. Move the protective card in front of the second carbon, if more than one copy is being made. Erase the errors on the carbon copy with a soft (or pencil) eraser first, then with the hard typewriter eraser used in erasing on the original copy.
5. When the error has been erased on all copies, remove the protective card, position the carriage to the proper point, and type the necessary correction.

SQUEEZING AND SPREADING OF LETTERS

In correcting errors, it is often possible to "squeeze" omitted letters into half spaces or to "spread" letters to fill out spaces.

1. *An omitted letter at the beginning or end of a word:*

   Error: an omitte letter
   Correction: an omittedletter

Corrective steps:
1. Move carriage to the letter *e*.
2. Depress and hold down the space bar; strike the letter *d*.

Note. On an electric typewriter, it may be necessary to hold the carriage by hand at the half-space point.

2. *An omitted letter within a word:*
   Error: a leter within
   Correction: a letter within

Corrective steps:
1. Erase the incorrect word.
2. Position the carriage at the space after the letter *a*.
3. Press down and hold the space bar; strike the letter *l*.
4. Release the space bar, then press it down again and hold it; strike the next letter.
5. Repeat the process for any additional letters.

3. *Addition of a letter within a word:*
   Error: a lettter within
   Correction: a letter within

Corrective steps:
1. Erase the incorrect word.
2. Position the carriage as if you were going to type the letter *l* in its regular position following the space.
3. Press down and hold the space bar; strike the letter *l*.
4. Release the space bar; then repeat the process for each remaining letter.

IBM SELECTRIC TYPEWRITER

When making corrections, you may locate the horizontal position of the typing element by using either the black line on the clear view card holder (circled at right) or the red arrow on the margin scale. If you use the card holder as your indicator, position the black line at the point on the paper at which you want to insert the new character. Then return to the line of type and insert the correction.

Crowding Letters

Error: the ordr today
Correction: the order today

To crowd the "e" into "ordr," erase the final "r." Backspace until the black line on the card holder is over the space formerly occupied by the final "r." Place the palm of the right hand on the top of the front cover. Reach under the cover and press LEFT against the carrier position post with your finger until the black line is moved back one-half space (as indicated in the illustration). Hold the carrier in this position and type the "e." Repeat the procedure for the "r."

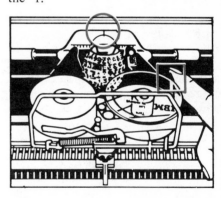

Spreading Letters

Error: He will send
Correction: He can send

To replace "will" with "can," first erase "will." Type "c" in place of "w" and type "n" in place of final "l."

Position the black line on the card holder over the position occupied by the first "l." Place the palm of the right hand on the top of the front cover. Reach under the cover and press left against the carrier position post with your finger until the black line of the card holder is directly between the "i" and "l." Type "a." Release the carrier and continue to type.

LIST OF ILLUSTRATIONS

LIST OF DRILLS AND TIMED WRITINGS